Latin American Voices

Integrative Psychology and Humanities

Luca Tateo, Department of Communication and Psychology, Aalborg University, Aalborg Øst, Denmark

Jaan Valsiner, Department of Communication and Psychology, Aalborg University, Aalborg Øst, Denmark

Floor van Alphen, Department of Basic Psychology, Universidad Autonoma de Madrid, Madrid, Spain

In the last decades, Latin America has been a productive and fertile ground for the advancement of theoretical and empirical elaborations within psychology, social and human sciences. Yet, these contributions have had a hard time to be internationally recognized in its original contribution and in its transformative heuristic power. Latin American Voices—Integrative Psychology and Humanities intends to fill this gap by offering an international forum of scholarly interchanges that deal with psychological and socio-cultural processes from a cultural psychological perspective.

The book series seeks to be a solid theoretically-based, though still empirical, arena of interdisciplinary and international debate, as well as a worldwide scientific platform for communicating key ideas of methodology and different theoretical approaches to relevant issues in psychology and humanities. It will publish books from researchers working in Latin America in the different fields of psychology at interplay with other social and human sciences. Proposals dealing with new perspectives, innovative ideas and new topics of interdisciplinary kind are especially welcomed.

Both solicited and unsolicited proposals are considered for publication in this series. All proposals and manuscripts submitted to the Series will undergo at least two rounds of external peer review.

More information about this series at http://www.springer.com/series/16145

Manuel Llorens

Politically Reflective Psychotherapy

Towards a Contextualized Approach

Springer

Manuel Llorens
Graduate Program in Clinical Community Psychology
Universidad Católica Andrés Bello
Caracas, Distrito Federal, Venezuela

ISSN 2524-5805 ISSN 2524-5813 (electronic)
Latin American Voices
ISBN 978-3-030-57791-9 ISBN 978-3-030-57792-6 (eBook)
https://doi.org/10.1007/978-3-030-57792-6

Translated and revised from the Spanish language edition: *Psicoterapia Políticamente Reflexiva: Hacia una Técnica Contextualizada*, by Manuel Llorens, © 2015 Editorial Equinoccio.

This Springer imprint is published by the registered company Springer Nature Switzerland AG
The registered company address is: Gewerbestrasse 11, 6330 Cham, Switzerland

I dedicate this book to the memory of
Deltry Musso, Juan Llorens and Marta Llorens,
the best teachers of psychotherapy,
life and politics
that I could have possible had.

Preface of the Series Editor

Psychotherapy as Permeable Developmental Arena

I got the final manuscript of this volume, *Politically Reflective Psychotherapy: Towards a Contextualized Approach*, in the middle of the Sars COVID-19 lockdown in Italy. It has been a strange coincidence: while I was forced in a state of social isolation, Manuel Llorens provoked my thoughts by showing that even the most apparently isolated and protected experience, that is, the psychotherapy session, is deeply affected by what is going on out there in a specific time and space. Psychotherapy is, in fact, much more permeable of what it appears.

Psychological sciences have been dramatically challenged by the COVID-19 pandemic and by its psycho-social consequences, revealing the effects of social, racial and economic inequalities. I felt the lack of preparation to deal with this kind of global phenomenon and the urgency of a serious theoretical and epistemological reflection, seeking advancements in the way psychology understands human psychic experience outside the Western-centric way of life. This volume is not about the Corona Virus, yet it may shed the light on this intricate connection of Science and Society.

We are living a time of political turmoil in different places in the world, and we are facing the revival of all sorts of nationalisms and extremisms, the genocide of indigenous population all over the planet or their epistemic silencing (Guimarães 2020). All this makes almost unavoidable for clinicians to address political issues.

However, clinicians do not really know how to do it. This volume, *Politically Reflective Psychotherapy: Towards a Contextualized Approach,* fills this gap and gives the theoretical and methodological coordinates to guide clinical intervention. Also, it intends to explore how psychotherapy is developed in a historical and political context, even though psychology has tried to disregard this fact.

This leads to the core feature of any psychotherapy. Is it meant to be only facing the individual or does the relationship with the environment include also the acknowledgment of the collective? Freud describes it in 1921 as follows:

> The contrast between individual psychology and social or group psychology, which at a first glance may seem to be full of significance, loses a great deal of its sharpness when it is examined more closely. It is true that individual psychology is concerned with the individual man and explores the paths by which he seeks to find satisfaction for his instinctual impulses; but only rarely and under certain exceptional conditions is individual psychology in a position to disregard the relations of this individual to others. In the individual's mental life someone else is invariably involved, as a model, as an object, as a helper, as an opponent; and so from the very first individual psychology, in this extended but entirely justifiable sense of the words, is at the same time social psychology as well (Freud 1921/1966, p. 69).

The recent pandemic has overturned many long-standing assumptions about global relations, local realities and individual life course as a result of which prominent fractures in contemporary society have become exposed. The combination of narrow-mindedness and intolerance remains submerged under conditions of the relative safety and comfort that affluence provides. When this bubble bursts, people realized that epidemics (including political tumults) were not something that happened only to "others": the poor, the black, the uneducated or the disadvantaged. Vulnerability and uncertainty are features of the human condition.

How do we make sense of such crises? Are we adequately prepared to understand political, social and interpersonal dynamics during such moments? Is psychology equipped to address all this? Manuel Llorens confronts these issues and takes a global view while underscoring the political conflict in Venezuela.

This is not the only one reason to be proud of hosting this volume in the *Latin American Voices* books series. The incredibly important message here is that psychotherapy is neither neutral nor apolitical. Llorens, indeed, puts under scrutiny the role of psychotherapy in serving the regimes in different latitudes and, by doing so, he calls for the "*the need to be politically aware in order to protect our field and those that seek our help*" (this volume, p. XX).

In my view, there is also another reason why psychotherapy is not apolitical: because it is ontologically developmental (Mihalits and Valsiner 2020). Any psychotherapy intervention deals with transformative processes that may help people to achieve a better quality of life. What is the human horizon of such a kind of intervention? Psychotherapy, in my view, implies a tension between the person and the imagined person, framed by an ideology behind. As any educational and developmental action (Marsico 2018), psychotherapy is also value laden. No neutrality is possible! Then, a reflective and contextualized approach to liberate psychology by its self-made false myths is very much needed. I am sure the reader will find in this volume the compass to navigate these uncertain waters.

Salerno, Italy
July 2020

Giuseppina Marsico

References

Freud, S. (1966). *The standard edition of the complete psychological works of Sigmund Freud, volume XVIII (1920–1922): Beyond the pleasure principle, group psychology and other works.* London: Hogarth Press.

Guimarães D. (2020), Dialogical multiplication: Principles for an indigenous psychology, Latin American Voices, 2, São Paulo, Brazil.

Marsico, G., (2018). The challenges of the schooling from cultural psychology of education. *Integrative Psychological and Behavioural Sciences*, *52*(3), 474–489. https://doi.org/10.1007/s12124-018-9454-6

Mihalits, D. S., & Valsiner, J. (2020). Dialectics of influence: How agency works. *Human Arenas*. https://doi.org/10.1007/s42087-020-00126-6

Foreword

During the last 50 years psychologists in Latin America have been striving to respond to the needs of its communities. Within this context many European and American theories were tested and found lacking, which stimulated the development of pioneering clinical practices which helped hone new concepts and effective interventions. Despite substantial advances within the Latin American psychotherapy, most psychologists in developed countries are still unaware of this emerging literature. Manuel Llorens' book *Politically Reflective Psychotherapy: Towards a Contextualized Approach* addresses this gap by providing us with a rich psychotherapeutic model in which he shares his ideas and the clinical tools that he and his group in Caracas, Venezuela developed to work with underserved communities.

Llorens was a founder, main researcher and clinical supervisor of a new and innovative graduate program in the Universidad Católica Andrés Bello, which was designed to address the needs of the residents of *el barrio*[1] of Antímano—the second largest barrio of Caracas with almost half a million inhabitants—and nearby communities. This graduate program was founded in 1998, when Venezuela was starting to experience one of the most dramatic transformations ever experienced by any contemporary nation. Venezuela, fueled by a roaring oil industry and solid democratic institutions, was the richest country in South America and every year it welcomed thousands of immigrants from all over the world. Today, in 2020, it is the poorest country of the Southern hemisphere, and it is governed by a dictator who has a warrant for his arrest in the United States for drug trafficking. Furthermore, over 5 million people have fled Venezuela during the last 5 years. This unprecedented mass migration is the largest experienced by any South American nation. Similarly, Llorens resides in Bolivia and many of the leaders and supervisors of the graduate clinical/community program are spread throughout the globe. Other Venezuelans like myself are unable to visit Venezuela because we cannot obtain the proper legal documentation to enter the country.

[1]Barrios are slums or shanty towns similar to Favelas in Brazil in which people take discarded lands (in which it is hard or dangerous to build) and build their homes with cardboard or wood. Most families in barrios have no access to basic services, such as water, electricity or gas.

The collapse of the Venezuelan political and economic system is not only the backdrop of *Politically Reflective Psychotherapy*, but it is also a central protagonist in this powerful text. In contrast to prevalent psychotherapeutic models that assume that science is universal and independent of circumstance, *Politically Reflective Psychotherapy* shows us how psychotherapy is crafted within a historical and political context that decisively influences psychotherapeutic ideas and interventions. Throughout this text Llorens describes how transformations in the Venezuelan society translated into clinical interactions and interventions. Not to include societies' socioeconomic and political dynamics would exclude a large part of peoples' experience from the psychotherapeutic process.

Llorens explains that regardless of clinicians' levels of political awareness our actions are woven into societies' fabric and extend beyond the walls of the consulting room, and thus every clinical action is a political statement. Llorens develops and details a psychotherapeutic model that reflects and opens space to discuss the political aspects that are inevitably embedded within the psychotherapeutic process. He develops and adapts psychotherapeutic tools to evidence and review clinicians "positioning" and "the distribution of power" in the therapeutic relationship that allow us to link the interpersonal psychotherapeutic work with the wider sociopolitical and economic context. This process allows clinicians and clients to address the structural conditions that may have not been noticed. However, Llorens does so as he helps his clients learn to cope with their individual symptoms.

Llorens' clinical approach is informed by psychodynamic ideas, yet he does not subscribe to one school of thought. His ideas are also enriched by cognitive behavioral techniques, the trauma literature and narrative approaches. In addition, Latin American psychologists Ignacio Martín-Baró and community psychologist Maritza Montero are prominent influences in his work, which is also enriched by excellent writers such as Ernesto Sábato and postmodern philosophers like Foucault and Derrida. Perhaps as a result of this unique combination of ideas and a commitment to serve marginalized communities, Llorens is able to develop a rich and effective psychotherapeutic model to respond to the needs of underserved communities in Caracas, Latin America and other parts of the world.

Some clinicians living in developed countries may wonder why it is helpful to learn from a book written in a different country. Llorens explains that a broader outlook encourages us to learn from different perspectives and deepen our understanding of ourselves. A wider view furthers our ability to identify, reflect and question our preconceptions, which may have inadvertently been limiting our clinical work. Consequently, *Politically Reflective Psychotherapy* allows us to examine psychology's legacy and gives us permission to question, explore and reinvent it according to our contextual realities and the needs of our clients. An enhanced awareness allows us to increase the efficacy of our interventions. The benefits of this approach are not limited to Venezuelans or South Americans; it can enrich clinician's psychotherapies throughout the world. In addition, the rise of the Black Lives Matters movement across the United States and the world reminds us that oppression and authoritarianism are not limited to Venezuela.

Furthermore, it is crucial to learn from different cultural and geographical communities because although the United States and Europe constitute only 10% of the world's population over 95% of all psychological ideas are tested with American or European samples and written by American or European researchers. As a result, psychology remains culture-bound, restricted in its origins, concepts, methods and its findings. Current psychological understandings only represent a small and limited fraction of the world's views; nevertheless, psychotherapy purports to be universally applicable. Llorens' book transports us beyond these borders and includes the voices of many who have never even been considered in the margins of any discourse.

A third reason is that the COVID pandemic has shown how we are all inextricably interconnected. What happens in one part of the globe can sooner or later influence us and we are more productive as we work together to solve global problems. The COVID pandemic, climate change or economic inequality can only be effectively addressed by an international collaboration. However, nationalist movements are growing in strength and pushing for the construction of walls that could isolate us from others. Nationalist trends are encouraging us to isolate and to dehumanize Others. In contrast, Llorens reminds us of the richness of discovering the Other or those who are different than we are. Far from being a threat, Others have unique qualities with who we can learn and grow.

In addition to eloquently describing the main assumptions of *Politically Reflective Psychotherapy* in the first two chapters, Llorens also examines how many of the pioneers in the field of psychology were inadvertently shaped by the prevalent assumptions of their times. For example, in clear detail, Llorens describes how Sir Francis Galton's theory of intelligence ended justifying preconceived ideas of the inferiority of "colored people" which then supported societies' racist views. The field of psychology is not immune from cultural assumptions. Yet when it ignores cultural influence as when it speaks in individual and intrapsychic terms it ends up perpetuating the current political and socioeconomic establishment.

In Chaps. 3 and 4, Llorens describes some of the dangers of developing a psychotherapy that is disconnected from its cultural context. Using lively international examples he illustrates the importance of listening to patients rather than lofty ideals. Llorens describes how psychology has repeatedly been weaponized to control and harm people. Psychologists have been involved in some of the most egregious crimes in history and Llorens summarizes over 15 international cases (e.g., China, Poland and Argentina). The incidents of torture by American psychologists in Guantánamo Bay Prison demonstrate that the United States is not free from these abuses. After the terrorist attacks on the twin towers in New York City and the Pentagon in 09/11/01 a group of psychologists supported by the American Psychological Association developed strategies to interrogate and torture prisoners in a Guantánamo Bay Prison. These illegal practices were justified because it was assumed that they could prevent future terrorist attacks or decrease the number of American military fatalities.

Furthermore, the power of psychology is evident in the numerous times in which it has been employed to counter and/or disavow any criticism of governments. For example, Llorens notes how the Venezuelan dictatorship has promoted itself as a progressive movement and used ideals of social justice to persecute the same people it claims to protect. Nevertheless, thousands of homicides are executed every year by the Venezuelan national police and mass graves attest to these crimes. Furthermore, throughout these chapters Llorens poses important questions that challenge the nature of psychotherapy. For example, is it possible to conduct psychotherapy in a space in which clinicians know that their opinions are dangerous and leave them vulnerable to persecution? Is effective psychotherapy conceivable in such an environment? How can psychologists survive economically and avoid becoming an instrument of the privileged few who can afford their services? Llorens explains that an understanding of the episodes in which psychology has been used as a weapon of repression can help us identify how clinical practices can run the risk of being perverted to serve authoritarian political projects. It can also help us open up the debate about the risks of training in a craft that attempts to develop independently from its political circumstances. Llorens' descriptions highlight the possibility that psychology again and again be used as a tool for political control unless we consider the cultural context.

One of the most dramatic case examples of this text is that of Franklin Brito, who was a government dissenter who died in a Venezuelan Military Hospital after being forcefully hospitalized for alleged "psychiatric" reasons. In fact, Brito was starting to draw international attention as he led a hunger strike in front of the offices of the Organization of American States. He was declared mentally unfit and the Venezuelan attorney general forcefully interrupted his protest to "protect" his health. He was sent to the Military Hospital where mental illness was used as an excuse to incarcerate him and delegitimize his political ideas. Llorens clearly shows how psychiatric language, procedures and institutions were used as a weapon to persecute and ultimately murder Franklin Brito.

Unfortunately, psychology has been used to pathologize political dissenters on too many occasions. Psychologists are often recruited by political elites to maintain their grip on power. In these circumstances, psychologists often use the language and credibility of science to reframe social problems as "paranoid protesters" or "psychopathic masses." In this way, problems cease to be poverty, abuse of power, corruption, political differences or social injustice and become individual pathologies. As Harvard psychiatrist and trauma researcher, Judith Herman, explains, the systematic study of social injustice—just as the investigation of trauma—requires the support of political institutions. Advances in the field of psychology can only occur when they are supported by a political movement powerful enough to legitimatize alliances between clinicians and clients. Unfortunately, in the absence of strong political movements for human rights, the active process of bearing witness inevitably gives way to the active process of silence. For well-meaning and politically "neutral" mental health providers, it is challenging to continuously hear the testimonies of social injustice which often leads them to be passive. Nevertheless, clinicians remaining idle in the face of injustice helps maintain power imbalances, thereby favoring the offender.

In the last four chapters of *Politically Reflective Psychotherapy*, Llorens provides many vivid clinical examples through which he illustrates in detail the psychological interventions that he and his group have designed and adapted from different approaches. One of the first psychotherapeutic tasks when working with clients facing social injustice is to identify and name the power dynamics present within the psychotherapeutic room which are derivative of political and socioeconomic forces. The same contextual macro-forces affecting nations are also expressed interpersonally in the consulting room. However, these influences are not only acknowledged and validated but clients are also taught strategies to more effectively manage them. As clients are more successful in managing their anxiety and depressive symptoms they are more effective in transforming their lives and contexts. The specific descriptions of Llorens' clinical examples make it difficult not to feel the pain and strength of his patients and the clarity in which they are described permits them to be generalized to different contexts.

Moreover, Llorens offers a stark warning about what can happen in societies in which psychologists listen to dogmas and ideals rather than to the voices of its communities and clients. One of Llorens' patients expresses this truth in her admonition, "what happened to me can happen to you tomorrow." She had not only lost her well-paying job but also her right to vote. As many democratic institutions in developed countries are increasingly strained by the pressure of nationalist and authoritarian forces, *Politically Reflective Psychotherapy* sheds a much-needed light which will help clinicians navigate through turbulent and excruciating political times.

Politically Reflective Psychotherapy does not limit itself to describing the risks of a politically neutral psychotherapy, it is mostly a testament to our strength and resilience. We can improve even under the worst of conditions. Through Llorens' rich clinical illustrations again and again we experience how psychotherapy can become an open and intimate space, where repressed voices can speak freely. As these voices are acknowledged, they sustain personal freedom and offer hope to individuals and communities. Within the psychotherapeutic process silenced experiences are validated and bear witness to struggles that would not have otherwise been heard. Llorens' text offers support to those who have survived oppression and helps them learn how they can be empowered and transform oppressive forces. This book is a powerful tool to assist people in liberating themselves from irrational ideas and from political control. *Politically Reflective Psychotherapy* is an invitation to join this transformative dialog and continue refining a more effective psychotherapy for all.

Boston, Massachusetts

Martin La Roche, Ph.D.
Associate Professor in Psychology
Harvard Medical School
Director of Mental Health Training
Boston Children's Hospital at Martha Eliot

Preface

From Carl Rogers' efforts to bring person-centered workshops to challenge Apartheid in South Africa to the psychoanalysts who had to flee Nazi persecution, from the writings of the School of Frankfurt to psychoanalyst's activism under the Latin American dictatorships, not to mention the deliberate use of clinical terms to dismiss dissidence in the Soviet Union and China, as well as the participation of psychologists and psychotherapist in torture, as in the recent controversy regarding Guantánamo or in the prisons of Yugoslavia and Uruguay, the dilemmas psychotherapy has faced in regard to politics have been complex and controversial throughout its history.

Yet, when I trained as a clinical psychologist, reflection on our craft's history or in regard to the social and political frame in which psychotherapy operates was never brought up. Consideration about the client's or the therapist's social, economic and political history, and how they influenced the therapeutic relationship were also often disregarded. As if the specific circumstances in which psychotherapeutic theory and practice developed had been filtered to be able to show a "pure," abstract discourse, free from the contingencies of a particular context.

These silences regarding the history of our task are especially problematic considering the fact that it is an activity that pretends to open space to recover that which has been silenced and repressed. The historical recuperation of the origins and political influences of our profession, that "archaeology of silence" as Foucault (1967) has called it, has evidenced how psychotherapy is as susceptible to repression, to forget part of its history, as some of those who seek our help. The reasons why a task dedicated to the recovery and elaboration of personal history tends to forget part of its own are, of course, thought-provoking in itself. To consider the political and social circumstances that helped mold psychotherapeutic thought can protect us from the frequent dogmatism in clinical training that tends to elevate proposals developed in specific contexts to universal truths. It allows us to return to our own particular contexts and listen to it in detail, perhaps for the first time.

My clinical formation began to be challenged over its lack of social and political reflection, thanks to the work of social psychologist Martín-Baró (1986). His proposal to think and develop a psychology that could be relevant to the unresolved issues of Latin America, rather than be content importing solutions that didn't quite fit, made sense in my clinical work that worked with clients who faced poverty, social violence and the political polarization that has marked Venezuela during the last three decades. I had to deal with dilemmas that my clinical training had not prepared me for. Too often case discussions and supervisions invited us to leave those issues aside and concentrate on the "psychological" elements of the case. I found, over and over again, how the challenges posed by our historical circumstances were avoided and silenced.

This book is an attempt to engage with the provocations proposed by Martín-Baró in the field of psychotherapy. It is an effort to examine our discipline and the way it has dealt with the political dilemmas of our clients. Along the way, Latin American community psychology, Liberation Psychology and feminism, as well as postmodern paradigmatic revisions of various theories have offered resources to deal with these issues. I share some of the tools that I have found useful along the way to comprehend what happens in a psychotherapy that focuses on its context, as well as the ethical and practical dilemmas that this brings along. I do not pretend to refer to one particular school of psychotherapy as I believe these issues are relevant across theories and should be addressed on a metatheoretical level. But psychoanalysis and systemic approaches appear more prominently in the examples of the book, as they have been more present in the Latin American clinical literature.

Psychotherapy's language, settings, professionals and logic have been used and abused by many governments in order to further their causes. Latin America has been a politically complex continent and important reflections have come out of the terrible experiences faced, for example, during the dictatorships suffered in Chile, Uruguay and Argentina, as well as the civil war in El Salvador. I will examine the use of psychotherapy to persecute dissidence in different latitudes to evidence the need to be politically aware in order to protect our field and those that seek our help.

Venezuela's political hardships have produced complementary material to what psychologists wrote in regard to the impact and consequences of political repression in other Latin American countries. But the authoritarianism represented by Chavismo in Venezuela has also been different in the sense that it evolved from a personalistic, military-led, but democratically elected government that had popular backing and flourished during a spectacular oil boom, to an economic crisis of historical dimensions led by the cruel dictatorship of Nicolás Maduro. The polarization that Chavismo has produced throughout the years in and outside of Venezuela has elicited intense passions and influenced the interpretation of many events. These political conditions have impacted therapy in many ways and have been a challenge to address. Politics did not creep into the therapeutic setting in Venezuela, it blew the door open, sat down and presided it as the elephant in the room.

So I will also describe how psychology, in general, and psychotherapy, in particular, has been recruited by Chavismo's discourse to further its power and persecute dissidence. I want to record and share many of the abuses that have been greatly obscured behind government's effective propaganda, and show how the struggle to attend to the population's urgent needs has had to navigate in the midst of intense political currents.

Finally, I propose a metatheoretical frame that I believe allows the incorporation of a series of tools developed, thanks to the critiques provided by Latin American community psychology, Liberation Psychology and feminism. Clinical examples of these issues and possible ways to address them will be shared.

I wrote the original draft of this book from 2007 to 2011. A first edition was published in Venezuela in 2015, thanks to the efforts of my university, the Universidad Católica Andrés Bello and the Universidad Simón Bolívar. But the book, like so many other things, suffered the consequences of the terrible economic crisis of the decade and, after a number of years in the waiting, finally came out as an edition of only 100 copies. Although it allowed me to open conversation on these issues in a number of sites in Venezuela, it suffered a rather underground existence.

The wonderful opportunity to publish it with Springer has allowed me to revise the original edition, including some interesting material that has come out in regard to these issues in the last few years, as well as include a more detailed chronicle of what has happened in Venezuela.

Psychotherapy is an activity based on dialogue, and therefore a book on psychotherapy needs dialogue to exist. One of the harshest consequences of the political disaster in Venezuela has been the increasing isolation universities have suffered. The invitation to edit a revised edition of this book in English is an opportunity to counter this isolation and participate in a wider conversation. I believe in the power of debate to inspire thought. In that sense, the desire behind the book is to open space for conversation, rather than pretend to have the last word.

Caracas, Venezuela — Manuel Llorens

References

Foucault, M. (1967). *Historia de la locura en la poca clásica Tomo I y II*. México D.F.: Fondo de Cultura Económica.

Martín-Baró, I. (1986). Hacia una psicología de la liberación. *Boletín de Psicología, 22*, 219–231.

Acknowledgements

I want to thank all of those who have been generous enough to share their personal lives with me in the course of our psychotherapeutic encounters. Few activities can equal the amount of learning that comes from listening, day in and day out, to the most intimate, marvelous, challenging and terrifying aspects of life that therapy allows. I have been blessed to participate in a profession that has exposed me to the variety of ways that life can be lived. The capacity to listen in silence that one eventually learns is, in many ways, an act of reverence. Silence can be a way of showing respect to those who allow us to present their struggles. Their names have been omitted and changed in order to protect their identities, but the spirit of their lives inhabits this whole book and I am deeply grateful to all of them.

In second place, sitting in silence is not a sufficient condition to be able to listen. I have had the wonderful opportunity of learning my craft from psychotherapists that I admire, as well as through work with enriching colleagues. Among them I want to first thank the team of psychologists who I worked with at the Parque Social Padre Manuel Aguirre, S. J. throughout the years. That project marked my professional outlook as no other. In particular, Pedro Rodríguez, Carolina Izquiel, Juan Carlos Romero, María Alejandra Corredor, Geraldine Morillo, Alejandra Sapene, María del Valle Westinner, John Souto, Maribel Goncalves, Rubén Regardiz, Francisco Sánchez, Mikhael Iglesias, Desiree Loreto and Guillermo Sardi have all been central to these ideas. Claudia Cos, Ana Herrera, Fernando Rísquez and Marta Llorens were essential to my development in psychotherapy and life. I would also like to mention my friends and colleagues Susana Medina, Sandro Mazzucatto and Carlos Alzualde.

To resist and grow in adversity is not possible in isolation. A number of groups and organizations have helped these ideas mature. I am especially thankful to the Study Group on Psychoanalysis and Society led by Alicia Leisse and its members, Claudia Álvarez, Yone Álvarez, Carmen Elena Dos Reis, María Adela Alvarado, María Fernanda Martínez and Margot Brandi.

REACIN[2], the network of researchers and activists in favor of peaceful coexistence led by Verónica Zubillaga, has been a very important site to continue to empower resistance to government horror. Encuestas Libres, led by Miguel Ron, was another team in which I was able to continue to think and share these interests. I am very grateful to the efforts of the members of both groups.

The teams of the NGOs Profam and Plafam, the Institute of Psychology of the Universidad Central de Venezuela, the School of Psychology of the Universidad Metropolitana, the Psychiatry Service of the Hospital Universitario and Avepsi have been generous providing opportunities to expand on these debates. I was able to further my exploration on politics and psychotherapy, thanks to the time I spent at Manchester Metropolitan University. I am particularly indebted to Ian Parker and Erica Burman. I was able to discuss some of the cases and issues presented here at the Tavistock Institute in London and at a Conference of the International Society for Traumatic Stress Studies. Thanks to Linda Young and the staff at Tavistock as well as the invitation extended by Vivian Khedari and Wendy D'Andrea.

Maritza Montero's work is a very relevant influence that is evidenced throughout the book. She has been incredibly generous through the years sharing her experience and offering incredible opportunities. Her legacy has been an inspiration to many generations of psychologists in Venezuela. A big hug to her.

The School of Psychology of the Universidad Católica Andrés Bello has been my home throughout the years. I am proud to have been part of its struggle to resist oppression and to develop a university that faces the terrible challenges our country continues to offer.

Martín LaRoche and I share many common perspectives on psychology, probably influenced by our pregraduate studies at that same university in Caracas. Finding him in recent years has brought along much energy and support. I am very grateful for his contribution to this book.

Finally, Carla De Santis has been my most powerful source of inspiration and collaboration throughout the years these ideas came to light. Her love continues to allow me to grow.

[2]Red de Activismo e Investigación por la Convivencia.

Contents

Chapter 1
The Roots of a Politically Reflective Psychotherapy in the Midst of Crisis

It was the afternoon of December 6, 2002, many consultants had failed to show up for their therapy session that day. We were going through difficult days toward the end of a difficult year in Venezuela. On Monday of that week, the National Workers Federation, the Venezuelan Federation of Commercial Associations and the political parties opposing Hugo Chávez, the then President, had called for a national strike. The opinions regarding the fairness and adequacy of the strike were divided, even among those that considered themselves of the opposition. Therapists like me were suddenly faced with a dilemma. If I canceled my practice that day, the consultants identified with government would not only have to deal with the abrupt suspension of their psychotherapeutic process, but they would also probably interpret my decision as a political stance that would probably enter into the delicate balance of our psychotherapeutic relationship. At the same time, those identified with the opposition could inversely think that we shared the same political viewpoints, and that I was tacitly pronouncing my support. But not canceling sessions that day had the same amount of implications. Not canceling could be interpreted by sympathizers to the opposition as defiance of the call to strike and possibly even as an act of betrayal. Meanwhile, those identified with "chavismo" could interpret it as an act of support of the government. An act as simple as closing or continuing to provide therapy was transformed, inevitably, for every psychiatrist and psychologist in the country, as an act of political positioning, whether you wanted it or not.

In any case, I had decided to continue to work those days. I had struggled for months to try to resist the intense political polarization that the country was experiencing. I rejected the growing rigidization of thought that divided every act in a "us versus them" logic. I actively opposed government and, at the same time, was actively critical of many of the opposition's strategies.

Three blocks from my consulting room, one of the city's squares where I had walked all of my life, had turned into a central meeting point for opposition forces. A group of high-ranking military officers had defected and taken to protest against government, camping out in Plaza Altamira since May, based on the military's right to political opinion and participation, as well as their right to "civil disobedience,"

M. Llorens, *Politically Reflective Psychotherapy*, Latin American Voices,
https://doi.org/10.1007/978-3-030-57792-6_1

both of which had been written into the new National Constitution sanctioned by chavismo at the beginning of Hugo Chávez's presidency. I did not sympathize with the military, and distrusted their protest, almost as much as I disapproved Hugo Chávez's government. While I sat in my office observing events with skepticism, a few friends called and invited me to accompany a group that was going to the plaza to protest. I didn't get the chance to decide whether or not to go, when an armed man opened fire. Television cameras captured the terrible event. A man began to walk up the plaza shooting blindly against the mass, murdering 4 and injuring 20 more. The scene was terrifying. Horror had invaded the country once more.

That event and others that followed that same week escalated the conflict. On one side, passionate expressions of solidarity toward protesters who had, on countless occasions, faced violence from an authoritarian state increased. On the other, sympathizers of chavismo closed rank, distrustful of a civic movement organized around a hundred or so high-ranking military officers and a national strike led in part by the country's business elite. The political and economic crisis lasted for over a month, threatening government and leaving the population without gasoline and many basic products. The confrontations escalated on both sides. Discussions began, at the university I work at, of what position we should take as an institution. In a general assembly with students, teachers and employees, the majority voted to suspend activities. The political interpretation of our shutdown was heated and had many implications. One that was particularly relevant for my work extended to the community center that offers lower income communities, neighbor to the university, medical, psychological, educational and legal services. We decided that the center should continue open, in spite of the university shut down.

Contrary to the first impression, this book does not pretend to offer a review of the political events in Venezuela. The intention is to show how a political crisis inevitably floods psychotherapeutic space with questions, dilemmas and adaptations. It intends to explore how psychotherapy is developed in a historical and political context, even though psychology has tried to disregard this fact. It pretends also to show some of the solutions that psychotherapy has tried throughout history to answer the political questions that social context has raised, and finally, it pretends to share reflections on how, from Venezuela and Latin America, some professionals have developed alternatives to deal with these dilemmas.

The effort to organize a psychotherapeutic approach capable of facing the cultural, economic and political challenges of our specific context began in our university before these events in 2002. Since the mid-90s a team of psychologists of the Universidad Católica Andrés Bello at Caracas began to meet, train, conduct research and debate on how to develop a psychotherapy that could impact the grave social problems our country was enduring. At the beginning, these efforts were seen by our psychological community with some distance and probably condescension. Clinical psychology and psychiatry was based (and in great part continues to be) on traditional theoretical models imported from the United States and Europe. The suggestion of rethinking traditional elements of clinical work (such as the idea of a "neutral" stance imported from the medical model) was seen with apprehension.

But, in the following years, a few factors favored the possibility of challenging traditional models. Social psychology had already taken steps in that direction. Latin American social psychology had been asking essential questions about the paradigmatic and epistemological perspectives that were relevant in our context (Montero & Montenegro, 2006; Montero & Varas Díaz, 2007). Some of the answers began to circulate beyond the narrow hallways of academia and began to spark interest in clinical psychologists who were thinking on how to expand our ability to help. The growth of NGOs that began to deal with the growing difficulties in the country, and attend to human rights issues not being attended by government, was another contributing factor. They helped render visible issues such as that of street children (Llorens et al., 2005), family- and gender-based violence, sexual abuse, as well as the growing levels of poverty and violence in the country (Briceño-León, 2005). These initiatives opened space for a number of clinical psychologists to work with issues outside of the medical establishment. These spaces challenged our work and helped question our theories and practices. Our country had passed from being considered the privileged example of South America, due in great part to the oil boom of the 70s and the stability of a 40-year democracy, to a rapid increase of levels of poverty and violence, as well as the dramatic events of social protest, nationwide looting, and two coup d'etats in the 90s. Growing poverty forced the country to attend to the needs of communities that had been gravely overlooked and abandoned by previous governments.

At the beginning of that decade, members of the School of Psychology began to develop a psychotherapeutic program in marginalized sectors of Caracas. In 1998, these initiatives were organized around a Clinical Community postgraduate program where we have been able to discuss and develop ideas that are presented in this book.

But, from 2002 on, the relationship between psychotherapy and politics ceased to be an issue tackled by clinicians with interest in social issues, and became a central matter of debate to all of the psychological community. For example, in 2003, the Psychoanalytic Society of Caracas (SPC) dedicated its VII Annual Congress to the theme of psychotherapy in the midst of the social crisis. Those events allowed therapists to raise questions about the challenges made to their practice by political tensions. An illustrative debate that arose was the controversy over whether psychoanalysts should or should not attend public marches or other political manifestations. Many defended—what might seem to be an obvious stand—that psychoanalysts are citizens and therefore have the right and duty to manifest their opinion. But, doubts appeared on how to deal with possible transferential difficulties that might surface in analysis with patients that saw their analyst's public political position. Or, as mentioned earlier, how to deal with the conversations and fantasies that appeared about the motivations analysts might have when suspending sessions during a period of political unrest. A number of analysts raised the worry that their public positions might compromise some analytic relationships, threatening their professional responsibility toward their patients, which, after all, is a valid concern.

Increasingly the consulting rooms, even in the private sphere, began to be filled with people who had been affected, someway or other, by the political crisis: either they had been fired for participating in the national strike, or had been persecuted in their workplace for standing up against some governmental disposition or had felt threatened for having a political position different to their community (Goncalves, Gutiérrez & Rodríguez, 2009), or a family member had distanced him or herself based on ideological differences, or had suffered some form of post-traumatic symptomatology due to political violence or because a family member had been injured or murdered during protests, as well as a long etcetera.

Finally, the case of Franklin Brito, a dissident who died at the Military Hospital after being forcefully hospitalized because of "psychiatric" reasons, blew up in the face of the psychological establishment. Brito was leading a hunger strike in front of the OAS offices (Organization of the American States) when it was interrupted by force to "protect" his health after the nation's district attorney declared him "mentally unfit" to defend his own economic rights, in a twisted legal interpretation. He was sent to the Military Hospital where psychiatry was used as an excuse to incarcerate him. The use of psychiatric language, procedures and institutions as a weapon to persecute dissidence was fully displayed.

In short, it is not that we began to reflect on the relationships between politics and our work, but rather that politics barged into our consulting rooms and installed itself in the middle of our work. It became impossible to avoid the questions posed by our circumstances.

Yet, these questions aren't new. It is not the first time that psychology, in general, and psychotherapy, in particular, have faced a political crisis that has challenged the aspiration of being apolitical. We seem to have forgotten that the Nazi movement prohibited and burned Freud's work, pretending to develop a "non-jewish psychoanalysis," as well as pressured many analysts to expel their Jewish consultants and finally forced Freud to leave his beloved Vienna to exile himself in London. The exile of the analysts of Berlin and Vienna contributed to many political ideas going underground and disappearing from psychological debate to avoid political persecution in their countries of refuge, especially in the case of the United States, as has been shown by Jacoby (1983). The Spanish Civil War, as we shall see, left its mark on the psychiatry of its time. The work of the psychiatrist Vallejo-Nágera, who was an advisor to Dictator Francisco Franco and helped organize "psychiatric" interventions in the Spanish concentration camps, pioneered the psychiatric profession in Iberoamerica. Psychotherapy suffered significant pressure, regulations and abuse by the revolutionary movements of the Soviet Union and China, to the point of being used as a weapon of political repression. In Argentina, the military dictatorship impacted clinical practice and, in some regrettable and shameful cases, was used to torture and persecute.

In spite of the dramatic extremes of these examples, psychotherapists suffer from what Judith Herman, specialist on trauma (1997), called "episodic amnesia" in regard to these events. As a discipline we have tended to forget, sweep under our historical rug, the idiosyncratic adaptations that power has, on occasion, imposed on the exercise of our vocation. My opinion is that this amnesia, as in the case of the traumatized individual, makes it difficult to elaborate our own history and therefore avoid blindly repeating some of our mistakes. But, leaving the clinical metaphor aside, it is not reasonable to argue that trauma explains our incapacity to include the political dimension. Rather, I believe this avoidance is based on some of our deep-rooted beliefs on which our discipline has developed. It responds to the paradigmatic bases of modernity on which we built our theories and the framework of our technique. These bases, which need to be reviewed, predispose us to a "neutrality" and "apolitical" positioning that evidence its limitations only when confronted head on by the challenges of power.

Some sort of "political psychotherapy" is not the alternative, as this would be tautological. Every action that affects society, in the public and private realms, has an effect on the distribution of power, and is therefore inherently a political action. Regardless whether the clinician believes it or not, his or her actions are woven into the life of society and extend beyond the walls of the consulting room. What we need is a way to favor the development of a psychotherapy that can reflect and open space to discuss the political aspects that inevitably relate to our task: tools to evidence and review our positioning, the use of our power in the therapeutic relationship, and to allow us to articulate the relation between our interpersonal work and the wider societal context.

1.1 Interrogated by Our Context

Even the geographical location of the place where psychotherapy takes place influences the type of practice that is developed (La Roche, 2019). In our case, the university is on the southwest of Caracas. We are neighbors to many large predominantly poor neighborhoods that grow toward the peak of the hills that circle the valley of the city. During the years of tense political polarization around the figure of Hugo Chávez, the city was symbolically divided into the east, which was predominantly opposed to government and of a higher socioeconomic position, and the west, predominantly chavista and of a lower socioeconomic status.

Our psychology center began in a small office lent to us by a community school at Antímano, one of those large poor neighborhoods (called barrios in Venezuela or favelas en Brazil) that borders the university. There, we organized a psychotherapeutic service where students conducted their clinical practice. A few years on we were lucky to move to the spaces of the university's newly built community center, called the Manuel Aguirre s.j., Social Park. From there we have been able to develop a psychological service that offers psychotherapy as well as a series of community projects directly inserted in a number of neighborhoods we work with, as well as develop the clinical practice of our postgraduate program on Clinical Community Psychology.

Our center quickly began to be filled with experiences of poverty, social exclusion, lack of a social and institutional support, family and community violence, discrimination, lack of access to education, and medical and legal services.

Yet, our theoretical and technical languages continued speaking mostly in individual and intrapsychic terms. These languages were often limited in their understanding and tools to deal with the overwhelming daily experiences of our consultants, leaving them and the therapists equally frustrated.

I remember the supervision of a young clinician who had recently began to work at an extension of our unit in another poor income neighborhood called La Vega. She met with me a week after beginning her work there, deeply impressed by what she had heard. She recalled how, before her first session, she had worried about encountering cases filled with the violence she suspected was present in the community. But, in the first few days, what unexpectedly ended up impacting her the most were problems relating to hunger. She told me how, in the very first session, a young woman, deeply depressed and desperate, shared that she had not eaten for a few days because she had used the little money she had made to feed her smaller siblings and cousins who lived with her. Before starting that session the nurses that work at the center, as a gesture of welcome, happy to have a psychologist on board, brought her a cup of coffee. She had inadvertently left the cup on the desk while inviting the new consultant in. She recalled that: "when she began to tell me such a terrible story I couldn't stop thinking about the coffee waiting on my desk. During the whole session I thought about the coffee getting cold and how it was absurd not to drink it, but I wasn't about to do it while listening to her hunger, and I wasn't going to offer it to her either, worried that it might disrupt our transference relation from the start." She knew that offering the woman the coffee was not a solution for a much more complicated problem that would only serve to calm the therapist's guilt. But at the same time, to drink the coffee in front of her was not all too empathic.

This entanglement demonstrates how the work with people who suffer in harsh contexts of injustice and poverty sheds light on details of therapeutic work that most probably would pass as otherwise irrelevant in other contexts. It helps raise questions and open dilemmas that in other circumstances are less probable. A simple act, like receiving a cup of coffee and not drinking it before the start of a session had set off a series of questions such as: What is my priority as a therapist under these dire conditions? What can I offer? What are my responsibilities, and what are its limits? Is it possible to use psychotherapy to offer help in a place overwhelmed by urgent needs and, if the answer is yes, how is one to open space to do it? How does the difference in social status between the therapist and consultant influence therapy and how can those differences be addressed? How is one to reflect on all these questions without feeling despair faced with a reality that seems to surpass psychology's ability to comprehend such radically different settings?

These types of experiences have forced us to rethink ourselves. They've made us stop and reflect on many preconceptions that rest on theoretical models and traditional practices. It has led us to reach out to the wide legacy psychology offers us, but with permission to question and reinvent, so it can help us think in novel scenarios.

1.2 Poverty, Violence and Power Inside the Consulting Room

What working within poor communities also helped evidence is that politics does not only refer to the forces fighting for governmental power, but also to how power plays out in our daily lives, in economic, cultural and institutional affairs. That which, following Foucault, has been called micropolitics (Pakman, 2011).

During my clinical training at the psychiatric ward of a local university hospital (Hospital Universitario de Caracas), we had the opportunity to listen to a regional coordinator of the Health Ministry as he shared government's suggestions on how to deal with mental health issues prevalent at that time. It was 1998, Chávez had still not won the first elections that would take him to the presidency, but the social and economic crisis was already evident. The bureaucrat presented the data on the levels of poverty and unemployment. But what surprised me was that, toward the end, this spokesman of public policy, concluded that psychiatrists should prescribe more antidepressants and anxiolytics to "help" the population deal with these troubles. Even more amazing to me at the time was that nobody seemed to be shocked by the suggestion. The general impression seemed to be: "psychiatry and clinical psychology can't do much to alleviate the wider national problems like poverty, so we have no other choice but to listen to this speech in order to return as fast as possible to our world of affects, intimacy and the intrapsychic."

At the same time, the conversation evidenced a typical psychotherapeutic maneuver that ends up classifying and labeling with medical jargon, complex societal problems, directing these "disturbances" to specialists who try to "resolve" them without acknowledging the essential causes. This, as has been signaled out, serves to leave those who suffer the most in even more oppressive circumstances, often being ultimately blamed as the "problem." Based on these arguments the problem ceases to be poverty and is dissolved into "depression" or "anxiety."

One should question if those maneuvers help open space for the intimate worlds of consultants or build trenches to escape from a world with too many complexities that overwhelm us.

So, including the political and social dimension refers not only to attending to how power operates in relation to government, but also to how power plays out in all our societal relationships: in schools, jails, neighborhoods, cities, private companies, families, etc. Politics refers to the dynamics of power and how they are embedded in all the facets of our lives. In that sense, it is essential in numerous problems related to psychological hardship.

Clinical psychology and psychiatry received, toward the end of the last century, a series of critiques related to their limitations in adapting their practices to the multiple social contexts where they operate (Beltrán, 2001; Cowen, 1983; Espín, 1993; Layton, Hollander, & Gutwill, 2006; Pakman, 1997; Parker, 2007; Pérez, 1998; Sarason, 1981). Its difficulty in dealing with urgent social problems, as well as the tendency to blame, stigmatize and leave in an even more vulnerable situation those that suffer from a deprived social condition, has been evidenced. Authors such as Anthony, Cohen and Kennard (1990) have noted that resistance toward mental health services often does not have to do with the patient's limitations, but those of the services, which are not attuned to their cultural framework. Community-based mental health systems are often blind to the very parameters they seek to address.

The attempt to adapt people to our worldview and our models instead of the other way around resurfaces over and over in the work with people in poverty. A rather funny example was shared by a Peruvian psychoanalyst, Rodríguez Rabanal (1991, 1995), who wrote two books based on his experiences opening a psychoanalytic center in one of the poorer communities in Lima. In a conference in Caracas in 1996 he shared some of those difficulties:

> We built two spaces but the majority of our adult patients resisted visiting us at those spaces and instead, asked us to go to their homes, because they feared being stigmatized as mental patients by their neighbors. Those sessions were complicated because, when a therapist works in his or her consulting room, if the patient doesn't arrive, he or she can use their time reading or writing or whatever. But in our case, we had to go to the homes of our patients. So when the poor community members -and I am not referring to their material poverty here, but the fact that the had to put up with us- felt the desire to escape their appointments, they had to flee from their homes! We called it the "candadazo" (lock up) because we'd arrive at their houses at the time of the session and a great big lock would receive us at the front door. And that would happen over and over again.

Faced with different economic, cultural and political contexts, our frameworks and the application of our psychotherapeutic models can begin to unravel, and confront our taken-for-granted assumptions, as in the case of Rodríguez Rabanal's example. Traditional concepts such as "resistance" take on a different meaning when well-intentioned professionals try technical pirouettes with psychoanalytic fervor by going to consultant's homes to conduct psychoanalysis. Professionals often, challenged by realities that defy theory, insist on their worldview. In the words of Espín (1993), describing the reactions professionals have when trying to work in cultural contexts different from theirs: "the students I was training could not work with clients who did not 'believe' in therapy, whose values and life experiences did not fit their own" (p. 409). Or in the words of Cowen:

> Because mental health services had developed within a predominantly white, middle class tradition, they were for the most part packed in the frills and ribbons of that tradition, which includes fixed, pre-scheduled, fifty minute sessions, held in well-appointed offices staffed by efficient, verbally facile reception personnel. Unfortunately, since such trappings are unnatural or even alien to major segments of society, they turned off many people off prospective services before those services could ever take hold. (p. 637)

In spite of the resonating critiques that have come from different sources, academic psychology still resists the systematic inclusion of social, cultural and political variables when formulating its understandings of emotional suffering. The possibility of articulating effective solutions, sensible to those dimensions, is even farther away.

Layton et al. (2006) have compiled a series of papers by analysts who reflect on their experience dealing with political and social issues in the consulting room. Therapists share cases in which events related to 9/11 and the Iraq war appear in the therapeutic conversation. The book evidences that the circumstances in Venezuela, though critical, are not unique and that these dilemmas appear around the world.

In the chapter written by the jungian analyst Samuels, who has explored these issues in various books (1993, 2001, 2006), he reports the results of a study in which he asked 621 therapists, of 7 different countries, about the presence of political issues in therapy and how they deal with them. He found that 56% of the therapists reported discussing political themes in therapy with their clients. Samuels shares that, in the open question that was added to the scale, therapists struggled considerably to explain how they handled these issues. In other chapters, Layton, Hollander and Gutwill share clinical viñettes that illustrate the appearance of political- and social-class-related material in therapy. These examples show the amount of anxiety generated in therapists, related to their doubts as to how to respond to direct demands by clients who want to discuss political and economic positions and values. These authors have called it "psychoanalysis' last taboo." The difficulties dealing with these exchanges are evident in all the examples presented.

Hillman (2009) asks himself why, after years of teaching and supervising psychotherapy, he had helped future clinical candidates reflect on their religious beliefs, economic status, family history, ethnic roots, emotions and ideals, but not on their political convictions. That omission results worthy of analysis. The avoidance of these themes is even more dramatic in Latin American countries where political crisis have been frequent and dangerous, and where high levels of poverty are predominant.

Many of our greatest social problems such as racism, sexism, inequality, militarism, delinquency, violence and corruption stand out by their absence in clinical literature. How little input our field has offered to these problems has been pointed out by many authors (Cowen, 1983; Martín-Baró, 1986).

Empirical evidence has been accumulated demonstrating the importance of many of these problems in the etiology of mental health problems (Evans, 2004). Family violence is probably the best example. The lack of attention to the importance of child abuse in the comprehension of many clinical symptoms was signaled out by a number of specialists for a long time before it finally began to be regarded as a crucial factor. For example, John Bowlby, not so long ago, expressed:

> It seems to me that as psychoanalysts and psychotherapists we have been appallingly slow to wake up to the prevalence and far-reaching consequences of violent behaviour between members of a family, and especially the violence of parents. As a theme in analytic literature and in training programmes it has been conspicuous by its absence. Yet there is now abundant evidence not only that it is much commoner than we had hitherto supposed but that it is a major contributory cause of a number of distressing and puzzling psychiatric syndromes. Since, moreover, violence breeds violence, violence in families tends to perpetuate itself from one generation to the next.
>
> …Ever since Freud made his famous, and in my view disastrous, volte-face in 1897, when he decided that the childhood seductions he had believed to be a etiologically important were nothing more than the products of his patients' imaginations, it has been extremely unfashionable to attribute psychopathology to real-life experiences. (2005, pp. 86–87)

Specialists for over 30 years now have been able to confirm the relationship between child abuse and emotional disturbance. These studies debunked myths like the one that stated that child sexual abuse was not harmful or at least not a central etiological factor (Myers, 1992). A huge amount of research, described by Salter (1995) as an avalanche, has confirmed the relationship between child mistreatment and depression, dissociation, personality disorders, eating disorders, revictimization, sexual disorders, interpersonal problems and post-traumatic stress (Andrews, Brewin, Rose, & Kirk, 2000; Briere, 1992; Busby, Glenn, Steggell, & Adamson, 1993; Dubner & Motta, 1999; Kernberg, 2001; Stone, 1989).

Work in this area has also shown that the avoidance of the cultural and political dimension of human relationships serves to obscure many of the factors that sustain abuse. The difficulty in registering the impact of violence not only hinders the ability to deal with its consequences but also to stop it, leaving victims even more vulnerable (Moltz, 1992). Herman (1997) has expressed how perpetrators actively promote denial and forgetting. They use their power to try to silence victims and, therefore, clinicians must actively forge alliances that protect patients and work to foster a social context that helps to challenge denial.

It is interesting to note that awareness of the importance of the political dimension and the dynamics of power that influence clinical practice has come from different sources in different latitudes. In the United States, through the work of authors like Herman (1997) and van der Kolk (2014), the influence of feminism and the struggle for equal rights and work with combat veterans have contributed to evidence many of these issues. In Latin America, the political struggles, that many countries have had to face, have been crucial. For example, Jorge Barudy, a Chilean psychiatrist who has come to similar conclusions, was highly influenced by his sympathy toward the socialist government of Salvador Allende and by the political persecution he endured during the Pinochet dictatorship. He writes:

> The existence of oppressors and victims doesn't completely explain the existence of organized violence. A third party is required, the others… The third party are those members of the family and of society incapable of offering protection to victims, because for them, the fact that a mother or father can torture, neglect or sexually abuse their children is unthinkable; or simply because they fear getting involved or prefer to avoid problems; or, what is worse, because they are ideologically complicit with the perpetrators. In this group of co-producers of abuse there are still many doctors, psychologists, teachers, judges, social assistants, etc., that minimize or deny the existence of violence or are not capable of establishing the relationship with the signs of suffering and behavioral disturbances of children. Some professionals are prisoners of their theoretical models and roles and need to be helped to be able to recognize the existence of this drama. (2000, p. 24)

The absence of the analysis of the social and political dimension contributes to continue to silence the problems of the most vulnerable sectors of society, from political prisoners to children living in violent households.

A clinical discourse inevitably developed in a particular historical context, blind to the parameters of culture on which it is based, tends too easily to propose its "truths" in perfect concordance with widely shared preconceptions and social prejudices (Burman, 2000; Pérez, 1998). The feminist movement has evidenced, for example, how patriarchy underlies "scientific" arguments that equate pathology with characteristics associated with femininity, and health with those considered masculine. Freud's penus envy and Adler's masculine protest are only two of many historical examples.

So he or she who has suffered political persecution, disadvantage or oppression runs the risk of being labeled sick and sent to treatment centers to "recover." The use of medical discourse that tries to identify "pathologies" originated inside the person helps obscure the political conditions that produce suffering in the first place. When the explanation is reduced to the individual, he or she then becomes responsible for his or her recovery, without considering interventions needed to resolve the external conditions that caused the problem. Family therapist Michael White has eloquently signaled the risks of traditional clinical language and how it helps to obscure how many psychological problems are related to structures of inequality (1995).

In the same vein, Waldgrave (1990), writing in New Zealand, has argued how therapists can naively be used by the state to clean up its image and hide the consequences of governmental policy. He writes ironically signaling out how striving to make people in poverty happy without referring to their political and economic contexts is a way of working to clean up the failings of the state. Curiously enough therapists consider this work to be "neutral."

It is useful to highlight how this dominant discourse is not only found in psychological theory, but is also part of the common sense that so many of those that come to our consulting room share. In our community practice, we often find people feeling ashamed of having to deal with the difficulties of their contexts, convinced that they are, in the end, the ones to blame. Blind to the enormous efforts that they have made in their attempts to resist oppression, or feeling looked down upon for not being able to reach the expectations of achievement sustained by the same context that didn't offer opportunities to reach them.

The forces of social exclusion, like that of poverty, are demoralizing, because after denying the resources to foster development it stigmatizes those excluded signaling them out as losers, incapable of reaching culturally dominant expectations.

The tendency in Latin American countries to import undigested theoretical models and practices further enhances these simplistic interpretations. These unnegotiated applications often end up leaving professionals tangled up and feeling futile, incapable of dealing with the complex social factors that sustain much of the psychological sufferings that enter our consulting rooms.

References

Andrews, B., Brewin, C., Rose, S., & Kirk, M. (2000). Predicting PTSD symptoms in victims of violent crime: the role of shame, anger and childhood abuse. *Journal of Abnormal Psychology, 109*(1), 69–73.

Anthony, W., Cohen, M., & Kennard, W. (1990). Understanding current facts and principles of mental health systems planning. *American Psychologist, 45,* 1249–1252.

Barudy, J. (2000). *Maltrato infantil Ecología social: prevención y reparación*. Santiago de Chile: Editorial Galdoc.

Beltrán, A. (2001). La práctica psicoanalítica y el contexto actual: una situación crítica para el analista. *Actualidad Psicológica. XXVI, 293,* 10–14.

Bowlby, J. (2005). *A secure base: clinical applications of attachment theory*. London: Routledge.

Briceño-León, R. (2005). Dos décadas de violencia en Venezuela. In H. Bello (Ed.), *Violencia, criminalidad y terrorismo* (pp. 90–121). Caracas: Fundación Venezuela Positiva.

Briere, J. (1992). Methodological issues in the study of sexual abuse effects. *Journal of Consulting and Clinical Psychology, 60,* 196–203.

Burman, E. (2000). Method, measurement and madness. In L. Holzman & J. Morss (Eds.), *Postmodern psychologies, societal practice and political life* (pp. 49–78). Nueva York: Routledge.

Busby, D., Glenn, E., Steggell, G., & Adamson, D. (1993). Treatment issues for survivors of physical and sexual abuse. *Journal of Martial and Family Therapy, 19,* 377–392.

Cowen, E. (1983). Community mental health and primary prevention. In I. Weiner (Ed.), *Clinical methods in psychology* (pp. 634–696). New York: Wiley.

Dubner, A., & Motta, R. (1999). Sexually and physically abused foster care children and posttraumatic stress disorder. *Journal of Consulting and Clinical Psychology, 6,* 367–373.

Espín, O. (1993). Giving voice to silence: the psychologist as witness. *American Psychologist, 48,* 408–414.

Evans, G. (2004). The environment of childoohod poverty. *American Psychologist, 59,* 77–92. https://doi.org/10.1037/0003-066X.59.2.77.

Goncalves, M., Gutiérrez, J., & Rodríguez P. (2009). Cuando el acoso se convierte en política: análisis del acoso laboral en despedidos del sector público entre 2003–2005. *Revista Venezolana de Psicología Clínica Comunitaria., 9,* 31–56.

Herman, J. (1997). *Trauma and recovery: the aftermath of violence—from domestic abuse to political terror*. New York: Basic Books.

Hillman, J. (2009). El paciente como ciudadano. *Revista Venezolana de Psicología de los Arquetipos., 3,* 72–78.

Jacoby, R. (1983). *Repression in psychoanalysis*. Nueva York: Basic Books.

Kernberg, O. (2001). Psicoterapia focalizada en la transferencia. Psicodinámica de pacientes con organización de personalidad borderline: una visión general. *Trópicos, Revista de Psicoanálisis, IX*(1), 73–95.

La Roche, M. (2019). *Towards a global and cultural psychotherapy: theoretical foundations and clinical implications*. San Diego: Cognella.

Layton, L., Hollander, N. C., & Gutwill, S. (2006). *Psychoanalysis, class and politics: encounters in the clinical setting*. London: Routledge.

Llorens, M., Alvarado, C., Hernández, N., Jaramillo, U., Romero, M., & Souto, J. (2005). *Niños con experiencia de vida en la calle: una aproximación psicológica*. Buenos Aires: Paidós.

Martín-Baró, I. (1986). Hacia una psicología de la liberació. *Boletín de Psicología, 22,* 219–231.

Moltz, D. (1992). Abuse and violence: the dark side of family, an introduction. *Journal of Marital and Family Therapy, 18,* 223–224.

Montero, M., & Montenegro, M. (2006). Critical psychology in Venezuela. *Annual Review of Critical Psychology, 5*. www.discourseunit.com/arcp/5.

Montero, M., & Varas Díaz, N. (2007). Latin American community psychology: development, implications and challenges within a social change agenda. In S. Reich, M. Riemer, I. Prilleltensky, & M. Montero (Eds.), *International community psychology: history and theories* (pp. 63–98). New York: Springer.

Myers, J. (1992). Where are all the family therapists? Abuse and violence within the families and family therapy's response. *Journal of Marital and Family Therapy, 18,* 225–232.

Pakman, M. (1997). *Construcciones de la experiencia humana, Volumen II.* Barcelona: Gedisa.

Pakman, M. (2011). *Palabras que Permanecen, Palabras por Venir: Micropolítica y poética en psicoterapia.* Barcelona: Gedisa.

Parker, I. (2007). *Revolution in psychology: alienation to emancipation.* London: Pluto Press.

Pérez, M. (1998). La psicología clínica desde el punto de vista contextual. *Papeles del Psicólogo, 69,* 25–40.

Rodríguez Rabanal, C. (1991). *Cicatrices de la pobreza: un estudio psicoanalítico.* Caracas: Nueva Sociedad.

Rodríguez Rabanal, C. (1995). *La Violencia de las horas: un estudio psicoanalítico sobre la violencia en Perú.* Caracas: Nueva Sociedad.

Rodríguez Rabanal, C. (1996). Presentation of his book "La Violencia de las Horas" presented at the Casa del Professor de la Universidad Central de Venezuela. Caracas, July 12, 1996.

Salter, A. (1995). *Transforming trauma: a guide to understanding and treating adult survivors of child sexual abuse.* London: Sage.

Samuels, A. (1993). The political psyche. London: Routledge.

Samuels, A. (2001). *Politics on the couch: citizenship and the internal life.* London: Profile Books.

Samuels, A. (2006). Working directly with political, social and cultural material in the therapy session. In L. Layton, N. Hollander, & S. Gutwill (Eds.), *Psychoanalysis, class and politics: encounters in the clinical setting* (p. 11029). London: Routledge.

Sarason, S. (1981). An asocial psychology and a misdirected clinical psychology. *American Psychologist, 38,* 827–836.

Stone, M. (1989). Individual psychotherapy with victims of incest. *Psychiatric Clinics of North America, 12,* 237–255.

van der Kolk, B. (2014). *The body keeps the score: brain, mind and body in the healing of trauma.* New York: Penguin.

Waldgrave, C. (1990). Just therapy. *Dulwich Center Newsletter, 1,* 5–46.

White, M. (1995). *Reescribir la vida: entrevistas y ensayos.* Barcelona: Gedisa.

Chapter 2
Science and Politics: The Influence of Modernity on Psychotherapy

2.1 Science and Politics

Social crisis have historically left psychology and science, in general, dumbfounded. The great physicists of the last century took their hand to their heads horrified by the use politicians made of their developments. Robert Oppenheimer is perhaps the most dramatic figure in the history of science and politics. The physicist, director of the project that developed the atomic bomb during the Second World War, wrote in 1947, at the Massachusetts Institute of Technology:

> ...physicists have felt the peculiarly intimate responsibility for suggesting, for supporting, and in the end, in large measure, for achieving the realization of atomic weapons. Nor can we forget that these weapons, as they were in fact used, dramatized so mercilessly the inhumanity and evil of modern war. In some sort of crude sense which no vulgarity, no humor, no overstatement can quite extinguish, the physicists have known sin; and this is a knowledge which they cannot lose.

Consequently, the American government took away all the trust it had deposited in the scientist, denying him access to the information of these top secret projects. In the midst of these debates, a senator of the United States government curiously suggested that politicians should have never allowed scientists to have access to information regarding the atomic bomb (Gardner, 1986). Years later, Oppenheimer commented on his own quote, saying that when he considered that physicists had known sin, he meant "the sin of pride... We had the pride to think we knew what was good for man" (Oppenheimer as cited by Day, 2016, p. 109).

On the other side of the Iron Curtain, Andrei Sakharov, the most important physicist of the Soviet Union during the Cold War, quit the comforts of his academic life to become one of the most vocal opposition leaders against the scaling of the nuclear confrontation and the Soviet regime, for which he was persecuted and jailed. Years after retiring from his government-funded research he reflected on his involvement: "That was probably the most terrible lesson of my life. You can't sit on two chairs at once" (cited by Lizhi & Ratnesar, 1999, p. 331).

M. Llorens, *Politically Reflective Psychotherapy*, Latin American Voices,
https://doi.org/10.1007/978-3-030-57792-6_2

Ernesto Sábato, an Argentinian writer, began his adulthood as a Latin American promise in physics research, recruited to work at the Curie Laboratory in Paris and later at the Massachusetts Institute of Technology in Boston. When the Second World War precipitated, a vocational crisis led him to abandon physics and write a lucid essay on the relationship between politics and science. In 1951, he published "Hombres y Engranajes" (Men and Gears), where he develops a series of reflections that are still relevant. He records the disillusionment of a project that had promised to solve all of earth's ills. His disappointment allowed us to comprehend that science does not guarantee the future and that it needs to be accompanied by ethical and political reflection.

Modern science has stumbled time and time again with politics, in a complex and uncomfortable relationship, evidenced from the start perhaps with the Inquisition's persecution of Galileo. Some of the questions that mental health professionals are making are related to that uncomfortable and complex relationship. We ask: where should we stand as professionals at the service of human needs?

Modernity conceived science as an apolitical apparatus, objective and distanced from mundane discussions about power, able to transcend them in order to reach universal, pure truth, uncontaminated by personal or collective interests. Science had to distance itself from any suspicion of political activism. It was to be the peak of the modern ideal, representing a place of pure reason. Modern science is thought to be a universal knowledge, independent of circumstance. Scientific activity substituted religious activity as the guardian of truth and universal law, free from gods and superstition. The ideal of the modern world became science. Technology, as a consequence, promised to conquer all of man's troubles such as sickness, war and inequality. With that, the possibility of dominating nature and obtaining definite progress and the consolidation of a better world became a conceivable possibility. At the end of the nineteenth and beginning of the twentieth century, modern science offered reasons to be optimistic about the future.

2.2 Sigmund Freud

Sigmund Freud incarnated the ideals of modernity. Influenced by different discourses, some that opened doors that later helped transcend it, he repeatedly expressed his commitment to modern science. In The Future of an Illusion, he attempts to explain the roots of religious and magical thinking, as well as offering science as the option. He uses a religious metaphor to talk about "our God Logos" (1927/1983, p. 2991) and states emphatically: "No, our science is not an illusion, as it would be to think that we can obtain what it can give anywhere else" (p. 2992).

Freud clearly expressed his desire to distance himself from political events as in a telling letter sent to Marie Bonaparte in 1933 in which he tells her how fortunate she is to be able to dedicate herself to her work without having to deal with the horrible events occurring in the world. He continues:

> People fear that the German nationalist extravagances in Germany may extend to our little country. I have even been warned to flee to Switzerland or France as soon as possible. This is nonsense, I don't believe there is any danger… (2002, in Jones, cited by Stanford, p. 119)

Psychoanalysis, of course, has been systematically reviewed and debunked by positivist science and philosophers of science like Popper and Bunge (Bunge, 1985; García de la Hoz, 2000). But that doesn't mean that Freud did not aspire to develop psychoanalysis as an exact science. The contemporary hermeneutic or narrative interpretations are ours; they don't belong to Freud's project that he describes very explicitly: "psychoanalysis is a method of research, an impartial instrument, like the infinitesimal calculus" (1927/1983, p. 2981).

Quantification, physicalism and mechanism belong to the modern ideal at the beginning of the twentieth century. Scientific knowledge aimed to discover universal truths, the most exact explanation of reality, external to the observer and capable of being impartially observed. Conceived this way, a continuing approximation to a more complete truth seemed plausible, free from debate and personal perspectives. Thus, scientists could distance themselves from the world, access a privileged observation point, free from personal beliefs and points of view, convinced of contributing to the progress and welfare of humanity. Coderch (2001), a Spanish psychoanalyst, in his epistemological review of Freud, underlines how psychoanalysis was conceived as one of the many instruments devoted to controlling nature, through reason. Freud's insistence on neutrality, abstinence, anonymity and objectivity all point in that direction.

These hopes tumbled as the twentieth century advanced. With the world wars despair begins to emerge in many writings. Doubts about the benefits and the absolute universalism of science begin to creep into the original optimism. In Freud, we find moving texts in which he appears weary and shaken by senseless violence right at the moment he had expected the splendor of the future to be at its peak. In 1915, he writes:

> My conversation with the poet took place in the summer before the war. A year later the war broke out and robbed the world of its beauties. It destroyed not only the beauty of the countrysides through which it passed and the works of art which it met on its own path but it also shattered our pride in the achievements of our civilization, our admiration for many philosophers and artists and our hopes of a final triumph of the differences between nations and races. It tarnished the lofty impartiality of our science, it revealed our instincts in all our nakedness… It robbed us of very much that we had loved and showed us how ephemeral were many things we regarded as changeless. (1915/2001, p. 307)

Along with Freud's and his contemporaries' disappointment about definite progress thanks to science, the war and the collective confrontation left many perplexed and feeling futile. During the Second World War, Albert Einstein tried to gather the leading intellectuals of the time to search for answers on the challenges posed by war. He exchanged letters with Freud, who he asked: why war? To which Freud famously answered:

> As you see, little good comes of consulting a theoretician, aloof from worldly contact, on practical and urgent problems! Better it were to tackle each successive crisis with means that we have ready to our hands. (Einstein & Freud, 1933, p. 51)

Freud offers a clear example about the difficulties modern thought has dealing with developing political events. Even though he tried to offer explanations of historical phenomenona through psychoanalysis in texts such as Totem and Taboo, The Future of an Illusion, and Society and its Discontents, he barely considered the influence of the analyst's social and political position in the psychoanalytic process and was ambivalent toward various political themes (Frosh, 2007). It is particularly notorious how discreet he was expressing his position in respect to the advance of Nazism and the growing abuses he had to endure as a Jew. In a letter written toward the end of his life, a sample of his opinion on these events appears. In response to an invitation to write an article in an English journal that was preparing a special issue on antisemitism, we answered:

> I came to Vienna when I was a child of four years from a small town of Moravia. After seventy-eight years of assiduous work I had to leave my home, I saw the scientific society that I had founded dissolved, our institutions destroyed, our Printing Press taken over by the invaders, the books I had published confiscated or reduced to pulp, my children expelled from their jobs. Don't you think that you ought to reserve the columns of your special number for the utterances of non-Jewish people less personally involved than myself? (Freud, 1938/1964, p. 301)

Besides briefly listing the abuses he and his family endured, he implies that someone unaffected might be in a better position to give their opinion on the subject. This calls our attention and not only helps comprehend how a theory developed as a psychological cure, but also as a social critique kept relatively silent regarding the events of Nazi expansionism that dismantled psychoanalytic institutions. Ana Freud's expressions and her desire to expel Wilhelm Reich from the psychoanalytic association, in great part, because of the dangerous politicization that he recommended in moments where she believed it wise to be cautious are well known (Frosh, 2007). In that same line the main psychoanalytic institute in Germany kept silent when faced with absurd decisions like prohibiting Freud's name and "jewish concepts" such as the Oedipus Complex, and even worse, the persecution of jewish colleagues, even though the euphemistically renamed "Section A" continued to be constituted by freudian analysts (Totton, 2000). In interviews conducted years later, Totton reports that these analysts believed to have continued to function as psychoanalysts during the Nazi era, even though they submitted to enormous contradictions in their practice.

They didn't express doubts about continuing to function as psychoanalysts even though, for example, law demanded they salute their analysands with the Nazi greeting, a fact they were able to evade often arguing that in the therapeutic setting, personal communication was not allowed.

A curious strategy is to evade arbitrary imposition in which the fascist imposition is rejected with a technical argument. Professionals of different schools of psychotherapy have used similar arguments over and over again to avoid the political dilemmas with which history has confronted their theoretical and technical beliefs.

But voices in other disciplines began to rethink this distant and innocent version of modern science. A precursor and key text belongs to Bertrand Russell, mathematician, philosopher and recipient of the Nobel Literature Prize in 1950, who foresaw some of the dilemmas in the scientific project in his piece Icarus, or the Future of Science:

> Men sometimes speak as though the progress of science must necessarily be a boon to mankind, but that, I fear, is one of the comfortable nineteenth-century delusions which our more disillusioned age must discard. Science enables the holders of power to realize their purposes more fully than they could otherwise do. If their purposes are good, this is a gain; if they are evil, it is a loss... Therefore, at present, science does harm by increasing the power of rulers. Science is no substitute for virtue; the heart is as necessary for a good life as the head. (Russell, 1924, para. 39)

Of course, Freud wasn't the only defender of psychology as a representative of modern science. Positivist thinkers would later see Freud as a very impure expression of that ideal. Freud, located between the nineteenth and twentieth centuries, represents a unique example of the integration of romanticism of the previous times and modern thought (Gergen, 1992). His thinking is as influenced by Darwin as it is be Goethe. His efforts to translate his reflections on the contents of the romantic sensibility (dreams and passions) to physical and biological terms made his writings a controversial combination, halfway between literature and science, of the twentieth century. The reception of the Goethe Prize in 1930 underlines, during his lifetime, the debate of whether the value of his work is mainly literary or scientific.

2.3 Sir Francis Galton

Galton (1822–1911) is another key figure in the history of scientific psychology. A distant cousin of Charles Darwin he tried to take evolutionary theory and transform it into a technological proposal for the development of English society. As a passionate defender of quantification in science, he dedicated his laboratory to the measurement of physical and psychological human characteristics. He developed measurements to try to evaluate numerous variables such as auditory capacity, the level of boredom produced by speakers and intelligence (Pervin, 1996). He is a precursor to psychometry and various statistics, like the correlation coefficient, with which we work to this day. But his intentions transcended mere descriptive curiosity. Following a Darwinian logic and with the idea that intelligence was hereditary, he developed "eugenesia," a technological proposal to systematically select the most apt and therefore assure, following these beliefs, the optimal development of society.

Eugenesia would pair with the prejudices of the times to defend with a "scientific" stamp the idea that there are "superior races." Stephen Gould has done extensive research documenting how scientific discourse was used in the nineteenth century to defend racist arguments. He showed how developments in measurements of the cranium and of intelligence in the twentieth century are based on cultural conceptions that served to defend different versions of discrimination. In the introduction, he writes:

> Determinists have often invoked the traditional prestige of science as objective knowledge, free from social and political taint. They portray themselves as purveyors of harsh truth and their opponents as sentimentalists, ideologues and wishful thinkers. Louis Agassiz (1850, p. 111), defending his assignment of blacks to a separate species, wrote: 'Naturalists have a right to consider the questions growing out of men's physical relations as merely scientific questions, and to investigate them without reference to either politics or religion.' Carl Brigham (1923), arguing for the exclusion of southern and eastern European immigrants who had scored poorly on supposed tests of innate intelligence stated: 'The steps that should be taken to preserve or increase our present intellectual capacity must of course be dictated by science and not by political expediency.' And Cyril Burt, invoking faked data compiled by the nonexistent Ms. Conway, complained that doubts about the genetic foundations of IQ 'appear to be based rather on the social ideals on the subjective preferences of the critics than on any first-hand examination of the evidence supporting the opposite view' (1996, pp. 52–53).

Eugenesia soon became prominent as the ideal for wide social programs that sought to effectively select those most apt physically and psychologically to facilitate their procreation (positive eugenesia) and to avoid the reproduction of the inferior extreme (negative eugenesia). Based on the supposed existence of empirical proof that could demonstrate the intrinsic superiority of a human group, debates on supposed biologically based differences multiplied. Numerous researchers stated that there was no doubt about the superiority of white over black, man over woman and among the Europeans themselves, like Gratiolet, who said that the German brain weighed one hundred more grams on average than the French brain. Hitler used the writings of the Director of the Anthropology Institute, Kaiser Wilhelm, who wrote Human Heredity and Eugenesia, to argue in favor of "ethnic cleansing" in his "Mein Kampf." The eugenesic project was also used by famous psychiatrists to elaborate "intervention" programs in concentration camps, such as the ones used by Franco during the Spanish Civil War, as we shall see in the next chapter.

In his book, Gould shows how the idea of differences among the races and sexes was widely shared during the Enlightenment, and how, based on those ideas, scientific projects were recruited to serve those prejudices. These took advantage of the privileged place of scientific opinion to, using the words of Condorcet: "make nature herself into an accomplice of the crime of political inequality" (cited by Gould, 1996, p. 53).

The quotes of renown scientists cited by Gould evidence a wide acceptance of social stereotypes. A researcher from Paul Broca's team wrote:

> In the most intelligent races, as among the Parisians, there are a large number of women whose brains are closer in size to those of gorillas than to most developed male brains. This inferiority is so obvious that no one can contest it for a moment; only its degree is worth

> discussion. All psychologists who have studied the intelligence of women, as well as poets and novelists, recognize today that they represent the most inferior forms of human evolution and they are closer to children and savages than to an adult, civilized man. They excel in fickleness, inconstancy, absence of thought and logic and incapacity to reason. Without a doubt there exist some distinguished women, very superior to the average man, but they are as exceptional as the birth of any monstrosity, as, for example a gorilla with two heads; consequently, we may neglect them entirely (1879, pp. 60–61; as cited by Gould, 1996, pp. 136–137).

Even though the disastrous historical consequences to which these ideas of racial superiority led have made it impossible for any author to continue to position him or herself as a promoter of eugenesia, its roots continued to appear in the writings of contemporary psychologists, as in trait theory. One of the most controversial figures was Raymond Cattell (1905–1998). Infatigable researcher, and creator of numerous psychological tests, including his famous personality trait questionnaire, the 16PF (16 Personality Factor Questionnaire), he published a number of books that proposed the political applications of his scientific ideas. In one vision, which he named "Beyondism" and developed into a series of books (1987) and articles (1973), he proposed a world plan that included things like: a democratic base to evaluate desires, but a technocratic machinery to satisfy and have them administered by specialists; a ministry of evolution that directs change from above.

Toward the end of his life, after being elected to receive an award from the American Psychological Association for his lifetime achievements, controversy reappeared regarding his underlying racist thought, to which he answered:

> The world was a quite different place when I was growing up in the 1920's and 1930's. Employment, housing, and the legal system were rife with racist beliefs and practices. The statements I made in my early 20's represented the Zeitgeist of the time, reflected in writings by H. G. Wells, George Bernard Shaw, Beatrice and Stanley Webb (founders of the Labor Party), and the eminent statisticians Ronald Fisher and Karl Pearson. The events of the following decade had a major impact on my view of racism, eugenics, war, and the world.
>
> I do believe in voluntary eugenics as a means to contribute to the evolution of the human race. For example, I believe that thoughtful, concerned people (regardless of race) should be encouraged to have more children… (1997, para. 10–11)

Psychology sought to conceive and present itself as distant from political debates, as it politically positioned itself. Even the recording of its history has been compliant drawing a convenient picture that serves to defend that image. Parker (2007) underlines a revealing example when recalling how texts on the history of psychology, beginning with the classic written by Boring (1929), used Wilhelm Wundt's figure to locate the start of scientific psychology. What this version leaves out is that, besides the numerous experimental studies on perception, this researcher was also a prolific theoretician on social processes, editing ten volumes of his Volkerpsychologie or "cultural psychology." "Boring," in Parker's words "stitched together a variety of different studies to show an unbroken lineage from Wundt to modern psychology, and this meant that many of Wundt's speculations about the processes had to be filtered" (2007, p. 19). Criticism of modern science has signaled out the naive preconceptions on politics and ethics that many scientists have defended. Their moral purity has been cast in doubt.

Modern scientists believed that the scientific method assured neutrality and objectivity, just as long as they stayed away from political participation. But, as authors such as Guba and Lincoln (1989) have shown, time and time again, science has failed to be neutral. What's worse, veiling their political positions as scientific ones, has attempted to absolve them of their responsibilities.

Even the most enthusiastic defenders of positivist science have recognized the impossibility of gathering a body of neutral knowledge under a purified vision. Mario Bunge, an important Argentinean philosopher of science, who has studied the epistemological bases of psychology has dealt with trying to develop science under the influence of social forces, while sustaining the possibility of objective research. In 1996, in Ethics, Science and Technique, he opens up the debate on values in modern science and writes:

> Our issue is rigorously contemporary. Youth are questioning the morality of science in almost all parts of the world, and, although less, the nonscientific character of our present moral codes. Some criticize the alliance between science and the establishment. Others even blame science for wars, unemployment, alienation and the destruction of nature. And all complain about the fact that man reached the stars before fixing its home. In sum, no one accepts for a fact that science is good, nor that dominant ethics are wise (1996, p. 73)
>
> The educated man of our times cannot believe that truth comes from that which is Good, with capital letter, abstract and unassailable, and, on the contrary, understands that truth is valuable in itself and in conjunction with other ideals, can contribute to produce welfare, or on the contrary, destroy it.
>
> Modern man, and in first place, the scientist, knows that he is not beyond good and evil, because they are a human creation. The fact one can use scientific results in a good or bad way does not prove that scientific activity and moral codes are independent. It just proves that they are complementary and that we can pervert or blind ourselves enough so as to use truth, that is a good thing, to serve individuals or groups whose ideals are incompatible with the welfare, development of culture, peace, freedom, self government and progress of the majority. (1996, p. 42–43)

Contemporary conceptions of science have undoubtedly evolved. Not even defenders of positivist science argue about the unquestioned benefits of the scientific project. But the debate is not over. The discussion is still heated among thinkers that consider that science, being a human affaire, is inevitably situated in the social and political context, on one side, and those on the other that, recognizing the influence of social forces, consider that they are avoidable and that we should continue to strive to develop an objective science, free of those contextual influences. As a representative of the first group we can quote the psychologist Sarason, who critiques clinical psychology developed from the medical model, which has contributed to the consolidation of conceptions that consider human problems independent from their contexts. She writes:

> The substance of psychology cannot be independent of the social order. It is not that it *should not* be independent but that it *cannot* be. But American psychology has never felt

comfortable pursuing the nature and consequences of the social order. Let the other social sciences wrestle with such matters! (…)

it is almost totally lacking in the sense of social history that makes one humble before the fact that as individuals and collectivities we are inevitably prisoners of time and place, that self-interest and public interest should not be assumed to be identical, that how self-interest is defined depends on where one is in the social order, and that to transcend time and place, even in small part, requires that one put into words what the socialization process, because it was so effective, made it unnecessary to verbalize. (1981, pp. 830–831)

As an example of this ongoing debate, in 1999 and 2000, a series of articles in the American Psychologist debated on the possibility of developing a "value free" psychology (Brewer, 2000; Kendler, 1999, 2000, 2004; Sheldon, Schmuck, & Kasser, 2000).

2.4 The Debate on Modernity in Psychotherapy

Even when some of the most recognized representatives of positivist scientific thought have begun to present a more modest and contextualized view of science, many beliefs continue to entrench progress in traditional practices of production of knowledge.

Psychotherapy, heir, and in many cases directly influenced by experimental studies on human behavior, is filled with attempts to sustain the image of professionals that can defend a neutral truth, offer an objective evaluation, uninfluenced by political, economic or cultural frames. English psychotherapist, Totton (2000), recorded many of the apolitical representations of psychotherapeutic thought, as well as the psychotherapeutic theories that have explicitly dealt with the impact of power relations. He states that the image most therapists have of themselves is that of a "psycho-technician," free from the politics of their time. He offers many examples such as the following one:

Phyllis Greenacre states very clearly the traditional psychoanalytic view on therapists' involvement in politics.

The need to avoid violation of the transference field by the establishment of other avenues of relationship with the patient demands a high degree of restraint and sacrifice on the part of the analyst. It demands, among other things, the sacrifice on the part of the analyst of conspicuous public participation even in very worthy social and political 'causes' to which he may lend his name or his activities. (Greenacre, 1954, pp. 681–682)

This view depends, though, on the idea that the 'political' and the 'personal' can be safely demarcated. It embodies a sense of what politics is, and of the private individual as in some sense insulated from it, which is deeply conservative. (p. 57)

Marcelo Pakman, family therapist, reports on the efforts that therapeutic practice has made to be considered by society as a scientific activity and the consequences that it has had on the ability to reflect on politics. He makes a series of very sharp observations of the reasons why therapists have tried to distance themselves from any association to the complexities of subjectivity and social practices (1995).

In 1997, he continued to consider the effect that the effort to conceive therapy as apolitical has brought to our practice:

> Let's list some of the strategies that psychotherapists apply on a regular basis…
>
> One of them is to distance themselves from the political dimension of oppression, elevating the perceptive threshold of suffering caused by it and reducing their role to 'just doing my job', or 'do what my role demands'. It is a way of defending their professional identity defined by a training that is often dissociated from the socioeconomic and cultural context where they routinely work. The use of this solution is amplified when the therapist's training has emphasized psychological theories centered on the "internal world", compatible -or seemingly compatible- with seeing themselves or behaving as interpreters of causal factors, or any other perspective whose basic suppositions tend to disregard social interaction as a main component of mental phenomenon…
>
> Another strategy goes one step further and consists of limiting our role in terms of technique, turning into 'specialists' in a narrow field of intervention, doing tests, evaluations of dysfunctional families, or working as a secondary support to the judicial or social welfare system. In this case, we seek comfort in a role defined by other institutions, rationalizing our role as a subspeciality and supported by training programs blind to contextual parameters. (p. 252)

The therapist trained in this tradition struggles with political and social issues that enter the consulting room, with the place he or she inevitably inhabits in the social sphere and with attributes that have different weights in the distribution of power such as gender, class, ethnic origin, religion, etc.

An article by the Brazilian psychoanalyst Kemper (1992) illustrates this. It begins by reporting that one of his clients was murdered. The tragedy disturbed the analyst to the point of leading him to question some analytical premises. He pondered on the banality of discussing things such as "terminable" or "interminable" analysis "when social violence and criminality irrevocably interrupted the psychoanalytic contract and setting" (p. 130). This interruption led him to reflect on critical texts on psychoanalysis and raise various complaints on the state of his country. In the end, he reiterates an old critique stating that psychoanalysis is an elite practice, since economic realities can interrupt it. Kemper is satisfied concluding that psychoanalysis is a practice that is only possible in a context where the client has a minimum of support so that it doesn't turn into an "inaccesible luxury." He recommends analysts to never lose their neutrality and be satisfied with helping the patients that do have access to analysis, because that is the place where he or she will be able to help some to be free of neurotic symptoms and acquire a new vision of reality and society.

His article reflects clearly some of the obstacles that keeps psychoanalytic thinking stuck inside their middle-class consulting rooms, despite of the continuous challenges and questions posed by the social circumstances in Latin America. His theoretical and technical dogmatism makes him return once again to dichotomy between subjectivity and the "outer" world, to technical prescriptions of neutrality that recommend that critical observations on social reality be left out of the "therapeutic conversation," and therefore lead to prejudiced conclusions about the analyzability of lower income populations, as well as entrenchment in a limited space of the few patients that are supposed to be questioning the same social reality he struggles to leave out of analysis.

Gutwill and Hollander (2006) write about various sessions in which politics appeared. Their reflections are honest and useful. In the following case, they write about a woman who has just sabotaged a strike and her therapist avoided exploring the event and its ethical consequences further:

> I believe that my decision not to say anything constituted an enactment in response to anxiety stimulated by transgressive wishes and their inhibition. I was agitated, but wanted to be "good" and obey the psychoanalytic rule: don't politicize my patient, don't coerce her, don't talk about politics. Mary had crossed a picket line, and I had not dared to cross the psychoanalytic line. (2006, pp. 98–99)

The example clearly illustrates the implications that the psychoanalytic rule has and its influence on the therapist's disposition. Along with Greenacre's ideas, that were previously mentioned, we see how the construction of a modern professional ideal leaves analysts unprepared to face political and social dilemmas that appear in their contexts and that of their clients.

The idea that psychotherapy, as well as science, is inevitably marked by the distribution of power in society, and that the therapeutic relationship will be influenced by beliefs associated to social class, race gender and political beliefs is still seen as suspicious by the majority of practitioners. The ideals of neutrality, objectivity, apolitical positioning and universality continue to be the beliefs that occupy firm ground in our profession's conception of itself.

But in different settings these dilemmas, as well as novel answers, have begun to appear. In Latin America, social psychology as well as clinical work with victims of violence, be they political or family violence, has influenced reviews of therapeutic thinking. An event developed by the Chilean Society of Clinical Psychology (2000) titled "Violence in Culture" reflects some of those reviews that this area has brought upon the psychotherapeutic practice. It is a sample of how attention to collective problems that produce much of the emotional suffering we later see in therapy helps question and renew the psychotherapeutic practice (Vilches, 2000).

In the United States and the United Kingdom, work of various therapists has also helped to question psychotherapy. In the introduction of the book Psychoanalysis, Class and Politics (Layton, Hollander & Gutwill, 2006), which compiles the work of 14 therapists with dynamic orientation, the authors write:

> Our entrée into this subject is as psychoanalysts concerned about how events in the social domain are making their way into the clinical setting with more regularity and how they are entering into the transference/countertransference relationship. All of the book's contributors have had a keen interest for some time in what we view as the last taboo in the psychoanalytic field: namely, how to theorize the complex relationship between psychoanalysis, class, and politics and deal with its manifestations in the clinical settings. (2006, p. 1)

I think social psychologists, naturally close to the historical and social context, have left seeds with which clinical psychologists can begin to rethink our craft. Ignacio Martín-Baró, a social psychologist, who, during the civil war in El

Salvador of the 80s tried applying psychology to comprehend and influence the course of the armed confrontation, challenged psychologists in Latin America to review our theoretical bases. The clarity of his thought as well as his bravery has left a significant mark on psychology that has helped us reflect on our place, confronted with historical events. His writings made him an uncomfortable presence for the Salvadorian dictatorship that, in 1989, murdered him, along with other fellow jesuit priests. In one of his papers, he wrote:

> What has been the contribution of psychology to the development of Latin Americans? I think that, besides a few honorable exceptions, psychology and Latin American psychologists have remained on the margins of the great movements and issues that worry our people. The worse part is this marginality cannot be blamed on conformism by the part of psychologists or insensibility toward the suffering of the majority, but rather to the intrinsic impotence of our own psychological thinking. (2002, p. 73)

In spite of the fact that the majority of our psychological work is attached to modern values of science, we will see how it is also true that a wave of psychologists and psychiatrist have begun to challenge these decontextualized and presumed apolitical practices, proposing alternatives that are situated and reflective (Avissar, 2016), that attempt to offer answers to questions like those posed by Martín-Baró, and the one made by Einstein to Freud when he wrote to him asking "Why war?".

References

Avissar, N. (2016). *Psychotherapy, society and politics: from theory to practice*. New York: Palgrave MacMillan.

Boring, E. (1929). *A history of experimental psychology*. London: The Century Co.

Brewer, M. (2000). Values, politics and psychology. *American Psychologist, 55,* 1151–1152.

Bunge, M. (1985). *Teoría y Realidad*. Buenos Aires: Editorial Suramericana.

Bunge, M. (1996). *Ética, ciencia y técnica*. Buenos Aires: Editorial Suramericana.

Cattell, R. (1973). Personality pinned down. *Psychology Today*. July, 7, 40–46.

Cattell, R. (1987). *Beyondism: religion from science*. New York: Praeger Publishers.

Cattell, R. (December 13, 1997). Open letter to the APA. http://www.cattell.net/devon/openletter.htm.

Coderch, J. (2001). *La Eelación Paciente-Terapeuta: el campo del psicoanálisis y la psicoterapia psicoanalítica*. Bacelona: Paidós.

Day, M. (2016). *The hope and vision of J. Robert Oppenheimer*. London: World Scientific Publishing.

Einstein, A., & Freud, S. (1933). *Why war?*. Paris: Institute of Intellectual Cooperation, League of Nations.

Freud, S. (1915/2001). On transience. *The Standard Edition of the Complete Psychological Works of Sigmund Freud, vol. 14, 303–307.* London: Vintage.

Freud, S. (1927/1983). El porvenir de una ilusión. In *Obras Completas*. Madrid: Biblioteca Nueva.

Freud, S. (1938/1964). Anti-semitism in England. In *The standard edition of the complete works of Sigmund freud* (Vol. XXIII). London: Hogarth Press.

Frosh, S. (2007). Facing political truths. *Psychotherapy and Politics International, 5,* 29–36.

García de la Hoz, A. (2000). *Teoría Psicoanalítica*. Madrid: Quipú Biblioteca Nueva.

Gardner, M. (1986). *El Escarabajo Sagrado*. Buenos Aires: Biblioteca Científica Salvat.
Gergen, K. (1992). *El Yo Saturado: dilemas de la identidad en el mundo contemporáneo*. Barcelona: Paidós.
Gould, S. (1996). *The mismeasure of man*. New York: W. W. Norton & Company.
Greenacre, P. (1954). The role of transference—practical considerations in relation to psychoanalytic therapy. *Journal of the American Psychoanalytic Association, 2*, 671–684.
Guba, E., & Lincoln, Y. (1989). *Fourth Generation Evaluation*. London: Sage.
Gutwill, S., & Hollander, N. (2006). Class and splitting in the clinical setting: the ideological dance in the transference and the counter transference. In L. Layton, N. Hollander, & S. Gutwill (Eds.), *Psychoanalysis, class and politics: encounters in the clinical setting* (pp. 92–106). London: Routledge.
Kemper, J. (1992). Brazil: mental health in social distress? The dialectic between inner psychic and external social reality. *International Forum of Psychoanalysis, 1*, 129–135.
Kendler, H. (1999). The role of value in the world of psychology. *American Psychologist, 54*, 828–835.
Kendler, H. (2000). Let's be realistic. *American Psychologist, 55*, 1154–1155.
Kendler, H. (2004). Politics and science: a combustible mixture. *American Psychologist, 59*, 122–123.
Lizhi, F., & Ratnesar, R. (1999). Andrei Sakharov. In D. Rather & W. Issacson (Eds.), *People of the century: one hundred men and women who shaped the last one hundred years* (pp. 330–333). New York: Simon & Schuster.
Martín-Baró, I. (2002). *Psicología de la Liberación para América Latina*. Guadalajara: Universidad de Guadalajara.
Pakman, M. (1995). Investigación e intervención en grupos familiares, una perspectiva constructivista. In M. Delgado & J. Gutiérrez (Eds.), *Métodos y Técnicas Cualitativas de Investigación en Ciencias Sociales* (pp. 359–377). Madrid: Síntesis.
Pakman, M. (1997). *Construcciones de la experiencia humana Volumen II*. Barcelona: Gedisa.
Parker, I. (2007). *Revolution in psychology: alienation to emancipation*. London: Pluto Press.
Pervin, L. (1996). *La Ciencia de la Personalidad*. Madrid: McGraw-Hill.
Russell, B. (1924). Icarus, or the future of science. https://www.marxists.org/reference/subject/philosophy/works/en/russell2.htm.
Sábato, E. (1951). *Hombres y Engranajes*. Buenos Aires: Emece Editores.
Sarason, S. (1981). An asocial psychology and a misdirected clinical psychology. *American Psychologist, 38*, 827–836.
Sheldon, K., Schmuck, P., & Kasser, T. (2000). Is value-free science possible? *American Psychologist, 55*, 1152–1153.
Stanford, S. (2002). *Analyzing freud: letters of H.D., Bryher, and their circle*. New York: New Direction Press.
Totton, N. (2000). *Psychotherapy and politics*. London: Sage Publications.
Vilches, O. (2000). *Violencia en la cultura: riesgos y estrategias de intervención*. Santiago de Chile: Sociedad Chilena de Psicología Clínica.

Chapter 3
The Desire for Freedom as a Symptom: Political Abuses Around the World

It sometimes seems as though the clinical disciplines have never had to endure wars or dictatorships, or ever been the object of persecution. Herman (1997) reminds us that psychotherapy has faced the same influences as all of society and that opening spaces to hear others can sometimes be considered a dangerous activity. She also argues that there are parallels between abuse that occurs behind closed doors in the private sphere, as in the case of family violence and situations of abuse in the public sphere, as in the case of political violence. In both cases, abusers use similar strategies that include blocking access to those that can testify the existence of abuse, question the credibility of witnesses and use power to avoid the communication of clinical findings.

Parker (2007) goes further, signaling how psychology has been used to pathologize dissent as well as reduce political process to psychological reasoning, being suspicious of any collective behavior that threatens the status quo.

In its gravest forms, psychiatry and psychology have been accomplices and agents of abuse of power, being used as a weapon to discredit victims and to repress calls for justice. The psychotherapeutic task has endured persecution and submission to abusive political regimes as well as the corruption of its goals, while turning into a tool for torture and repression. Examples from around the world will be discussed. It is not a complete list, but a sufficiently extended one to evidence psychotherapy's vulnerability and how power can distort its practice.

3.1 China

It is probable that the most explicit distortion of the desire for freedom being turned into psychopathology through the use of psychological jargon has occurred in China. In regimes guided by totalitarian ideology that insist on having found the ultimate answers to the problems of human existence, any discomfort, complaint or critique is discarded as madness. A forensic psychiatric text, published in 1983 is a good example (Liu Anqiu, cited by Munro, 2002):

M. Llorens, *Politically Reflective Psychotherapy*, Latin American Voices,
https://doi.org/10.1007/978-3-030-57792-6_3

> Under the dominant influence of pathological thinking and other symptoms of psychological disease, mentally ill people may engage in behavior that sabotages the proletarian dictatorship and the socialist state. In terms of form and consequence, these acts constitute crimes of counterrevolution. The most commonly encountered pathological states involving counterrevolutionary behavior by the mentally ill are delusions of grandeur and delusions of persecution. (p. 90)

And further along it continues:

> The person concerned carries out the counterrevolutionary behavior in a brazen and flagrant manner and with no sign of scruples or misgivings. In a publicly confrontational manner, he or she will hand out leaflets in broad daylight and deliver speeches on the main road or at street corners. Naturally, some mentally ill people may act in a more covert manner than this; yet as soon as they're caught, they admit to everything quite frankly and unreservedly. (p. 92)

From the beginning of the Chinese Revolution all disciplines including psychology were reviewed and supervised. In a text that analyzes changes in Chinese psychology from 1949 to 1956, the authors (Chin & Chin, 1969) detail how all disciplines had to submit to a Marxist-Leninist revision as well as one based on Mao Tse-Tung's doctrine.

The submission of all psychological thought to political correctness in Chinese terms was gradual, reaching its peak during the Cultural Revolution that began in 1966. But some authors had already proposed changes. For example, general psychology texts should follow a certain scheme:

> The first part should show that the specific interest of psychology is the study of the development and training of communist workers, based on the differentiation of the processes of the socialist conscience. The study method should be historical materialism, as well as class analysis, presented from the point of view of the workers. Social reality, specially productive work, forms and develops the psychological organization of man and offers him the knowledge, technology, will power and conscience… The specific characteristics of the qualified communist worker were described in detail and proposed as a model for all citizens of the new China: he is a patriotic man, decided and capable of thinking, talking, acting in a qualified manner as a to-mien-shou (able to do anything), that feels love towards the party and towards labor, is respectful and confident in himself, is sociable and has revolutionary optimism, and finally has a international proletarian vision. (Chin & Chin, 1969, p. 48)

Psychopathological taxonomies were subjected to communist logic, which used psychiatric diagnoses that pathologized attitudes and behaviors contrary to the ideals proposed by the "new communist citizen." The first curious example of this can be seen in the significant increase of neurasthenia. In a study conducted in 1959 it is reported that 60% of non-hospitalized patients were diagnosed with this label. 86.7% of these patients were workers that did intellectual labor, which was considered suspect by the Chinese regime. Texts described this "pathology":

> Intellectual labor caused a "tension in the spine-brain nervous system". This did not occur because of "too much intelectual work" but because of "too little manual labor". As a cure, a great amount of intellectual workers were placed in manual labors and their condition seemed to get better. (Chin & Chin, 1969, p. 74)

Proposed treatments combined the use of drugs, group work and political harangues. In the words of the authors: "Personal optimism, considered a central element in the cure, was linked to revolutionary optimism and the task of building of socialism. National advances were exalted to increase individual revolutionary fervor" (p. 77).

There are records of explicit political persecution using psychiatry. Chen Lining, who was considered a political dissident from 1960 to 1966 and later, with the political change represented by the Cultural Revolution, came into power, reported having been qualified as a mental patient and subjected to torture through supposed therapeutic methods:

> During my political persecution at the Hunan Provincial Mental Hospital, I was subjected to numerous bouts of drug interrogation, given electroconvulsive therapy more than 40 times and insulin-coma shock therapy altogether 29 times, and was fed large quantities of chlorpromazine. They treated me like an experimental object and it was all a disguised form of physical torture. It was extremely painful, (Munro, 2002, p. 67).

After more than 15 years of ideological control of psychology, things got dramatically worse with the beginning of the Cultural Revolution. Between 1966 and 1970 all universities were shut down. University professors were sent to special institutions for their re-education and, in the words of Rubén Ardila, who writes the prologue of Chin & Chin's book: "In 1970, they returned to their previous posts convinced of the advantages of the university regime" (1969, p. 12).

Many psychiatrists were also removed from their hospital posts, labeled "bourgeois academic authorities" and sent to camps to do manual labor and to "learn from the peasants." The clinical literature was reduced to political doctrine and many psychiatric patients were re-evaluated by 1966 and passed on to the category of "political lunatics," for which they were taken to trial and forced to confess of having pretended to be ill, guilty of "counter revolutionary crimes." The majority of the patients were later jailed or executed. Official stats for that time report that 73% of the total patients in the hospitals of Shangái between 1970 and 1971 were considered "political cases." Official reports registered these tremendous distortions that affected psychiatry and psychology for ten years (Munro, 2002). Another testimony from a political prisoner recorded by a human rights organization attests:

> Summer 1969. After I was arrested as a counterrevolutionary, I was interrogated three times. I did not want to accept any charge for a crime that I had not committed, nor did I want to name any person as having committed any crime. Therefore I was sent to Jiangwan Number 5 [in Shanghai]. This place was known as the "Institute for Diagnosing Mental Disorder" —the setting of my most terrifying experiences during my entire 16 years of imprisonment.

> The whole "institute" was a large cage from within which one could not see the skies. Inside this large cage there were many small cages, which were only half as high as an average person. One could only squat or lie in them, and I had to crawl in and out of mine. They were no better than chicken houses. All those detained in the "institute" were suspected of mental disorder, but being there would truly drive a mentally normal person insane. There, one could constantly hear frightening screams. The wardens tried to stop people from screaming and, when failing to do so, would administer drugs to cause people to lose consciousness and thus become silenced. Once awakened from the drug, one felt very dull, depressed and uncomfortable.
>
> People sent to this institute were mostly those who had committed serious counter revolutionary crimes such as shouting anti-Mao slogans in public. In order to avoid sentencing of death, these people pretended to be mentally abnormal by screaming nonsense, only to be cruelly beaten and drugged. They were allowed to go out of their small cages to be "aired" once a day, and were given two meals of very thin porridge each day.
>
> Whenever the wardens appeared, I would tell them that I was not mentally disordered and that I would like to talk to them about my problems if only they would let me out of the "institute." Usually, people insisted on their lunacy in order to receive a reduced sentence. Therefore, when I very soberly proclaimed that I was normal, they truly believed me to be a madman. (Munro, 2002, pp. 77–78)

The orwellian barbarities of the Cultural Revolution returned to more common absurdities in the decade of the 80s; yet, the contamination of psychiatry and psychology persisted. In the mid-80s, the Ankang were created, known as institutes of "Peace and Health." These new centers were created for "mental patients" that were arrested by the police and later sent for psychiatric custody. A police encyclopedia, quoted by Munro (2002), lists the categories of those arrested:

> The first are those commonly known as "romantic maniacs" [hua fengzi], who roam around the streets, grab food and drink from others, expose themselves naked, or look unkempt and disheveled, and so have an adverse effect on social decorum.
>
> The second are those commonly known as "political maniacs" [zhengzhi fengzi], who shout reactionary slogans, write reactionary banners and reactionary letters, make anti government speeches in public, and express opinions on important domestic and international affairs…
>
> The taking of mentally ill people into custody is especially important during major public festivals and when foreign guests arrive for visits, and it should be appropriately reinforced at such times. (Munro, 2002, pp. 121–122)

These rather curious arguments that intend to distinguish from a "real" and a "clinical" political dissident that leads to the former being arrested and the latter sent to "treatment" have been abundant in clinical practice for over 50 years. It has led to the conclusion, in studies such as the one developed in 1972 that "the reason why most patients become mentally ill is connected to the class struggle, and the fundamental causal factor in the majority of cases is that the patients still retain a bourgeois worldview and methodology" (Munro, 2002, p. 204). These texts state, without a doubt, that the cure is to be found in the elimination of ideas that defend private property and the implementation of the ones that defend public property. Recent reports of human rights organizations show that there has been an increase in the use of political indoctrination sessions that exhort patients to cure themselves studying the works of Mao and adopting a "proletarian" political view for the treatment of mental disorders since 1996 (Munro, 2002).

This historical record was made visible in 1999 when various international scholars denounced the forced hospitalization of religious activists belonging to the Falun Gong movement. Members of this organization, that practice a version of traditional Chinese mysticism, have reported the hospitalization of more than 300 of their fellow members. This wave surged after the Falun Gong made a silent vigil in Beijing to which more than 10000 people went, making it the largest public manifestation since the events in Tiananmen Square in 1989. Among those detained and sent to hospitals, there were university professors, government officials, peasants, house workers and judges, who helped to spark a controversy in the psychiatric world (Lee, 2001; Lyons, 2001; Lyons & Munro, 2002). Three of those arrested died presumably as a direct consequence of the mistreatment received in those "mental health" institutions. A report on the extension and severity of the human rights violations against Falun Gong members lists testimonies of people who have been abused in the name of recovery. The terrible state of the mental health apparatus in China seems to persist today (Liu, 2003), even though the first law on mental health was finally proclaimed in 2013. Reports are still found of the commitment of political dissidents to psychiatric institutions (Chinese Human Rights Defenders, 2016).

3.2 Soviet Union/Russia

Psychiatry's, and, in particular, psychoanalysis' relationship with the Soviet Union was complex and varied, as Miller chronicles in his marvelous book, Freud and the Bolsheviks (2005). The first Russian contacts with Freud's work were enthusiastic. Russian was the first language to which The Interpretation of Dreams was translated (1904/1983), and the psychiatrist Nikolai Osipov was a dedicated follower of Freud, with whom he exchanged letters. In 1910, a small community of Freudians was already organized in Russia, a date in which Osipov travels to Vienna to visit Freud. But perhaps, the most notable link to Russia was that of an aristocratic Russian patient, treated initially by the celebrated psychiatrist Bekhterev, who traveled to Europe accompanied by Leonid Drosnés, founder in 1911 of the psychoanalytic society in Moscow (Angelini, 2008). He would go down in psychoanalytic history with the pseudonym of the Wolf Man, to protect his identity in Freud's case presentation (1914/1983).

The Bolshevik Revolution would change the early course of psychoanalytic development. Initially open to psychoanalysis, it would become increasingly critical of it, until finally prohibiting its practice. Osipov ended up emigrating worried about ideological persecution.

But after World War I, a group of 15 members set up a Psychoanalytic Society, which in 1922 joined the International Psychoanalytic Association. They even received support from government, publishing under the State Editorial House and for the opening of an elementary school financed by the State. In 1921, the Psychoanalytic School of Moscow, explicitly inspired by psychoanalytic thought and co-directed by Vera Schmidt and Sabrina Speilrein, was inaugurated with 30 children. In 1922, the State Institute of Psychoanalysis of the University of Moscow was founded. And in Kazan, far from Moscow, a young psychologist, later a reputed neurologist, Alexander Luria, also founded a Psychoanalytic Society. But, already in 1923, high governmental circles began to cast doubt on psychoanalytic practice. A number of debates regarding the school arose in which "the study of the social origins of child development and the problems of social classes" was recommended (Miller, 2005, p. 116). In the rest of academic psychology, the intellectual purge had begun. That same year, the director and founder of the Institute of Psychology of Moscow was dismissed. The obligation to base any psychological reflection on historical materialism began to be proclaimed by many professionals. According to Miller, what happened to psychoanalysis was similar to what happened to other areas of thought:

> To sabotage a potential rival (be it an institution, an individual or a group of ideas), delegitmize it and later incorporate it to its own benefit, became a common governmental practice. Psychoanalysis experimented one of the early waves of this assault, that would later engulf other professions. (p. 140)

Faced with pressure, most professionals tried to continue their work trying to avoid political dilemmas. That did not result in an effective strategy in the end. Even Lenin began to make public declarations against Freud's ideas, attacking them with fierce moralism with which ideology began to persecute any deviation from convention. According to Klara Zetkin's memoirs, Lenin stated:

> I mistrust those who are always absorbed in the sex problems, the way an Indian saint is absorbed in the contemplation of his navel. It seems to me that this superabundance of sex theories which for the most part are mere hypothesis, and often quite arbitrary ones, stems from a personal need. It springs from the desire to justify one's own abnormal or excessive sex life before bourgeois morality and to plead for tolerance towards oneself. This veiled respect for bourgeois morality is as repugnant to me as rooting about in all that bears on sex. (Zetkin, 1929, para. 12)

Trostky, meanwhile, had a much more open opinion and was curious about psychoanalysis. Which initially fostered some protection toward these professionals, but later, after the persecution of Trostky, left them even more exposed. The most brutal repression did not come until the 30s and produced a few curious anecdotes. Lev Vigotsky and Valentin Voloshinov (whose name is considered to be Mikhail Bakhtin's pseudonym) showed interest in psychoanalysis and published articles related to the theory (Angelini, 2008). Wilhelm Reich visited Moscow in 1929 for two months. His observations on the country were considered controversial and simplistic, not by foreign psychiatrist but to those in Moscow. Some criticized him for rendering invisible to the persecution they were being subjected to, and others for overestimating the importance of psychoanalytic activity in the country.

In 1930, during the first congress on human behavior, allegiance to the principles of historical materialism was declared (Jiménez, 1994). From this date on, not only

Freudians but also all expressions of academic psychology that diverged from marxism were persecuted. Even Pavlov was attacked for being too mechanistic. By 1927, he had resigned to his Physiology course as a result of the imposition of party members in the Academy of Science and the expulsion of some of his collaborators. Even though he maintained a tense relationship with power, he was tolerated and received financial support up until his death in 1936. But he was strongly criticized and it was not until 1950 that he was restituted for political reasons as an intellectual hero. He, who had been persecuted, was now rescued as an emblem. Even Vigotsky, probably the only one to develop a coherent theory derived from materialism, was also condemned and reconsidered only after the death of Stalin.

In the 30s, legislations regulating private life, such as marriage, divorce and abortion, began to appear. Prostitution and homosexuality were persecuted and stricter moral vigilance was established. Alexander Zalkind, who in 1928, was appointed as chairman of the Planning Commission for Pedagogical Research, part of the science directorate of the Ministry of Education, attempted to develop a Marxist-Leninist version of Freud's work. He considered that the path toward a utopian society was intertwined with the development of new sexual norms (Etkind, 2018). Zalkind twisted Freudian ideas to promote the need for stricter sexual supervision of citizens. He wrote about how desire should be geared to "the collective" rather than toward a sexual partner, how sex should be less frequent and jealousy was to disappear. He wrote a moral guide book titled "Twelve Commandments," which stated, among other things, that sex between different social classes was a type of perversion: "sexual attraction to a class-hostile, morally repugnant object is as corrupt as being sexually attracted to a crocodile or an orangutan" (Zalkind, cited by Miller, 2005, p. 160).

But even Zalkind was later persecuted for having used psychoanalysis. By 1930 publications such as one by Stoliar denounced the promoters of psychoanalysis, and a Stalinist witch hunt began (Miller, 2005).

Other historians agree that the development of psychiatry and psychology was not affected immediately after the Bolshevik Revolution of 1917 (Korolenko & Kensin, 2002). It was finally Stalin himself who completely prohibited psychoanalysis in 1936, considering it a morally depraved ideology that stimulated individualism, hedonism and a bourgeois lifestyle. Freud, Adler and Jung's books were destroyed (Totton, 2000). A direct quote from Stalin expresses the idea that the unconscious is dangerous for society because it escapes from conscious control. The fragment is a classic expression of the desires and anxieties of totalitarian scheme:

> There is nothing in the human being which cannot be verbalized. What people hide from themselves, they hide from society. There is nothing in Soivet society that cannot be expressed with words. There are no naked thoughts. There exists nothing at all except words. The unconscious doesn't exist because it is not feasible to control it through our consciousness. Everything of importance is under the control of consciousness, which means that it is under the control of society. (Stalin, 1949, cited by Korolenko & Kensin, 2002, p. 54)

Stalin's text reduces psychological process to whatever fits into political doctrine. If Soviet dogma dictates that all society is under the control of central powers, then the phenomenon of the unconscious cannot exist. In this line of ideas, the possibility that emotional disturbances exist in a perfect society is contradictory. So mental sickness had to be much less frequent in the Soviet paradise than anywhere else. This led to the conclusion stated by many psychiatric texts that alcoholism and drug addiction were non-existent in the Soviet Union. In the few cases where the existence of alcoholism was recognized, it was attributed to the remains of the capitalist mentality that continued to infect socialism (Korolenko & Kensin, 2002). Theories on psychological origin of emotional disorders were prohibited and many psychiatrists were considered dangerous and sent to be re-educated.

Idiosyncratic arguments appeared to explain dissidence. On the one hand, lack of interest in the party and the state was seen as an indicator of psychopathology and, on the other, the use of Marx's and Engels' theories to criticize government were considered cases of "philosophical intoxication," of pathological origin. A new series of labels were used to describe the different dissident thoughts, such as "reformist delusional ideas," "poor adaptation to social environment" and "over estimation of his own personality" (Bloch & Reddaway, 1985; Totton, 2000).

Between 1949 and 1965, the poet and mathematician, Alexander Volpin was hospitalized no less than five times for his political positions; his last hospitalization was a consequence of having requested a visa to visit the United States. This last event aroused the first collective protest against these practices through a petition signed by 99 of his colleagues. Yet Miller (2005) specifies that it was not until the 70s when Soviet government began to systematically use psychiatry as a weapon of psychiatric repression. The opening up of spaces for dissidence under Khruschev and the condemnation of Stalinism led to using psychiatry to conceal government persecution. The situation would deteriorate. The term "sluggish" or "slow progressive schizophrenia" was introduced by the psychiatrist and Communist Party member, Snezhnevsky, that allowed for a wide and diffuse category to label a long list of political dissenters. Among the signs and symptoms considered in the "disorder" were: euphoria, hyperactivity, optimism, irritability, explosive behavior, sensibility, infantile behavior, inadequate emotionality, hysterical reactions, dissociation, obsessive and phobic behavior. This diagnosis is cited by various authors as the most common label used to persecute dissidence (Bloch & Reddaway, 1985). Its imprecise definition allowed psychiatrists an absolute discretionality. Spencer (2000) concludes that thousands of lives were affected by the wrongful use of the label that kept stigmatized victims in psychiatric records that excluded them from possible jobs and state licenses.

Bloch and Reddaway's report concludes that those subjected to these abuses were, in majority, human rights activists, along with nationalists, potential emigrants and defenders of religious beliefs. They also state that only a small group of psychiatrists participated directly in these abuses, probably guided by ideological reasons (a quarter of doctor's study program in the Soviet Union was devoted to political themes) and as a strategy to further themselves in the state-controlled medical hierarchy. The great majority, however, participated indirectly, keeping silent and executing forced hospitalization and medication orders even while telling patients that they didn't agree with the decision. Some dissidents later reported (Bloch & Reddaway, 1985) that these doctors excused themselves telling them that it was best for all, since the option would have been sending them to jail.

In 1971, Vladimir Bukovsky, political dissident, denounced these abuses to the World Psychiatric Association. The organization decided not to suspend the USSR, alleging that it would only isolate them even more. Bukovsky passed the next seven years of his life in jail, after which he was sent to exile (Bloch & Reddaway, 1985). The continued imprisonment of political prisoners in psychiatric institutions led to a protest campaign conducted by the British delegation of the Psychiatric World Association that reached the congress of Honolulu, where these abuses were finally condemned in 1977.

In 1981, the psychiatrist Anatoly Koryagin published an article in the Lancet (Koryagin, 1981) documenting the existence of 16 special hospitals for political dissidents. In response to the article, the authorities arrested him and sentenced him to 12 years in prison. He conducted numerous hunger strikes during which he was force-fed and psychotropic drugs were administered to keep him sedated. His release and deportation was negotiated in 1983.

That same year, sensing their imminent expulsion from the World Association, Soviet representatives opted to withdraw from the organization.

These reports gradually led to a review of the improper use of psychiatry as a weapon of political repression. It wasn't until 1989 when the Soviet delegates of the World Association recognized the systematic abuse of psychiatry in their country. These discussions significantly influenced the Declaration of Honolulu and the Declaration of Madrid that delineated the ethical standards for the exercise of psychiatry in the world (Munro, 2002).

Korolenko and Kensin (2002) describe how psychiatric practice in the Soviet Union was characterized by: (1) isolation from other specialities like psychology and sociology; (2) isolation from other countries; (3) lack of control over psychiatric services; (4) reduction of knowledge in the population about mental problems; (5) use of psychiatric terminology in mass media to offend and humiliate political adversaries; (6) excessive use of psychiatric diagnosis; (7) limitation of the mental rights of the patients; (8) exploitation of psychiatric patients under the category of "occupational therapy."

Marks and Savelli (2015) quote the rather humorous anecdote of an Ukranian psychiatrist who, puzzled by the reforms proposed by Mikhail Gorbachev during glasnost, began to believe that the leader was suffering from "sluggish schizophrenia," since he seemed to be exhibiting the symptoms of reformist ideas and a struggle for truth. The authors mention the anecdote as an example of how many psychiatrists might not have used those diagnosis cynically to persecute dissidents, but rather, as a consequence of their training, really believing that those labels constitute a mental disorder.

In 1992, the director of the Serbsky psychiatric institute, Tatyana Dmitriyeva, publicly recognized the role that hospital played in those abuses. These declarations appeared related to the spirit of the times. Bukovsky, who had been labeled a "psychopath" by authorities after making his official complaints in 1971, returned to the hospital as a gesture of personal and social closure.

One would like the story to end there. But the legacies of authoritarianism often continue even after clear advances in human rights. After the ascent of Vladimir Putin to power in 2000, Dmitriyeva, who is currently a member of the government party, took back her statement of 1992 alleging that the reports of abuse had been greatly exaggerated. In 2007, Larissa Arap was interned by force in a psychiatric clinic after publishing an article in a newspaper related to Gary Kasparov's opposition movement, regarding cases of child sexual abuse in a boarding school. The report was replicated in many sources including BBC News, the Russian London Newspaper, the Chicago Tribune and La Nación de Argentina. On her release she reported to have been forcefully detained and drugged without consent. In 2013, Reuters reported that Mikhail Kosenko was arrested after protesting on the eve of Putin's inauguration of a new six-year term. The judge ruled that he committed those acts of protests in a state of insanity and sentenced him to indefinite detention and compulsory treatment in a psychiatric institution (de Carbonell, 2013). On 2017, Newsweek reported that Crimea Tartar protesters were being confined to psychiatric institutions as punishment. The head of the Independent Psychiatric Association of Russia quoted that "psychiatry is now part of frequent procedure in criminal trials where there is no concrete evidence to substantiate the charges" (Roache, 2017, para. 8).

3.3 Hungary, Poland, Yugoslavia and Czechoslovakia

Even though there are less references about the Soviet Bloc countries of Eastern Europe, recent studies have begun to emerge reporting important restrictions for research and psychotherapy practice during the years of Soviet control (Ajkay & Sipos, 2000; Kokoszka & Sitarz, 2000; Sebek, 1996). Marks (2018) details how different expressions of treatment survived either officially or undercover behind the Iron Curtain. A curious and diverse array of therapeutic experiments can be found. Versions of psychoanalysis—including a "socialist psychoanalysis," suggestion, work therapy, rational brands of therapy and even a long standing research project on the use of LSD for therapy—can be found in Hungary, Poland, Yugoslavia and Czechoslovakia.

Hungary has an interesting history led by Sandor Ferenczi in this respect, previous to Soviet occupation. As a key member of Freud's psychoanalytic inner circle, he helped to strengthen its presence in Budapest, opening the first psychoanalytic school outside of Vienna in 1913. The brief Soviet Republic of Hungary opened the doors even more for psychoanalysis in 1918. It offered Ferenczi, after years of rejection from the medical community, a post at the University of Budapest. But, the so-called White Terror that soon toppled the government expelled him from the Hungarian Medical Association after only 133 days and relegated him and many other Jews from universities. Yet Ferenczi's labor left a legacy that has been picked up by later efforts. The psychoanalytic association continued to function up to the first year of the Second World War, even though their meetings were closely monitored by the political police (Vikár, 1996). Only the Nazi invasion in 1944 prohibited meetings, and the Jewish analysts were persecuted, sent to concentration camps or murdered ipso facto. At the end of the war, the association met again, in 1949, but this time the communist party proscribed psychoanalysis in Hungary, and the persecution continued until 1956. The study of all of psychology was considered suspicious and psychotherapy as something irrelevant (Ajkay & Sipos, 2000).

The formal study of clinical psychology only begins, in great part, thanks to the efforts of Ferenc Mérei, who dedicated his life to training in psychotherapy. In 1975, the International Psychoanalytic Association (IPA) approved the membership of various Hungarian analysts and in 1989, its association regained membership to the IPA. Harmatta (1992) details the difficulties of his work as a therapist under supervision of the state. He describes a small community of analysts that, in his words, sustained the only psychoanalytic practice in the communist countries of Eastern Europe. He comments it was tolerated but continually attacked. Those that dared come in contact with psychoanalysis risked being shunned from the medical community. But, at the same time, these activities allowed the development of an "internal exile" where many intellectuals went to build alternative spaces to the dominant discourse. The author reports that he had the exceptional privilege to have access to specialized journals from abroad, attend clients and even take the phone off-the-hook during sessions.

This context generated a series of peculiarities of the therapeutic alliance, since, in part, people went to therapy to escape social control and often continued to assist after achieving considerable improvement, because of the space of freedom perceived by clients and therapists. Harmatta also comments that political themes were the main taboo, and that the majority of people, analysts and clients dissociated the political dimensions of their lives, a phenomenon that also occurred in the consulting room. Finally, he comments his reaction when one of his patients reported that he had been interrogated by the medical director of the clinic, soliciting a detailed report of what they had been doing in therapy. This event rekindled the anxieties of the client and the therapist of living under the constant scrutiny of the state.

> While I listened to the patient, I felt both tension and relief all at once. I was surprised by the sense of relief. The creepy feeling, however, that I was being observed and secretly watched, had suddenly disappeared. Now I knew I was under surveillance. (p. 135)

Harmatta decided not to introduce any complaint regarding the event. Years later he was surprised to ponder on how natural the decision to remain silent had been, knowing that filing a grievance would have been taken as defiance to authority. He decided to keep quiet and continue working as inconspicuous as possible. The anxieties reported are an example that helps reflect on the challenges totalitarian contexts exert on the therapeutic relationship.

In Poland, the Nazi and communist persecution was similar but harsher. Kokoszka and Sitarz (2000) report that 180 of 270 registered psychiatrists died during the Second World War and that psychoanalysis was prohibited afterwards. It left a legacy of backwardness and limited the possibility of research and professionalization.

A fascinating account on the treatment of drug addiction in Yugoslavia chronicles psychiatrist's reaction to the appearance of a young drug-consuming subculture in the 70s and their comprehension of it, in the midst of a Tito's socialist dictatorship (Savelli & Marks, 2015). Some psychiatrists concluded that the growing use of drugs in the late 1960s was influenced by western culture, the hippie movement and rock and roll. A prominent psychiatrist agreed with the interpretation that drug use and youth subculture was a reaction of disappointment toward western values. Curiously enough, he considered that explanation to be also true in Yugoslavia, signaling western influence as to blame for the younger generation's disillusionment, even though, according to various reports, many were sons and daughters of communist party officials.

Yugoslavia's relative independence from the Soviet Union allowed psychiatry to have much more ties to the West and avoid blatant ideological interpretations of psychological theory. Authors have recorded the use of psychoanalytic concepts in diverse settings. An idiosyncratic assimilation of these concepts to the Yugoslavian brand of socialism, which endorsed what was known as workers' self-management, is reported.

Many mental health professionals were allowed to train in the West and they brought back psychological ideas on personal freedom and self-fulfillment. Antic (2016) reports how mental health professionals were actively recruited by Yugoslav government to help build their brand of government. In their separation from Stalinist Russia, Yugoslavia adopted the idea of self-management and psychiatrists were recruited to develop re-education programs for those signaled out to be of Stalinist inclinations.

These programs, such as the ones developed in the Goli Otok prison, were brutally repressive. Goli Otok was conceived as a prison on an island designed to bring back comrades to the correct ideological path. With psychoanalytic inspiration, prisoners were pressured into confessing in minute detail any fantasy or thought in the name of "self-management." The idea was to re-educate and later incorporate the prisoners into the state, so those that seemed to progress in the program were given small roles in the conduction of the prison. There was a complex hierarchy of prisoners so that everyone participated in the "re-education" of everyone else, which in the end made everyone suspicious of everyone, breaking up any sense of possible community. If a supervisor seemed to be soft on a co-prisoner, he would also be suspicious of not advancing in his personal process. Torture accompanied other strategies and there are reports of prisoners having to walk through halls where fellow prisoners beat them with sticks. Those that did not hit hard enough were then made to walk through the hall themselves. New prisoners were welcomed by older prisoners by being beat and spit on. Those that did not seem to "improve" were subjected to exhausting physical labor and the harshest conditions possible.

Some prisoner's reports show how this system led them to feel guilty of not only having been victimized but also having participated in the victimization of others. It was a bizarre combination of "psychoanalytic" inspired personal reflection, guided by an authoritarian logic. Prisoners were subjected to group sessions where they were to revise their fantasies, dreams and confess all their "filthy hidden thoughts" (p. 190). In Antic's words:

> Goli Otok's eerie focus on self-exploration, which went hand in hand with physical torture and brutally harsh labor, made it a rather unique institution in the communist world. (p. 188)

In parallel, Antic suggests that work in consulting rooms was also influenced by the authoritarian framework. He quotes Vladislav Klajn, a proponent of "socialist psychoanalysis," who stated that analysts needed to be more "authoritative" in some cases to be able to "force active participation" (p. 189). This "analyst" was also a leading figure in the police force.

In Czechoslovakia, Sebek (1996) comments some of the difficulties confronted in regards to the clandestine practice that he and a group of fellow psychoanalysts developed under the communist regime. He describes how psychoanalysis was considered suspicious and private practice was prohibited, which is why an undercover community of practitioners emerged. He reports how anxieties surfaced in therapeutic work regarding those circumstances. They took preventive measures like keeping the network clandestine and by being careful whenever accepting a new client, avoiding those with impulsive tendencies that could put the treatment and the therapist at risk.

He reports a case when a client turned his therapist into the authorities. Besides this instance, the fears of being betrayed appeared in therapy and got intertwined with transferential issues. He mentions that certain states of confusion due to fear suffered by therapists and clients seem similar to those reported by psychoanalysts in Argentina during the dictatorships. One of the most difficult tasks, according to Sebek was to establish the ethical frames with which to sustain the analytic position. In his reflections, he uses Winnicott's concept of false self to understand some of the adaptive mechanisms that he and his compatriots used frequently to preserve a private space of thought protected from the regulations and government impositions. His experience and reflections led him to underline the importance of finding a secure space to be able to enter into therapy.

Curiously enough, psychiatric research on LSD proliferated in Czechoslovakia (Kaczorowski, 2018). In the 50s psychiatrists began experimenting with the effects of the drug on hospitalized patients and then, using it themselves. The head of the experiments Jiñ Roubíĉek invited a series of artists to express their trips visually. One of his student assistants was Stanislav Grof, who was to later pioneer research on altered states of consciousness.

A local pharmaceutical plant began producing LSD providing the substance for thousands of reported psychedelic sessions. Kaczorowski (2018) reports that, once the U.S. banned the substance, Czechoslovakia became a main source of illegal trafficking. In the 70s the country followed suite and banned the substance, but it had already made its mark and continued to be used by many of the youth's clandestine counter culture.

3.4 Germany

The Nazi experience was extreme in its many versions of horror, and clinical practice was no exception. Psychoanalysis in particular, and psychiatric practice in general, was disturbed by Hitler's ascent to power. Being Jewish, Freud's life and the history of psychoanalysis were directly influenced by those events.

After being given full power by the Reichstag in 1933, Hitler began the Nazification of all cultures. The Berlin Institute that had functioned as a pioneer of psychoanalysis, granting attention to the neediest, was put under the control of a right-wing political activist named Mathias Göring, a cousin of Herman Göring and founder of the Gestapo (Danto, 2005). The institute had served as the center of psychoanalytic development in Germany, thanks to the participation of analysts such as Otto Fenichel, Wilhelm Reich, Melanie Klein, Karen Horney, Franz Alexander, Helen Deutsch and Ernst Simmel.

When the institute entered the "leveling" process, Freud's work was banned along with concepts like the Oedipus complex (Totton, 2000). Simmel was arrested and later freed. Freud and Adler's books were burned. History reports Freud remarking "What progress we are making. In the Middle Ages they would have burned me. Now, they are content with burning my books" (cited by Gillam, 2012, p. 78).

Some authors that have chronicled these events have reported how the psychoanalytic group of the institute discreetly changed its name to "Section A" and have written that:

> Both analysts and analysands lived in potential fear of each other. Patients frequently were afraid that the analysts would betray confidences. Psychoanalysts were concerned about being denounced by their patients... it is difficult to conceive of an ongoing psychoanalysis in the setting I have briefly described (Chrzanowski, 1975, cited by Totton, 2000, p. 102).

The psychoanalyst Marie Langer (Griffiths, 2006), who was a leftist activist in Vienna during the ascent of the Third Reich, after which she escaped to join the International Medical Brigade during the Spanish Civil War, suffered personal difficulties during her psychotherapeutic practice. She left us with this moving testimony of Germany in 1934:

> ... they had arrested an analyst, when a patient that was working for the opposition was detained by the Gestapo at the entrance of his consulting room. Informed of this event, the authorities of the Wiener Vereiningung met and decided that, in order to preserve analysis, the psychoanalytic society and its members were prohibited to exercise any illegal political activity or offer therapy to anyone in that situation. This put the members of the

> Vereiningung in a conflict of loyalties, not only regarding their political ideology, if they had one, but also regarding their professional ethics. Three dead end streets were left in regard to patient activists: interrupt their treatment, prohibit them to continue with their political activity or to accept, in an implicit alliance, the continuation of the analysis, without speaking too much of the subject. I imagine that my didactic analyst decided on the last option; which I am thankful for, as well as for the fact that, a little later, we in friendly fashion terminated it (Langer, 1972, p. 260).

Langer's situation in her training institute evidences the trauma therapeutic activity was subjected to as well as the limitations to freedom of thought. Her political activity continued undercover but in 1936 she was arrested for "working in favor of peace." According to her account, a friend comments the episode in her analysis and Langer receives a "friendly" warning by the institute's didactic analysts: "I understood one had to choose between psychoanalysis and social revolution" (1972, p. 260). This episode contributed to her emigration to Spain and later to Argentina, where we will meet up with her again.

Let us not forget about Jung's participation in Nazi Germany. In 1933 he was named vice president to the General Medical Council of Psychotherapy by President Göring (Danto, 2005; Samuels, 1993). He was also the editor of the council's journal, *Zentralblatt für Psychotherapie und ihre Grenzgebiete*, that published explicit antisemitic and pronazi papers that, among other things, invited all doctors to study *Mein Kampf*. He himself published articles such as "the Aryan" in which he stated that the German unconscious had more potential than the Jewish unconscious. Jung was explicitly critical of Freud for trying to reduce the comprehension of the German people to concepts that, according to him, and referring to the sexual determinants proposed by Freud, were only relevant to the Jewish population (Masson, 1997; Samuels, 1993).

Academic psychology was soon affected by Hitler's ascent to power. The historian Mandler (2002) reports how the congress of the Psychological Society of Germany was postponed from April 1933 to October after Hitler's election as Chancellor on January of that year. In those months the society suffered important changes, mainly because of the resignation of various academics that rejected the prohibition of Jews at the congress. After these exclusions, the event had no opposition and changed the main theme, which was originally the unconscious, to the "German contemporary situation." The main presentations made numerous references to the new government and, according to Mandler, praised among other things "the great psychologist, Adolf Hitler."

Some important psychologists showed resistance, most notably Wolfgang Köhler, founder of Gestalt psychology. Faced with the requirement of giving the ritual "Heil Hitler" salute before each class, he decided to inform after each salute that it was an obligation of his post that in no way represented his agreement with the ideas it expressed. He struggled to avoid the expulsion of his Jewish colleagues, among which was Kurt Lewin. His 1933 resignation was rejected but he finally was able to resign from the university in 1935.

The most dramatic report comes from the very center of psychiatric practice. Nazism turned it, to use Danto's (2005) phrase, into the worst paranoid nightmare imaginable. Let us recall how the ideas of eugenics were central to much of the Holocaust's ideology. In his meticulous historical review, Strous (2006) details the central position of psychiatry in the mass murders committed. The first expressions of this appeared long before the Second World War. At the beginning of the Nazi regime, psychiatrist Ernst Rudin was elected president of the International Federation of Eugenics Organizations and the German Society for Racial Hygiene. He ordered for mass sterilization of those suffering from psychiatric and hereditary disturbances, reaching between 300,000 and 400,000 victims, of which 60% are calculated to have been psychiatric patients.

Then, the process of T4, which implemented massive "euthanasia" for mental patients, began. A total of 70,273 psychiatric patients were murdered in the name of racial hygiene through the program. The exact number was calculated by Strous, thanks to the medical archives that were meticulously classified by the doctors that participated in the process, which reveals that it was not an undercover operation, but rather an expression of the belief of doing what was considered to be the right thing. Some psychiatrists wrote in defense of these murders justifying them. Dr. Alfred Hoche published *Permission to Destroy Life Unworthy of Living* in 1920, stating that: "the right to life must be earned and justified, and not dogmatically assumed" (p. 33, cited by Strous, 2006). This text was widely quoted by doctors in the Nazi regime.

Among those assassinated there was a large group of children who were starved to death, because it was considered a cheaper procedure. It is important to emphasize how this cruelty cannot simply be attributed to the delusions of a small group. The murder of more than 70,000 patients required the ideological complicity as well as the passive acceptance of many hospitals and health workers. Strous reports letters of protest and decisions to avoid cooperation as examples of a few expressions of resistance. Complaints went unheard, even though there are no records of punishment for those that resisted.

The last record of horror was conducted by the psychiatrist Irmfried Eberl, infamous for heading a concentration camp. He was the director of Treblinka since it opened on 1942 and records reveal how he directly supervised the gas chambers, using a white robe in his rounds to "calm" future victims, thanks to his medical presence (Strous, 2006).

3.5 Spain

In Spain we find another notable case of psychiatric abuse. Part of its notoriety stems from the fact that its main author was Antonio Vallejo-Nájera, now known as the "Spanish Mengele," who was also one of the most reputed world psychiatrists at the time. Professor of Psychiatry at the University of Madrid after the Spanish Civil War and author of numerous texts that are classical clinical references such as Treaty on Psychiatry (1944), he conducted a series of "experiments" on war prisoners at Francoist concentration camps. During the war, Vallejo-Nájera was the director of the psychiatric services of Franco's army and worked in the concentration camp at San Pedro de Cárdena. The conditions of the camp have been described as inhumane. It has been considered a laboratory for what were later to become the Nazi concentration camps of Dachau and Buchenwald (Bandrés & Llavona, 1997).

Vallejo-Nájera proclaimed himself to be a eugenic thinker, as well as an admirer of the Inquisition and argued that Marxism, as well as ideas that questioned catholicism, had genetic and psychological roots. During the war years, he published two treatises titled: Eugenics of Hispanicity and the Regeneration of Race (1937) and Eugamia (1938). He proposed that individuals in Spanish society should be classified by caste, according to the moral quality that the person expressed during the war. At the San Pedro de Cárdena camp he worked along with German researchers trying to describe the characteristics of political enemies. The work was based on the hypothesis of a high incidence of mental weakness and antisocial psychopathy in the "political democratic-communist fanatics" (Vallejo-Nájera, 1938; cited by Bandrés & Llavona, 1997). The prisoners were subjected to a long list of measurements and psychological testing that is detailed in the report *Biopsiquismo del fanatismo marxista*. The evaluation of the prisoners formerly belonging to Abraham Lincoln National Brigade led the psychiatrist to conclude that they were people without spirituality, with histories of personal failure, alcoholism, suicidal tendencies and promiscuous sexual lives. In no place does he consider that his findings might be influenced by the fact that they were imprisoned in a concentration camp, for example, in regard to suicidal thoughts. A report on a women Spanish soldier titled *Psique of the marxist fanatic, psychological research on marxist female delinquents* evidences the use of psychological jargon to justify a long list of prejudices and stereotypes that argue about the essential weakness of women in general, considering it on par to the functioning of animals (Bandrés & Llavona, 1997).

On the basis of these "findings," Vallejo-Nájera designed programs to "transform" the Marxist fanatic, which included making them march, sing songs in favor of Franco and six-week courses on religion that the prisoners continually failed and made the teachers to repeat them over and over again. Recent testimonies have denounced that families were separated and children were given to profanquista families following the doctrine of Vallejo-Nájera (Tremlett, 2002; Vinyes, 2002).

González Duro (2008) chronicled the development of psychiatry during and after the Spanish Civil War, underlining how the franquista persecution contributed to the backwardness of the discipline slowing down the first advances it had had during the Republic.

3.6 United States

During the 50s, the CIA began a project called MK-ULTRA that destined up to 25 million dollars (Whitaker, 2000) to do research on mind control. The project was conducted by Sidney Gottlieb, an eminent psychiatrist, who presided the American and Canadian Psychiatric Association, was a prestigious professor at the University of McGill and participated as a jury in the Nuremberg Medical Tribune: Ewen Cameron. Many of the studies were done at the Allan Memorial Institute, a psychiatric hospital in Montreal. The testimonies of many of those "treated" by Cameron and the death under suspicious circumstances of one of the collaborators provoked an inquiry that detailed a long list of cruel acts and torture practiced on mental patients (Albarelli Jr., 2009).

Gottlieb explored different techniques of brainwashing with federal money in prestigious settings such as Mount Sinai Hospital, Columbia University and the University of Chicago, along with 54 colleges and universities and 12 hospitals and clinics (Whitaker, 2000). He also set up an experimental whorehouse with one-way mirrors where unsuspecting citizens were drugged and observed. Experiments with LSD, cocaine and mescaline were developed at the universities. Elsewhere, Cameron explored extravagant interview strategies (such as constantly blowing air into interviewee's eyes, sensory deprivation or making them repeatedly listen to tapes of their own recollections of their most painful memories, which he called "psychic driving"), electroshock, medication and the use of LSD to disorient patients, in order to try to provoke memory loss and implant new ideas. In the 80s, a series of civil demands opened up to the public the records of these inhumane practices that were implemented on patients that had been put in the care of Cameron (Thomas, 2001). Patients originally hospitalized for symptoms such as anxiety attacks ended up with permanent damage and vegetative functioning.

In his book documenting MK-ULTRA Thomas reports how Gottlieb financed and organized "an unprecedented system of torture," powered by doctors with shared values and financed with government funds. Many of the experiments inflicted considerable harm to patients. The program did not come into public view until 1977, thanks to an article in the NY Times. In the 80s a family of seven patients took CIA to the court and obtained a settlement.

One of the amazing facts about the MK-ULTRA affair is the amount of academic and health institutions involved, as well as the leading participation of a central figure in the psychiatric world such as Cameron. Weinstein, a psychiatrist whose father was one of the patients damaged by Cameron (quoted by Whitaker, 2000), chronicled and reflected on the gravity implications for the mental health apparatus:

> It is the silence and resistance to truth that makes us all vulnerable. I am haunted by the silence of my colleagues who worked at the Allan Memorial Institute in the 1950s and did not speak up; I am appalled by their continued silence in the 1980s when the truth emerged. Medicine has a history of engaging in evil undertakings when the motivation can be reframed so that the outcome is couched under the rubric of 'for the greater good'. (p. 285, cited by Whitaker, p. 161)

North American psychology was involved again with cloudy military affairs more recently in Guantánamo. Even though the American Psychiatric and Medical associations prohibited the participation of their members in any of the military interrogations in Guantánamo Bay Prison, built to incarcerate military enemies, the American Psychological Association (APA) resisted to do so for a few years. Finally in 2008, after years of debate, the prohibition was approved.

Psychologists were present in 2002 when the first prisoners from Afghanistan arrived at the base and later formed Behavioral Science Consultation Teams that counseled the Army on how to build rapport with the prisoners. But the reports that began to appear confirmed that some of the "techniques" included stripping a prisoner naked, injecting intravenous fluids to force them to urinate on themselves, exercising them to the point of exhaustion and making them roll over and perform dog tricks (Levine, 2007), "beatings, extreme temperature, painful forced positions, rape disguised as body searches and nudity" (Gray & Zielinski, 2006). Other reports denounced that many of the psychologists came from the SERE program (acronym for Survival, Evasion, Resistance, Escape) of the American Army designed to train soldiers to resist torture. Many of the techniques used to train American soldiers to deal with torture were then used against prisoners of Guantánamo to torture them.

Based on these accusations, a study was organized in 2005 by the APA president Ronald Levant along with Gerald Koocher, who had previously also been president of the association, as well as the editor of the journal Behavior and Ethics. The study group was suspected from the start since six out of ten researchers belonged to the Army, some of them were experts in brainwashing and interrogation techniques, including the colonel who introduced the SERE techniques in Guantánamo. Professor of Bioethics Steve Miles called the committee "a Monty Python" skit. The final report was widely criticized by the press and human rights groups because of its vagueness and the incapacity to take a stand on the acts of torture reported (Levine, 2007).

In relation to these discussions a new visit to the base was set up, this time conducted by the president of the APA, alongside the president of the American Psychiatric Association, who was invited by the Pentagon. The psychiatrists again were critical and prohibited any of its members from participating in any interrogation, while the president of the APA was more accommodating declaring that it was "an important opportunity to continue to provide our expertise and guidance for how psychologists can play an appropriate and ethical role in national security investigations" (cited by Levine, 2007).

As pressure against allowing psychologists to do these "enhanced interrogations" mounted, Koocher was quoted as saying that ethical declarations such as the Geneva Convention are "toothless protocols." He redefined the ethical imperative not as "do no harm" but only to try "do as little harm as possible" (Kimmel, 2012, p. 62).

By the end of 2008, members of the APA voted to prohibit psychologists from operating in detainee centers where international law is violated. Proof has continued to show that psychologists were central in the development, supervision and implementation of these practices specifically through a consultation team called

Mitchell, Jessen & Associates that received millions of dollars. In 2014 the Senate voted to declassify key sections of a report detailing the CIA's post 9/11 interrogation program. Mitchell and Jessen are signaled out as the masterminds of the program. Though not members of the APA, reports have identified how the APA colluded to allow psychologists to collaborate actively with these detention centers. The release of evidence has forced the APA to dismiss some of its senior members involved in the scandal (Ackerman, 2015). Mitchell has since published a defiant book where he acknowledges his involvement in interrogations and details the acts of torture that go from sleep deprivation to waterboarding (Mitchell & Harlow, 2016).

3.7 Argentina

We have been able to comprehend the consequences of the dictatorships suffered in Argentina on psychotherapeutic activity through many accounts. Various authors (Hollander, 2010; Puget, 1987; Totton, 2000) describe how analytic processes of political activists were shut down when state terror exercised by the Military Junta began to disappear and terrorized the population, not to mention the persecution of progressive psychoanalysts. Puget describes how fear and panic filtered through analytic relationships promoting corrupt pacts between analysts and analysands to not refer to political and social issues. Hollander interviewed eminent analysts who were politically engaged and described how they continued functioning with significant amounts of denial and dissociation that allowed them to downplay the threats of being targeted.

We meet up again with Marie Langer who was mentioned in the section on Germany. Emigrating to Argentina, after a stint in Spain, she became a pioneer of the psychoanalytic movement in the south, becoming one of the founders of the Argentine Psychoanalytic Association. Historical events once again placed her in the position of having to question the relationship of politics to psychoanalysis and the decisions of her colleagues.

She advocated in favor of the public positioning of the Argentine Psychoanalytic Association after the uprising called the "Cordobazo" in 1969 against the dictatorship and criticized the psychoanalytic institutions for taking distance from social events:

> If all attempt to criticize and evolve is reduced to "resistance", analysis turns into an accomplice of the establishment, adaptive in the worst sense of the word and constitutes a rationalization of the analyst's dogmatic attachment to the past and to the advantages of the status quo that the established order offers …
>
> to isolate oneself and deny social historical processes, far from representing a neutral stance (on the part of the analyst), is rather an active way of taking position… in a country in social crisis, facing events of national commotion, our shared destiny must be talked about in therapy -sometimes as an urgent issue-, along with dealing with external events regarding transferential issues and the relationship with internal objects. The omission of the social

> sphere is maintained by a unconscious complicity between the patient and the analyst, as a result of both of their resistances and counter resistances. (1972, p. 265)

She also criticizes the tendency to reduce any explanation of social events to intrapsychic variables stating that: "the psychoanalytic interpretation can complement our sociological and political comprehension, but loses its meaning if it is given in isolation" (p. 20). Like Totton she warns against psychoanalysis' tendency to interpret any reflection of political reality as a form of resistance and all activism as a form of acting out.

Hollander, who extensively interviewed Argentinian, Chilean and Uruguayan psychoanalysts who suffered during the military dictatorships (2010), and Staub (1989), who studied the Argentinian Dirty War, conclude that analysts were reduced to the position of silent witnesses even though their therapeutic practice was deeply affected. She agrees with the idea that neutrality contributed to the analyst's silence :

> This public posture existed in spite of the fact that psychoanalysts and other mental health professionals were specific targets of the military dictatorship. They were viewed as containers of their patients' secrets and thus an important source of potential information on the subversive opposition to the social order. Within this general environment of intimidation, many psychoanalysts, like the citizenry in general, withdrew defensively into an isolated social and professional life. They supported the leadership of their psychoanalytic associations, which refused to take a publicly critical position against the extreme human rights violations of the state. This stance was justified on the grounds of "professional neutrality". It was argued that psychoanalysis was a scientific enterprise, a profession whose study and treatment of psychic reality needed to be separate from social and political activities and pressures. (2006, p. 157)

Hollander also chronicled the experiences of those brave analysts that, against the current, were vocal in challenging the psychoanalytic institution, advocating in favor of a much more active exchange with the social sphere, leading to the formation of the group "Plataforma" that broke off from the Argentinean Psychoanalytic Association in 1971. These analysts questioned technical dogmatism, published a collection of their reflections under the title "Cuestionamos" (we question) and created Research and Training Centers that formed students in clinical and social theory. As the authoritarian military governments turned into hardline dictatorship with the coup d'etat of 1976, many of these analysts were signaled out as radicals with ties to student activists, having many of them to flee the country.

One of the first to flee was Marie Langer who appeared on the Argentine Anticommunist Alliance's death list in 1974. Others struggled to continue their work in an increasingly threatening atmosphere. Hollander (2010) writes about an analyst whose 18-year-old son was tortured and murdered and of another prominent analyst who had to jump out of a window and barely escaped arrest.

Puget (1987) also records the impact of the dictatorship on therapeutic relations. She states that denial was the most frequent response for those who were not directly targeted. She also reflects on the ways individuals adapted, along with the impacts it had on couples and groups. She mentions, for example, how in groups, members who were active dissidents were often silenced or isolated as if "contaminated." In her own words, she stated:

> The practice of psychoanalysis in a period of social commotion caused by state terrorism creates grave difficulties. I propose the following hypothesis: we eliminate certain representations related to the social reality from our perceptual field, which leads to misinterpretations of materials related to it. In some cases this was because we declared ourselves impotent or "without theory" to comprehend it. In other cases, failure was more directly linked to fear. In other words we pushed this material aside using a certain type of rationalization that justified our failure as an excuse. (p. 29)

Jacques Derrida gave a conference on the human rights abuses committed during the last Argentinean dictatorship, criticizing the timid proclamation of the psychoanalytic society that had intended to make a complaint. He referred to bulletin 144 of the International Psychoanalytic Association (IPA) and the declarations given during the thirty-first Congress of the IPA in New York. Those declarations pretended to take a stance regarding the human rights abuses that were happening in Argentina and the impact it was having on psychoanalytic practice there. The association declared its opposition to "the use of psychiatric and psychotherapeutic methods to deprive individuals of their legitimate freedom; to an individual receiving psychiatric or psychotherapeutic treatment based on political considerations; to the interference with professional confidentiality for political purposes" (cited by Derrida & Nicholson-Smith, 1991, p. 201). But the philosopher criticized the declaration because of its timidness and vagueness, a declaration that avoided mentioning Argentina explicitly:

> Under given conditions, once a protocol has been established, naming can become a historical and political act, responsibility for whose performance is inescapable. This responsibility that the IPA has ducked at a particularly grave moment in history -the history of psychoanalysis included. Henceforward, should psychoanalysis wish to take the measure of what is happening in Latin America, to measure itself against the state of affairs down there reveals, to respond to what threatens, limits, defines, disfigures or exposes it, then it will be necessary, at least, to do some naming. This is the first requirement for an appeal: a call to call that which has a name by its name (1991, p. 231).

Through his remark, Derrida, without being a psychoanalyst seemed to have put his finger on psychoanalysis' anxiety facing these types of dilemmas. He goes beyond his criticism of the document mentioning that it is symptomatic of the relationship between psychoanalysis and politics.

> … the less psychoanalytical and ethical-political discourses become integrated in the strict sense of which I refer, the easier it is for some apparatuses to integrate or appropriate others -for political or police agencies to manipulate the psychoanalytical sphere, for the powers of psychoanalysis to be abused, and so forth.
>
> The implications of this overwhelming fact, though overlapping, may be said to fall into three types.
>
> The first type concerns the neutralization of ethics and of the political realm, an utter dissociation of the psychoanalytical sphere from the sphere of citizen or moral subject in his or her public or private life. Why deny that this fracture line runs through our entire experience, sometimes clearly visible, sometimes less so, affecting all our judgements large

> or small, every day, and every instant; and this whether we are analysts ourselves or merely non-analysts concerned about psychoanalysis? This incredible dissociation is one of the most monstrous characteristics of the *homo psychoanalyticus* of our time. It is a ghastly deformity which gives us the aspect of mutants; sometimes it is terrifying, sometimes comical, and sometimes both at once. (p. 214–215)

He also criticized psychoanalysis for not contributing its tools to think and discuss about the collective problems that not only affect coexistence, but often, as in the case of Argentina, deeply affect the discipline.

Totton (2000) quotes Jimenez (1989) on similar difficulties that also appeared when working as an analyst under Pinochet's dictatorship. This author mentions how the sociopolitical reality operated as a counter transferential weight and how he made efforts to take distance from historical events in order to open space up for therapy. Kernberg (1998) makes similar remarks when he mentions the debates that appeared in the psychoanalytic society in Chile during Allende's government.

Political events have not ceased to "invade" the tranquility not only of Argentina, but of all Latin America. Psychoanalyst Silvia Bleichmar, more recently wrote *Dolor País* (2002), exhorting all professionals, especially academics, to take active political positions. Referring to universities after many years as a professor in Argentina and Spain, she criticized the tendency to increasingly organize training on technical considerations that are distanced from the social context.

3.8 Uruguay

In her interviews, Hollander (2010) chronicles how the 60s represented a fertile moment for the integration of medical, psychological and social scientific considerations in an exciting atmosphere of social transformation in Uruguay. But a coup in 1973 brought a dramatic stop to those possibilities.

Cajigas Segredo (2002) mentions that, during the dictatorship that lasted from 1973 to 1984, even though a group of psychologists were committed to resist oppression, others collaborated. University professors were fired because they were considered a threat to government, and private universities were pressured into developing a technocratic program to substitute a university involved with society. The teaching of psychoanalysis was relegated and considered subversive as behaviorism was imposed.

Quoting reports of the Red Cross, Cajigas Segredo describes how psychology was systematically implemented in Uruguayan prisons as a tool to intimidate political prisoners. A prison cynically named Libertad (Freedom) was expressly designed with the input of psychologists to increase prisoner's suffering. Stover and Nightingale (1985) confirm through two prisoner testimonies that a psychologist and a psychiatrist were among those conducting torture. A Red Cross visit confirmed that prisoners were subjected to administration of drugs as well as social and sensory deprivation to produce profound distress.

Prisoner testimonies report how they were received by psychologists at their entrance to the prison and then subjected to abuse using the same taped conversations they had had with the professionals. Any form of privacy was eliminated and prisoners were only called by numbers or insults and never by their names. It was prohibited to be touched, not even during family visits. They were not allowed to sit or lie down except when sleeping, so prisoners had to pass all day standing up. Family visits were supervised and any expression of affection was prohibited. If this happened the prisoners were punished with months of solitary confinement and had their visits suspended.

3.9 Brazil

Villela (1998) writes about the complicity of psychoanalytic institutions and the dictatorships of the 60s and 70s. Slightly different from the experience in Argentina and Uruguay, the author argues that, in Brazil, psychoanalysis had continued to be a practice limited to the elites. This circumstance might have contributed to the incredible succession of events that occurred in relation to an analyst that belonged to the torture squadrons of the political police.

Villela signals how an article written by Marie Langer in 1973 in the journal *Cuestionamos* is the first reference to the issue. The author reveals how doctor Amílcar Lobo worked with the army on teams whose task was to obtain information from political prisoners. Lobo was a candidate of the Psychoanalytic Society of Río de Janeiro. He simultaneously worked at the Casa de la Muerte (House of Death) in Petrópolis under the nickname Carneiro. The most ironic fact of the whole ordeal is that he was an analytic patient of the society's president Dr. Cabernite. It was later known that the case was made public, thanks to the anonymous denouncement made by Helena Besserman who sent a letter to the IPA. The president promptly denied all accusations, the society defended itself as neutral in respect to the political circumstances and the IPA president accepted the denial. A graphological study of the anonymous letter was made and Besserman scolded, having her full membership to the psychoanalytic society delayed. In a public conference in 1980 two other analysts mentioned the issue, as a result both were expelled from the Río de Janeiro Psychoanalytic Society.

The case remained unresolved for almost a decade when the dictatorship finally fell. In 1986, Helena Besserman and one of the expelled analysts brought victims of Lobo to the society's annual meeting where they testified on the analyst's active participation in their torture. In 1989, Amílcar Lobo wrote a rather apologetic autobiography where he confesses his crimes. In various newspaper interviews he excuses himself saying that his task as a physician was to avoid the prisoners from dying after the torture sessions (Villela, 1998). The psychoanalytic society did not offer any public apology until 1986 and Cabernite's license was finally revoked in 1992, almost 20 years after the affair.

Curiously enough Cabernite had been analyzed and trained by Werner Kemper, a German psychoanalyst who had been an active member of the "aryanized" Berlin Institute during the Nazi regime. In 1948, with the support of Ernest Jones, he moved with his wife, also a psychoanalyst, to become Rio de Janeiro's first training analyst (Russo, 2012).

In 1995, the International Psychoanalytic Society finally discussed the investigations that confirmed Lobo's participation in acts of torture without producing any sanction.

These events transcend the silence that quietly accepts an abusive state and refers to active complicity during state terror. Events like this demand to reflect on the beliefs and practices that contribute to maintain the silence of professionals whose main task is to work against the forces of repression and forgetting.

3.10 Cuba

In 1979, the American Psychologist published an article written by the director of a national group of psychology of the Health Ministry of Cuba. The text was a result of a visit to the island made that same year by psychologists of the American Psychological Association (García, 1979). It tries to show the characteristics of cuban psychology at that time resulting in an interesting portrait for what it shows as well as what it conceals. The author, one of the first psychologists who graduated at the University of La Habana after the revolution, chronicles the creation of the first schools of psychology in 1962 and the development of professional activities sponsored by the state: 40% of the 700 registered psychologists were working for the Ministry of Health. The theoretical orientations are hard to pinpoint, so the author mentions that "western psychotherapies (including those psychoanalytically inspired, systemic and behaviorist theory) are being analyzed from a Marxist-Leninist perspective to design intervention techniques adapted to the conditions of Cubans and their new ideology" (p. 1092). Even though the new ideology already was 20 years in power, the theoretical results of those analysis are not mentioned. What is mentioned repeatedly are the few psychological problems that the author considers to be present in the country. Some behavioral problems "that are generally not severe" (p. 1093) in childhood are mentioned, along with "exceptional" cases of delinquency, child abuse, autism, to complete a rather curious list. The author emphasizes that "drug problems are inexistent" (p. 1093). The techniques used are also hard to fathom, even though the modification of ideas, values, attitudes and behaviors is mentioned, which sounds a lot like indoctrination. "Sports therapy" is used often with the youth that need to develop the capacity for team work and build trust among themselves. The article does not present one reference in regard to these practices and the cases of the use of psychiatry and psychology to persecute political dissidents are completely absent.

A later article (Bernal, 1985) refers to García's text and adds that by 1980 there were 350 registered psychologists on the island, with particular growth in the area of health and school psychology. He also mentions the lack of doctoral level psychologists that was beginning to be attended to with a few candidates that had continued their studies in the Soviet Union and the German Democratic Republic. The most distinguished psychologist mentioned is Fernando González Rey who made relevant contributions to the field of personality psychology and moral development. The author also mentions that western and North American psychology are rarely used, which evidences backwardness in relation to methodology and recent developments in the rest of the world.

González Rey (1995) writes a much more complete version of the development of psychology during the Cuban Revolution. He recalls how the study of psychology in the 60s, which he called a period of "necessary dogmatism," was undoubtedly influenced by a search for a Marxist interpretation and the visit of prominent Soviet professors. But still, he considers that the group of professors of the school of psychology of the University of Havana were able to work with a certain amount of freedom. In the 80s, González Rey and other prominent Cuban psychologists were allowed to attend the meetings of the Sociedad Interamericana de Psicología (Interamerican Society of Psychology) and begin to establish links to Latin American critical perspectives, which led to the development of the society's congress in Havana in 1987. In his perspective, psychology was fertile and creative up to the 90s when more conservative representatives of the party impose the new university dean with a more orthodox and rigid direction and many of his generation of professors, including him, abandon Cuba. Confessing his deep identification with the ideals of the Revolution he recognizes the terrible influence of an omnipotent state on the functioning of academic institutions, as well as the flagrant persecution of anyone accused of "ideological deviation." He lived the rest of his life in Brazil.

In 1991 Vladimir Bukovsky, the Soviet psychiatrist that had denounced the psychiatric abuses in the Soviet Union, published a book that documents the abuses in Cuba, establishing comparisons. Even though there are many similarities regarding the use of psychiatric institutions and strategies to persecute and torture political dissidents, he mentions that Cuba advanced to abuse with much more speed and less restraint. They didn't seem to feel the need to invent new diagnosis as many of the cases of torture never received a clinical diagnosis (Bukovsky, 1991). The process of publicly denouncing the abuses in Cuba has been even harder than in the USSR since the country retired from the World Psychiatric Association in 1983 as a measure of solidarity to the complaints made against the Soviet Union.

Brown and Lago (1991) collect the reports of NGOs like Amnesty International and Human Rights Watch, as well as the testimony of 30 Cubans that denounced having been tortured in psychiatric hospitals after being detained for political reasons. The center signaled out is the Havana Psychiatric Hospital, specifically in the Cabó-Serviá and Castellanos ward. The interviewees reported of having been arrested for political reasons and then taken to the hospital without any explanation and without receiving any information on how long they will be deprived of their freedom. Incarcerated in stacked halls with psychotic patients and criminal population, there are repeated reports of rapes and beatings, either by other patients or by the nurses, the use of electroconvulsive therapy without the use of anesthesia, the use of psychoactive medication to keep prisoners sedated and disoriented, as well as floors filled with excrements and trash that no one cleaned up. During the visit, Amnesty International investigated these reports, and they were allowed to visit the Cabó-Serviá ward, but the Castellanos ward was said to non-exist in spite of the numerous patients whose hospital registers confirmed had been inpatients there. Amnesty International reported to have been surprised about the precarious conditions of the psychiatric wards in comparison with other hospital installations that seemed new and well kept (Amnesty International, 1988).

Robert Bahamonde was one of the cases investigated by Brown and Lago (1991). He was an educator and agronomer at the University of Havana, who participated in the Cuban Commission of Human Rights and National Reconciliation. His political activism in Cuba as a critic earned him numerous arrests. The first was in 1971 after writing a letter to Fidel Castro in which he suggested the use of material incentives to better the production at the plantation where he worked. He was "hospitalized" a number of times in the before mentioned psychiatric ward.

Another case refers to the psychiatrist Samuel Martínez Lara who graduated in Cuba but conducted postgraduate studies at the University of Berkeley in California. In 1982, the chief of State Security in the hospital he worked at (Calixto García Hospital) asked him to show a medical history of one of his patients. When Martínez failed to comply to his request, he was arrested and accused of having been recruited by the CIA during his stay in California. In 1987, he started an undercover publication and was co-founder of the Cuban Party for Human Rights. In 1989, he was arrested and accused of being "dangerous to socialist society" and having "contempt toward Fidel Castro." He was convicted to conditional freedom until the next year when he was arrested again and transferred to the Havana Psychiatric Hospital; during his trial two psychiatrists testified to having diagnosed him with a "psychopathic personality disorder." In 1991, he was expelled from Cuba.

José Luis Delgado was 18 when he tried to obtain asylum in the Embassy of Colombia in Cuba. He was arrested and sent to a psychiatric hospital where he was threatened with rape and beatings, was subjected to many electroconvulsive therapy sessions without anesthesia and heavily drugged with psychotropic drugs. After which he was convicted and sent to prison for six years. Once he was released, he gave an interview to a reporter from the international agency, Reuters, sharing his experience and that of other political prisoners he met while in jail. He was arrested again and sent to solitary confinement in a cell known as the "rectangle of death" for 18 months. In April of 1989 he was finally able to escape the island.

Trying to recollect the history of psychology in Cuba we meet again with Marie Langer. In the special volume of the English journal Free Associations (Puget, 1989) dedicated to her work, her visits to the island are mentioned. Puget describes how in 1985, during a meeting of intellectuals in Havana, Fidel Castro ordered his Minister of Health to get in contact with Langer to "introduce psychoanalysis officially in Cuba, 'I want some of that here'" (p. 41). The anecdote is revealing in many ways. It evidences the absence of psychoanalysis until that point, but perhaps even more dramatic, the arbitrary imposition of authoritarian opinion as opposed to academic debate. It wasn't through exchange of researchers or any other professional means, but through Castro's whim that psychoanalysis arrived in Cuba.

Rossiter, Walsh-Bowers and Prilleltensky (2002) were able to speak to 28 Cuban mental health workers as part of a comparative study between the ethical squemes underlying the profession in Cuba and Canada. The focus of the paper was the exploration of the weight of the historical context in the construction of the ethics of the discipline and the demonstration of the important differences that an ethical perspective can have from one context to the other. But the working conditions of the psychologists in Cuba are also evidenced. The article, in general, tries to sympathize with the Cuban situation, praising in various moments the collective conception of work and the reports of the professionals that explain their work through Cuban communist rhetoric such as "we are a society that is rooted in a Marxist-Leninist ideology… I think this also helps us to promote these values" (2002, p. 542). But the strict vigilance of the professionals and their fear is evident in the interviews. The authors recognize that the interviews are affected because open dialogue was interrupted by the pressure to adapt. They also mention:

> There was some indication that judgements about adherence to the values of the revolution interact with hierarchies in employment contexts (i.e. bosses or supervisors) in ways that heighten the perception of risk involved in speaking openly… Indeed we were constantly aware in our interviews of the possibility of putting our respondents at risk by encouraging them to be open. (p. 545)

The article, along with a contemporary record of the strict supervision that mental health professionals are subjected to in Cuba, is a telling sample of how external observers eager to find in Cuba an option to capitalists systems deal with the contradictions that emerge. The authors excuse themselves in various passages of "not being poor" and recognize that their findings might be a bit "romanticized" (p. 548). They certainly don't denounce with the same vehemence they do in other papers, the political abuse of the exercise of psychology that is perpetrated there.

3.11 South Africa

A paper that documents the evolution of critical perspectives of psychology in South Africa (Painter, Terre Blanche, & Henderson, 2006) also allows us to see some of the collusions psychologists made with discriminatory practices under the Apartheid. The text begins with a quote that is revealing in itself, showing how the "technical" practice of the psychologists that believed to be going on with their tasks is clearly oppressive for those whose rights were being curtailed. A South

African poet named Breyten Breytenbach that passed seven years in jail because of his opposition to the regime, writes:

> He had me go through the gamut of outdated tests, the Rorschach blots and blobs, squiggles and various I.Q. examinations. Naturally I was never informed about any of his deductions. I was the guinea pig. These perverted practitioners of the spurious science of psychology do not have as their first priority to help the prisoner who may be in need of it. They are the lackeys of the system. Their task very clearly is to be the psychological component of the general strategy of unbalancing and disorienting the political prisoner (Breytenbach, 1984, p. 90, cited by Painter, Blanche, & Henderson, 2006).

Even though the point of the article is not to signal out these practices, but to chronicle the development of critical psychology, they show how psychologists collaborated actively with the Apartheid offering their "findings" about the intellectual inferiority of blacks and on occasion were "neutral" witnesses of the inequality and acts of discrimination, clearly serving an abusive system. Rather than racist, the authors conclude that these psychologists systematically avoided the theme of race, adopting a medical model that allowed them to be silent accomplices of the tragic history of injustice.

The history of our science is abundant with active participation in abuse and allegations of neutrality that appear as clear examples of what Arendt aptly called "the banality of evil."

References

Ackerman, S. (2015, July 14). Three senior officials lose their jobs at APA after US torture scandal. *The Guardian*. https://www.theguardian.com/us-news/2015/jul/14/apa-senior-officials-torture-report-cia. Accessed March 11, 2020.

Ajkay, K., & Sipos, Z. (2000). Hungarian clinical psychology and psychotherapy. *Changes., 18* (2), 83–90.

Albarelli, H., Jr. (2009). *A terrible mistake: the murder of Frank Olson, and the CIA's secret cold war experiments*. Walterville, OR: Trine Day.

Amnesty International. (1988). *Cuba: recent developments affecting the situation of political prisoners and the use of the death penalty*. New York: Amnesty International.

Angelini, A. (2008). History of the unconscious in Soviet Russia: from its origins to the fall of the Soviet Union. *International Journal of Psychoanalysis, 89,* 369–388.

Antic, A. (2016). The pedagogy of worker's self-management: terror, therapy and reform communism in Yugoslavia after the Tito-Stalin split. *Journal of Social History, 50,* 179–203.

Bandrés, J., & Llavona, R. (1997). Psychology in Franco's concentration camps. *Psychology in Spain, 1,* 3–9.

Bernal, G. (1985). A history of psychology in Cuba. *Journal of Community Psychology, 13,* 222–235.

Bleichmar, S. (2002). *Dolor País*. Buenos Aires: Libros del Zorzal.

Bloch, S., & Reddaway, P. (1985). *Soviet psychiatric abuse: the shadow over world psychiatry*. Boulder Colorado: Westview Press.

Brown, C., & Lago, A. (1991). *The politics of psychiatry in revolutionary Cuba*. New Brunswick: Transaction Publishers.

Bukovsky, V. (1991). On the outskirts of the empire. In C. Brown & A. Lago (Eds.), *The politics of psychiatry in revolutionary Cuba*. New Brunswick: Transaction Publishers.

Cajigas Segredo, N. (2002). Contribuitions of psychology to social transformation in Uruguay. *International Journal of Group Tensions, 31,* 53–77.
Chin, R., & Chin, A. (1969). *La psicología en China Popular*. Bogotá: Editorial Pluma.
Chinese Human Rights Defenders (2016, May 5). Forced Psychiatric Commitment of Dissidents Continues as Police Act Above Enacted Law (4/29-5/5, 2016). https://www.nchrd.org/2016/05/chrb-forced-psychiatric-commitment-of dissidents-continues-as-police-act-above-enacted-law-429-55-2016/. Accessed February 28, 2020.
Chrzanowski, G. (1975). Psychoanalysis: ideology and Practitioners. *Contemporary Psychoanalysis*, *11*, 492–499.
Danto, E. (2005). *Freud's free clinics: psychoanalysis & social justice, 19181938*. New York: Columbia University Press.
de Carbonell, A. (2013, October 8). Putin critic sentenced to detention in a psychiatric ward. *Reuters*. https://www.reuters.com/article/us-russia-protest/putin-critic-sentenced-to-detention-in-psychiatric-ward-idUSBRE9970OY20131008. Accessed February 20, 2020.
Derrida, J., & Nicholson-Smith, D. (1991). Geopsychoanalysis: "… and the rest of the world". *American Imago, 48*(2), 199–231. www.jstor.org/stable/26303831. Accessed March 14, 2020.
Etkind, A. (2018). *Eros of the impossible: the history of psychoanalysis in Russia*. New York: Routledge.
Freud, S. (1904/1983). La Interpretación de los sueños. En *Obras Completas*. Madrid: Biblioteca Nueva.
Freud, S. (1914/1983). Historia de una neurosis infantil (Caso del 'Hombre de los Lobos'). En *Obras Completas*. Madrid: Biblioteca Nueva.
García, L. (1979). Psychology and health care in Cuba. *American Psychologist, 35,* 1090–1095.
Gillam, S. (2012). *Sigmund Freud: famous neurologist*. Hawaii: ABDO.
González Duro, E. (2008). *Los Psiquiatras de Franco: los rojos no estaban locos*. Barcelona: Ediciones Península.
González Rey, F. (1995). Sociedad y psicología en Cuba: avanzando en uno de sus caminos de investigación y construcción teórica durante tres décadas. *Revista Interamericana de Psicología, 47,* 195–210.
Gould, S. J. (1996). *The mismeasurement of man*. New York: W. W. Norton & Company.
Gray, G., & Zielinksi, A. (2006). Psychology and U.S. psychologists in torture and war in the Middle East. *Torture, 16,* 128–133.
Griffiths, E. (2006). Psychic glimpses. *Latin American Perspectives*, *33*, 177–178.
Harmatta, J. (1992). Psychic liberation under political tyranny. *International Forum of Psychoanalysis, 1,* 135–139.
Herman, J. (1997). *Trauma and recovery: the aftermath of violence—from domestic abuse to political terror*. New York: Basic Books.
Hollander, N. (2010). *Uprooted minds: surviving the politics of terror in the Americas*. New York: Routledge.
Jiménez, B. (1994). Cambios sociopolíticos y desrrallos históricos en psicología. In M. Montero (Ed.), *Construcción y Crítica de la Psicología Social*. Barcelona: Antrhopos.
Jimenez, J. (1989). Some reflections on the practice of psychoanalysis in chile today—from the point of view of the relationship between psychoanalysis and society. *International Review of Psycho-Analysis*, *16*, 493.
Kaczorowski, A. (2018). A communist LSD trip: the story of Czechoslovak acid. PrzeKrój. https://przekroj.pl/en/society/a-communist-lsd-trip-aleksander-kaczorowski. Accessed March 9, 2020.
Kernberg, O. (1998). *Ideology, conflict and leadership in groups and organizations*. New Haven: Yale University Press.
Kimmel, P. (2012). Unsafe, illegal, unethical and ineffective. In Cooper, S. & Ratle, K. (Eds.) *Psychology serving humanity: proceedings of the 30th international congress on psychology*. London: Taylor & Francis Group.
Kokoszka, A., & Sitarz, M. (2000). Contemporary psychoterapy in Poland. *Changes, 18,* 24–34.
Korolenko, C., & Kensin, D. (2002). Reflections on the past and present of Russian psychiatry. *Anthropology and Medicine, 9,* 51–64.

Koryagin, A. (1981). Unwilling patients. *The Lancet, 317,* 821–824. https://doi.org/10.1016/S0140-6736(81)92691-X.

Langer, M. (1972). *Cuestionamos: documentos de crítica a la ubicación actual del psicoanálisis.* Buenos Aires: Granica Editor.

Lee, S. (2001). Who is politicizing psychiatry in China (letter)? *British Journal of Psychiatry, 179,* 178–179.

Levine, A. (2007, January/February). Collective unconscionable: how psychologists, the most liberal of professionals, abetted Bush's torture policy. *Washington Monthly.*

Liu, M. (November 24, 2003). Finding peace of mind. Newsweek

Lyons, D. (2001). Soviet style psychiatry is alive and well in the People's Republic (letter). *British Journal of Psychiatry, 178,* 380–381.

Lyons, D., & Munro, R. (2002). Dissent as a symptom: why China has questions to answer. *British Journal of Psychiatry, 180,* 551–552.

Mandler, G. (2002). Psychologists and the international socialist access to power. *History of Psychology, 5,* 190–200.

Marks, S. (2018). Suggestion, persuasion and work: psychotherapies in communist Europe. *European Journal of Psychotherapy and Counselling, 20*(1), 10–24.

Marks, S., & Savelli, M. (2015). Communist Europe and transnational psychiatry. In M. Savelli & M. Marks (Eds.), *Psychiatry in communist Europe* (pp. 1–26). New York: Palgrave MacMillan.

Masson, J. (1997). *Against therapy.* Londres: Harper Collins Publisher.

Miller, M. (2005). *Freud y los bolcheviques.* Buenos Aires: Ediciones Nueva Visión.

Mitchell, J., & Harlow, B. (2016). *Enhanced interrogation: inside the minds and motives of the Islamic terrorists trying to destroy America.* New York: Crown Publishing.

Munro, R. (2002). *Dangerous minds: political psychiatry today and its origin in the ao era.* Nueva York: Human Rights Watch. https://www.hrw.org/reports/2002/china02/. Accessed April 20, 2020.

Painter, D., Terre Blanche, M., & Henderson, J. (2006). Critical psychology in South Africa: histories, themes and prospects. *Annual Review of Critical Psychology, 5.* www.discourseunit.com/arcp/5. Accessed February 15, 2008.

Parker, I. (2007). *Revolution in psychology: alienation to emancipation.* London: Pluto Press.

Puget, J. (1987). The state of threat and psychoanalysis: from the uncanny that structures to the uncanny that alienates. *Free Associations, 13,* 84–140.

Puget, J. (1989). Marie Langer, 1910-1987. *Free Associations., 15,* 39–43.

Roache, M. (2017, September 7). Political psychiatric abuse returns to Russia and ex-soviet states, critics say. *Newsweek.* https://www.newsweek.com/russia-putin-psychiatry-punitive-crimea-uzbekistan-prison-jail-kremlin-moscow-661179. Accessed February 21, 2020.

Rossiter, A., Walsh-Bowers, R., & Prilleltensky, I. (2002). Ethics as a located story: a comparison of North American and Cuban clinical ethics. *Theory & Psychology, 12,* 533–556.

Russo, J. (2012). The social diffusion of psychoanalysis during the Brazilian military regime: psychological awareness in an age of political repression. In J. Damousi & M. Ben (Eds.), *Psychoanalysis and politics: histories of psychoanalysis under conditions of restricted political freedom* (pp. 165–184). New York: Oxford University Press.

Samuels, A. (1993). *The political psyche.* London: Routledge.

Savelli, M., & Marks, M. (2015). *Psychiatry in communist Europe.* New York: Palgrave MacMillan.

Sebek, M. (1996). Aggression in society and on the couch. *Free Associations, 6,* 477–492.

Spencer, I. (2000). Lessons from history: the politics of psychiatry in the USSR. *Psychiatric and Mental Health Nursing, 7,* 355–361. https://doi.org/10.1046/j.1365-2850.2000.00297.x. Accessed April 20, 2020.

Staub, E. (1989). *The roots of violence: the origins of genocide and other mass violence.* Cambridge: Cambridge University Press.

Stover, E., & Nightingale, E. (1985). *The breaking of minds and bodies: torture, psychiatric abuse and health professions.* New York: Freeman.

Strous, R. (2006). Hitler's psychiatrists: healers and researchers turned executioners and its relevance today. *Harvard Review of Psychiatry, 14,* 30–37.
Thomas, G. (2001). *Las torturas mentales de la CIA*. Barcelona: Ediciones B.
Totton, N. (2000). *Psychotherapy and Politics*. London: Sage Publications.
Tremlett, G. (2002, November 1). Marxists are retards. *The Guardian*. https://www.theguardian.com/world/2002/nov/01/spain.gilestremlett. Accessed April 20, 2020.
Vallejo Nájera, A. (1937). *Eugenesia de la Hispanidad y Regeneración de la Raza*. San Sebastián: Española.
Vallejo Nájera, A. (1938). *Eugamia: selección de novios*. San Sebastián: Española.
Vallejo Nájera, A. (1944). *Tratado de psiquiatría*. Barcelona: Editorial Española.
Villela, L. (1998). Cale-se, the chalice of silence: the ethics of psychoanalysis and the return of the repressed in Brazil. *Journal for the Psychoanalysis of Culture and Society, 3,* 167–173.
Vinyes, R. (2002). *Los Hijos Perdidos del Franquismo*. Barcelona: Plaza y Janés.
Vikár, G. (1996). The Budapest school of psychoanalysis. In P. Rudnytsky, A. Bókay, & P. Giampieri-Deutsch (Eds.), *Ferenczi's turn in psychoanalysis*. New York: New York University Press.
Whitaker, L. (2000). *Understanding and preventing violence: the psychology of human destructiveness*. Boca Ratón: CRC Press.
Zetkin, C. (1929). *Lenin on the women question*. Marxist Internet Archive. https://www.marxists.org/archive/zetkin/1925/lenin/zetkin2.htm. Accessed April 20, 2020.

Chapter 4
From Humanistic Murder to Ecological Mining: The Case of Venezuela

I found one report of politically motivated interference of a public hospital long before the onset of the Boliviarian Revolution. The psychoanalyst, Serapio Marcano, wrote a book (1987) where he retells the experience of the enormous pressures and obstacles the project faced in redesigning the psychiatric hospital, El Peñón, in the 70s. The text chronicles the attempt to transform the hospital from a traditional clinical service to one framed in a community perspective. The effort to make the hospital's organizational structure more horizontal was met with distrust by the official health administrators. Identification with leftist ideals was most probably part of the tensions at a time that, even though there was a democratic government, the fight against leftist guerrilla movements had been violent. The administrators decided to block the attempts to reform the institution and imposed a director of training with more traditional ideas. The author also reports having been a target of threats, coercion, the undercover taping of some of his conversations and the substitution of those in charge of the hospital with less qualified but subservient personnel. The attempt to lead a more community-oriented center was accused of being an attempt to politically indoctrinate. Finally, the hospital was shut down, and many of the professionals were fired. But there is no comparison with the dimension in which psychology and psychiatry have been recruited by Chavismo to further their hold on power.

4.1 Recruiting Mental Health Experts to Quiet Dissidence

The election of Hugo Chávez in December of 1998 and his proposed Bolivarian Revolution promised to bring more equality and the defense of the most vulnerable. But his coming to power soon polarized the country and intense political conflicts were unleashed that haven't subsided in more than 20 years. Profound institutional transformations occurred which included the rewriting of the Constitution, the

M. Llorens, *Politically Reflective Psychotherapy*, Latin American Voices,
https://doi.org/10.1007/978-3-030-57792-6_4

inclusion of the military as an active political actor and the continuous accumulation of power by Chávez.

In the early years, a rapid escalation of conflict between Chavismo and the opposition, made up of many of the forces that previously had a hold on power, generated a deep polarization in society. In many cases, government pushed to provoke that polarization, while in others it responded with an increasing amount of abusive measures to try to quell it and impose its agenda.

One of the most distinctive characteristics of the political process in Venezuela, in my opinion, is that Chavismo adopted a host of populist and progressive flags as a justification of their hold on power, but simultaneously has been an explicitly militaristic movement, not shy on using force to impose itself, what researcher Vásquez has aptly termed "compassionate militarism" (2010). Chávez, of course, was a former member of the Armed Forces who attempted a military coup in 1992. The often-used phrase of a "peaceful but armed revolution," expresses this particular mix.

The Boliviarian project is a rather unorthodox brand of socialism, termed "Twenty First Century Socialism," sprinkled with a lot of traditional Latin American military "caudillismo," which is a historical tradition of authoritarian leaders that control the country through military force. Chavismo quickly began to accumulate power and control any possible institutional resistance, gaining strength through popular support at first, and later by imposing its force when popular support waned.

In its effort to impose its ideological vision, social science, in general, and psychology, in particular, were adopted. In Venezuela, we find examples of abuses of psychiatry and psychology that we have chronicled in other parts of the world: the use of idiosyncratic diagnosis to disqualify the opposition, psychiatric wards and psychotropic medication to incarcerate and sedate dissidence, as well as the use of psychological jargon to justify human rights abuses. But what seems rather new is the curious and constant use of the language of critical perspectives of social science and progressive movements to counter and/or disavow any criticism. Chavismo has, to a point that is dumbfounding, dedicated great effort to construct a discourse that promotes itself as progressive while at the same time, in a very perverse manner, persecute those same subjects that it claims to defend.

Let us chronicle some of the efforts to co-opt psychology and abuse it for political purposes. Early on in the political confrontation I was offered a first-hand glimpse of these attempts in December of 2002 during a national strike that was called upon by the workers of the state-owned oil company (PDVSA), the national workers organization (Corporación de Trabajadores de Venezuela) and the main association of industrial owners (Fedecámaras). Tension had been building up in the country since December of 2001 after the National Assembly gave Chávez power to write new laws without the need for its approval, a legal figure introduced into the recently written Chavista Constitution. In the following months, massive protests erupted around the country, especially in the capital of Caracas. In April, these protests led to a huge march toward the center of the city, which resulted in 19 deaths in circumstances that have not been cleared up to this day. Chávez was ousted by opposing military leaders for 2 days, after which he returned to the presidency offering apologies and promising to negotiate with the opposition.

Having endured such a crisis just 6 months back, the national strike threatened to deepen the country's instability. With that in mind I was invited as a representative of the community health center of my university, along with other psychologists and psychiatrists to meet at the offices of the Panamerican Health Organization. The invitation was granted by the psychiatrist Jorge Rodríguez who I knew very well, having shared time with him during my clinical training at the University Hospital. After graduating we continued working together at the postgraduate program of Clinical Community Psychology of the Universidad Católica Andrés Bello. Rodríguez is the son of a left-wing political leader who participated in the guerrilla movement, and was arrested in 1976 accused of participating in the politically motivated kidnapping of William Niehous, an American who was the Vice-President of Owen-Illinois. During his arrest, Rodríguez's father was murdered after being tortured. These details are relevant, since Jorge Rodríguez soon escalated in the Chavista hierarchy passing from administrator of a public hospital to lead the National Electoral Council, later to the Vice-Presidency, and has also been Mayor of Caracas and Minister of Communications. His sister, Delcy, also accumulated a significant amount of power, holding the post of Vice-President from 2018.

Having very different opinions on Chavismo, we had been able, up to that point, to maintain a friendly relationship in which we were able to debate and discuss our different viewpoints. The invitation to that meeting, made officially by the Ministry of Health, was extended on the premise that the government wanted to explore the viewpoints of various experts on mental health to organize possible preventive responses for societal reactions to the mounting political tensions. I assisted with caution but committed to offer the help we were able to give from our community center if the proposal was reasonable. In the meeting, there were other professionals who I knew and respected from other universities and centers.

After a rather brief round of listening to our perspectives, a series of questions repeatedly began to focus on only one point: our opinion on the impact of television and if it was to be blamed for the responses of a large part of the population who was protesting against the government. The insistence that we pronounce ourselves on this issue and that we hand them stats that could demonstrate the emotional disturbance caused by mass media on children evidenced the hidden agenda of the meeting. Government was planning on using "scientific" arguments regarding the dangerous effects of media on citizen's emotional stability to further the restrictions and persecution against media. All of our responses, such as the fact that it is not possible to produce simple epidemiological data that can isolate a variable such as the effect of mass media on emotional disturbances that appear in the consulting room, were met with the insistence that we pronounce ourselves. After the motives of our presence were made sufficiently clear, all of the invited professionals got up and left. But the meeting was a signal of things to come in the field.

Psychology and psychiatry were consistently reduced to a rhetorical tool used to further Chavismo's ideological claims and dismiss any criticism. Psychologists and psychiatrist were either ideological comrades, or were systematically distanced from any government program or institution. An interview with a psychiatrist who worked in the Ministry of Science expresses feelings of guilt for having been forced to censor publications that had been approved because they were written by academics who were critical of government (Alzualde, 2017).

In several occasions, government invited different experts on different fields to events or committees only to use their presence as a rubber-stamp for their decisions. One of the most dramatic examples was the National Commission to Reform the Police (Conarepol) that was created in 2006. The commission was created as a response to the exponential increase in violence in Venezuela that by that year had reached the level of around 50 murders per 100,000 inhabitants, which was one of the highest rates in the world. The situation turned into a national crisis when three teenagers were kidnapped by thieves dressed in police uniform. The three youngsters and an adult who was driving were found murdered 2 months later, sparking protests that extended throughout the country. When the case was finally resolved, four active police officers were charged with having been part of the kidnapping.

The commission was formed by professionals linked to security from different institutions and universities. It was a welcomed initiative for its relevance, as well as the plurality of voices that were initially invited, a number of which I know personally. The commission worked for 9 months elaborating a diagnosis and a set of recommendations to reform the security apparatus in the country. Much of this initiative was led by a Human Rights activist, Soraya El Achkar, who had previously led an NGO that accompanied families of victims of police brutality called Red de Apoyo por la Justicia y la Paz. She was assigned to lead the National University of Security, an institution designed to train a new type of community police officer aware of the importance of human rights.

As the commission began to advance with specific suggestions to weed out corruption, counterbalance the arbitrary power of the police institutions and challenge the stronghold of the military, obstacles began to appear. The experts began to resign from a commission that evidenced its ineffectiveness.

Members of the commission expressed that a "counterreform" was activated that systematically undermined any possibility of real change. The commission, in their words, was used to: "be exhibited in times of police crisis, put makeup on it and religitimate it" (Ávila, in press, p. 216). By 2010 hopes were clearly thwarted as the militarization of public security had taken complete control of police institutions (Zubillaga & Hanson, 2018). A police reform that was designed to develop a citizen-directed force, based on a human rights perspective, ended up being a militarized, corrupt force.

From 2012 to 2014, Chávez and his successor, Nicolás Maduro, removed all civilians in charge of different national security organizations like the National Boliviarian Police and the National Security University and substituted them with ex military officers (Smilde & Hanson, 2014). In January of 2014, Soraya El Achkar was removed as the director of the previously celebrated new university for the police and the direction was given to a military officer who had participated in the coup d'etat with Chávez in 1992, even though the institution was, according to its original vision, to be guided by civilians with a proven trajectory in human rights.

The consequence is that, a decade after the commission was created, homicides have continued to increase, reaching 70 murders per 100,000 inhabitants, and the police has become a systematic and lethal protagonist of them, committing a quarter of those homicides, according to numbers issued by the government—more than 4000 murders a year since 2015 (Zubillaga & Llorens, in press).

Soon the panorama that Casique (2009) had warned about became evident. She reported on the difficult relationship between intellectuals and Chavismo since 2001, including those that had ideological sympathies with the government. Juan Barreto, for example, who holds a Ph.D. in sociology and was a Deputy under Chavismo and Mayor of Caracas until 2008, stated in an interview in 2007, cited by Casique, that "there are decisive times when the leader has to control all decisions. It is the time for democratic caesarism, understanding that the leader is the synthesis of the ethical-political moment of society" (p. 7). It seems, though, that the ethical-political synthesis that Barreto defended seemed to last too long since he broke off from Chavismo in 2012. Casique argues that the intellectuals invited to the revolutionary process were not included to help reflect upon the process and provide original ideas but were strictly to defend the revolution and silence the critics. Any dissident opinion was promptly silenced.

Jorge Rodríguez, who we mentioned earlier, not only continued in Chavismo, but became a central figure. I was surprised to see him jump from hospital administrator to one of the directors of the National Electoral Council, considering that he had no previous experience in the electoral field. It was also surprising and revealing that, afterward, he jumped from being the President of the country's electoral council to becoming the Vice-President of the government when he was supposed to be a neutral arbitrator toward working as the chief of the electoral power.

But in regard to our subject, we heard again from Rodríguez, when he inaugurated a talk show on the state television channel called "Politics on the Couch" (Ciudad CCS, 2016). It is a television format that has become a whole genre in Chavismo. Chávez was famous for his own television show called "Hello President" in which he rambled live for 8 hours or more every Sunday. The program where he showcased his incredible capacity to talk for many hours, sing, tell jokes and, of course, insult his political adversaries was one of his trademarks. Other chavista leaders followed suit and Rodríguez added his psychiatric training to this unique mix of television talk shows.

On the program he acts as a condescending teacher diagnosing all of the opposition as psychotic, along with the ex-president of Colombia. For example, Henry Ramos Allup, leader of one of the main opposition parties, according to him, presents: "pathological behavior, aggression, intolerance, infallibility, is irritable, manipulative, has ideas of persecution, is untrustworthy, fickle, wreckless, impatient, careless, depressive, an egomaniac, authoritarian and deceitful." It is a rather curious list, from which he concludes, after showing short samples of the politician's public appearances, of being a "psychotic" (Rodríguez, 2017). He then goes on to explain, using an electronic blackboard, in a pseudo-didactic fashion, what a psychosis is. He goes on to discuss his "differential diagnosis" to distinguish between, according to him, a schizophrenia, a bipolar disorder or a dementia.

Rodríguez concludes that "psychosis is the opposition's disturbance" (Rodríguez, 2017). Even though he has also claimed that it suffers from an antisocial personality disorder (El Nacional, 2015), the use of pseudo-psychiatric jargon to insult the opposition is blatant.

In 2017, after another massive wave of protests exploded again in the streets of Venezuela, government organized the International Forum of Violence and Psychological Operations that was put on in the chancellor's office with psychologists invited from France, Brazil, Guatemala, Mexico, Argentina as well as psychologists from Venezuela who sympathize with Chavismo. The forum was televised on state television and the Minister of Communications at the time inaugurated the event promising to produce a psychological diagnosis of the country (Rosales, 2017; Torres, 2017). In the forum, opinions defended ideas such as that student protesters were naive and being used "by a genocidal empire that is building irregular armies" (Flores, 2017). I tried to attend but was informed that the event was open only to sympathizers.

The forum and a series of interviews given by the psychologists that belong to the group that organized it have insisted on the argument that a large part of the population has protested as a result of psychological warfare. In the following months, government officials gave a series of interviews to the international press, in response to multiple manifestations of international organizations that included the Organization of American States and the European Union insisting on being a victim of psychological war directed by the world against Venezuela (Paullier, 2018).

I was able to interview Fernando Giuliani (personal communication, July 1, 2017), a community psychologist of Uruguayan origin, who was one of the organizers of the forum, and asked him what evidence had the group been able to gather to conclude that the protesters had been manipulated and not simply responding to the grave economic crisis and the abuse of their political rights. Giuliani responded referring to events that occurred in Chile and Argentina during their dictatorships. When I acknowledged that those events had been terrible, but that did not prove that the mass of protesters in Venezuela were manipulated, he acknowledged that they didn't have any concrete proof. When I asked him if this was not a dangerous use of psychological jargon that helped government to dismiss millions of protesters in the streets, there was no answer.

4.2 Psychotic Dissociation and the Diagnosis of Dissidence

A rather extravagant example of the invention of a psychiatric diagnosis was proposed by a former Minister of Health, Erik Rodríguez (unrelated to Jorge Rodríguez), an epidemiologist, who coined the term "psychotic dissociation" in the book published by the Ministry titled: "Psychotic Dissociation: the ideological weapon of the Venezuelan counterrevolution" (2005).

The diagnosis was created by him to describe what he stated to be disturbed behaviors presented by masses who had been manipulated by the mass media into rejecting the government. He diagnosed a large part of the population as suffering from this "psychotic dissociation" which he describes in the following text:

> This is how we created the label psychotic dissociation to define the behavior of the middle classes affected by the mass media, especially television, that created the antichavista ideology. It was on the basis of these elements that the sociological category called psychotic dissociation, that reflects one or various components of three medical categories (dissociation, psychosis and disturbed behavior). (p. 39)

A rather bizarre document, filled with pseudo-scientific jargon, published by the Ministry, and funded by the state pretended to explain away through "psychopathology" the behavior of a large part of the population that rejected government's authoritarianism. The document consisting of 58 pages was massively distributed and the phrase "psychotic dissociation" was repeatedly used on state television as a main argument to disregard protests.

The vague use of language that passes from the clinical to the sociological, assigning a mental disorder to a specific economic class is a remake of classical psychiatric abuse seen in communist countries. In this section, Rodríguez again attempts to define his concept:

> Even though it is true that we are not looking at a dissociation, a psychosis or a disturbed behavior as such, we can understand that the symptomatology that constitutes these entities or psychopathologies helps define or construct a category with which we will define the behavior of people that manifest an unusually violent and irrational behavior beginning in 2002.
>
> To approach the identification of this collective behavior we define it as psychotic dissociation, because we observe this psychopathological trilogy (dissociation, psychosis and disturbed behavior). Based on the definition of this collective behavior we proceeded to observe and analyze what was the fundamental inducing factor that explained that such an important sector of Venezuelans, mainly of the middle classes, had been affected. All of the transdisciplinary studies agree that private mass media, especially television, was the inoculating agent. A later study revealed that those inoculated and transfused were those that had been most influenced by the consumerist publicity that is shown on those mediums.
>
> The term psychotic dissociation does not appear in the Diagnostic and Statistical Manual of Mental Disorders (DSM-IV), but we start off establishing that some psychological entities such as dissociation, psychosis and disturbed behavior (oppositional defiant disorder and antisocial disorder) constitute components that are psychological references to the label of psychotic dissociation. (p. 34)

It doesn't seem necessary to pick apart this very outlandish text, in which three psychopathological categories appear to be vaguely mixed together. Psychological contents are said to be "transfused," without mentioning the fact that the "transdisciplinary studies" that are alluded do not appear referenced and we do not know of their existence.

Erik Rodríguez's continuous appearance on state television explaining his "scientific" findings was so ridiculous that they produced amazement, laughter and indignation in a large part of the mental health professionals. For a moment, it was difficult to know if such a stunt had to be taken as a serious threat or simply disregarded. But the term was used repeatedly to argue in favor of the persecution and eventual shutting down or take over of all independent television channels and newspapers.

Soon health became one of the battlegrounds of the revolution. All public workers began to be systematically subjected to ideological control, particularly those related to the Ministry of Health. An ideological debate on the administration of the health system would have been logical and possibly fruitful event. But what occurred was the use of the health system to try to control the population.

In several clinical programs, we began to receive reports of students having been advised by their supervisors not to discuss political issues with their patients in therapy. Health professionals began to be fired for holding opinions contrary to the government, and cases of harrasment based on political positions began to be reported (Núñez, 2003; Goncalves & Gutiérrez, 2005).

Perhaps the most public examples were the declarations of the Health Minister, Roger Capella. After the opposition conducted a recollection of signatures to solicit a referendum to revoke the mandate of the president in 2004 (a figure that is constitutionally valid), the Minister declared that all medical personnel that had signed it would be considered a conspirator and a terrorist and that they should all be fired. These intimidatory practices and politically motivated dismissals had been reported for a while before his declarations, but he offered a public confession of the practice from a high-ranking government officer, admitting that any expression of disagreement with government was going to be punished (El Nacional, March 27, and April 16, 2004a, 2004b).

Since then pressure to public workers has continued with more violence. There are abundant examples like that of ex-Minister of Oil and Energy captured on camera who, in a large meeting with all the personnel, warned: "We are outraged when we find people who are light (referring to people are not wholly committed to the revolution). Anyone who forgets that we are in a revolution will be reminded by beatings" (Reyes, 2006).

After Hugo Chávez died in 2012 and his successor Nicolás Maduro took over the control of the country after winning a dubious election by less than 1% of the votes, a grave economic crisis overtook the country that included one of the highest and longest hyperinflations in world history (Hanke, 2019). This provoked, among other many consequences, the complete collapse of the health system. Psychiatric patients, in particular, suffered from grave deprivation of medicine and the most basic hospital implements such as clean sheets and food (Casey, 2016). Worldwide reports have circulated and documented the situation, such as the one in the Washington Post that reported 14 inpatients died at the Peñón Psychiatric Hospital since 2016 because of "poor conditions and a want of medication" (Krygier & Faiola, 2019), which is a huge number considering its maximum capacity is of 40 patients. These reports repeatedly mention how doctors are afraid to offer their testimony due to fear of reprisal.

The reports of our colleagues who work in the public system are horrific. For example, a clinical psychologist who supervises students that develop their first clinical practices in a state hospital reports that the psychiatric service is so abandoned that patients can go without any doctor supervision for days. One patient in the service died after cutting herself and later acquiring an infection in those same wounds because of the lack of hygiene in the service. She infected her wounds with her own feces. Another died after having a grave infection go untreated, even though he denounced to the press that he was not even receiving analgesics and was in terrible pain (Sarmiento, July 8, 2019).

As professionals in the public sector continue to resign, they often struggle between feeling that their work is futile in such precarious situations and the feeling that, if they leave, the patients will be completely abandoned. Doctor's and other health workers in consequence report huge amounts of burnout. A literary web page that publishes chronicles on life in Venezuela posted the story of a pediatrician who had a nervous collapse from the stress of seeing so many youngsters die on her floor. "I'm exhausted from only being able to help them die," she expresses in despair. The footnote at the end of the text reports of her suffering. It states that the name of the doctor and of the hospital was changed to avoid retaliation (Fernández, 2018). Amnesty International has denounced how doctors have been threatened, fired, arrested and tortured for filing complaints in regard to hospital conditions (Buada, May 22, 2019).

In recent years, part of the research team I belong to that is documenting many of these issues has recollected testimonies of communities that have been ravaged by violence, either committed by delinquent gangs or by security forces (Zubillaga & Llorens, in press). In one of these communities, the psychiatrist, a member of our team, has been threatened with arrest, because he diagnosed a large number of community residents and teachers of the community schools with PTSD. Government officials have warned him to shut up about the events we have been recording.

4.3 The Franklin Brito Case

In 2009, the most terrible case of psychiatric abuse came into public view. Franklin Brito was a biologist who had dedicated his life to agriculture and to teaching at a local high school, along with his wife, in a rural town where he had 290 ha of land.

His farming had been proving fruitful until a conflict began with the Mayor. Brito filed a report on a way of resolving a plague that had been affecting the crops of the region. His recommendations were considered a better approach than one that had been suggested by the Mayor's office whose project of importing chemicals was rejected in consequence by the Corporación Venezolana de Guayana (a governmental office that financed projects in the region). In revenge, the Mayor began harassing Brito and his family (Vásquez, 2019).

At first he was fired from his teaching post. His students rallied in favor of Brito, signing a letter asking him to be reinstated. But all protests went unheard. Afterward his farm was invaded. The invasion was allegedly based on new enabling laws that Chávez had personally emitted, giving poor farmers the right to occupy unproductive, abandoned lands. Brito's lands were neither abandoned nor unproductive. The invasion appears to be part of the local government's revenge.

Franklin Brito began a series of protests to bring attention to his situation. He and his family organized vigils outside the presidential palace and, in 2005, he cut of his little finger in front of the Supreme Court. The extreme protest caught the attention of Chávez who decided to intervene. But the solution offered to Brito was to hand him back his lands unofficially, without restoring him the papers that granted ownership. A solution that Brito rejected. In 2007, the Supreme Court sentenced that the lands be returned to Brito. But the sentence was never executed and Brito denounced that he was offered money and blackmailed to convince him to stop his protest.

He began a series of hunger strikes that led to a final protest in front of the offices of the Organization of American States (OAS) in 2009 that lasted more than 3 months. By this time his case had become notorious and the image of this 1.90 m tall man weighing less than 60 kg a recognizable image on the news. As a consequence, a government official, the Defender of the People, a figure in the bolivarian Constitution that is supposed to defend the rights of the citizens, declared that Brito was mentally unfit, and that he had to be taken into custody to protect him from himself (Rodríguez, 2013). In short, government arrested Brito arguing that he was mentally disturbed and that they were "protecting" him. Sixty police officers arrived to take him to the Military Hospital.

He was taken to the psychiatric ward where he received an initial evaluation. The doctors at the service concluded that he was not suffering from a mental disturbance and rejected his hospitalization. In response to which, he was forcefully hospitalized in the ophthalmology service.

Eight evaluations were done by the psychiatric service, each one rejecting any finding of mental problems. Yet, a month into this hospitalization, the Attorney General, Luisa Ortega Díaz, declared that he was "mentally incapacitated" to make his own decisions (VTV, January 14, 2010). They had to bring in a psychiatrist from another hospital, Angel Riera, who in his Twitter identifies himself as a "Medical Revolutionary Psychiatrist," to sign a report that stated that he suffered from a "paranoid personality" and a "delusional disorder" (Rodríguez, 2013).

Brito was sedated and force-fed. He was in custody under the watch of the National Guard and no visits were allowed. The requirements that oversee any involuntary hospitalization according to the norms of the World Health Organization, such as an independent evaluation, access to the possibility to appeal or the approval of a family member, were never met. So Brito's hospital bed was clearly a prison.

In February, a group of psychologists organized a petition to free Brito, supported by the Venezuelan Psychological Federation and other psychology-related associations. Forums in different universities and protests in front of the Military Hospital were conducted.

In March, María Teresa Urreiztieta, a psychologist and university professor, who had been supporting Brito and his family was able to speak on the phone with him. She commented in a university forum that Brito told her:

> I am being held prisoner, now. I have three, not two, National Guards at my door. I am ok, but stuck here. They say I am sick. Since they weren't able to make up any crime they made up that I had to get well before I am free to leave. I will take this to the end for my family and my dignity. (Pilato, 2010)

On January, the International Court of Human Rights had dictaminated that Brito had to be evaluated by an independent doctor. Since the court order had been ignored, Brito, began in March a thirst strike, in which he rejected any food and water, dropping to 43 kg, finally forcing authorities to accept the visit of a Red Cross doctor. After the visit, he was force-fed again. Once he began to recover his normal body weight the director of the hospital decided to give him his medical discharge. But the court that dealt with his case rejected the doctor's order.

Seeing no solution to his imprisonment Brito, once again, decided to go on another hunger strike that led to his death on August of 2010, after 8 months of being forcefully held in the hospital. The ordeal did not end there for Brito's family; 5 months after his death, the national ombudsman, or Defender of the People, charged them with "incitement to suicide" (Vásquez, 2019).

The case was highly disturbing for me, as we watched, in what seemed to be slow motion, the weight of a highly distorted system turned against the will of a man who had decided to defend his rights and dignity at all costs. His stubborn appeal for a legal resolution seemed to defy government logic. They tried to appease, blackmail, threaten and coerce him. They were willing to buy him out and pay him to go silent and do everything except officially accept that he was right and government officials were wrong. Brito rejected any solution that was not a formal legal sentence in his favor.

In a certain sense, in the logic of Chavismo, Brito was mad. In a very corrupt system in which problems are resolved informally through coercion or exchange of favors, the desire to reach a legal, transparent solution seems close to madness. Power was willing to bow to Brito's complaints unofficially. But it wasn't willing to publicly recognize that it had done wrong. To expect power to recognize its mistakes was too much. Government preferred to set up a charade to deny Brito's claims.

But the case was also disturbing from the point of view of the reaction of the psychiatrists and psychologists in the country. In particular, I knew a few of the professionals that worked in the psychiatric ward at the Military Hospital. I spoke to them several times urging them to publicly declare what was happening to Brito inside the hospital. They answered that they were doing what they could. They resisted immense pressure to accept him in the psychiatric ward and they kept their honest stance declaring Brito sane each time they were forced to repeat an evaluation. But they conceded that they weren't willing to publicly denounce the use of their hospital and the name of psychiatry to abuse Brito's rights. They were comprehensibly scared of what the consequences might be. When we protested outside of the hospital and invited them to join us, they rejected our invitation.

But, the rest of the country's mental health system was also timid. Even though we were able to organize an official protest supported by the Venezuelan Federation of Psychologists, we weren't able to get the psychiatric association to sign it.

The protests held outside of the hospital were never more than a small group of professionals and students. Most gave us vocal support but were not ready to publicly protest the abuse of the profession. Was not public protest something distanced from what clinical psychologists do?

I was even more dismayed by the fact that our university's clinical psychology program continued to develop its clinical practice at the Military Hospital during these events. I pleaded with the supervisors and authorities arguing that we could not continue teaching in those spaces as if nothing was happening. How could we teach an ethical, politically aware practice of our profession in a center where the rights of someone were being so dramatically abused in front of the whole country? Is it possible to conduct psychotherapy in a space where one knows that some opinions are dangerous? Can, for example, a lower ranking officer, as those that are often treated in the Military Hospital, truely be invited to share his conflicts with his superiors and speak freely of his anxieties, while another man is being held hostage by the government for expressing his opinions? Is psychotherapy conceivable under such circumstances? I believe that a reasonable training, at the very least, must pose those questions and not continue as if everything was normal.

The most frequent response was that they understood the gravity of the situation but what were they to do? Was that not something that had to do with human rights, and courts of laws, and not with clinical psychology?

I found that these responses were an eye-opener. Our professional identity, the definition of our task in technical terms, is often used as a defense against the conflicts politics bring to our field. It is a way to deny complicated dilemmas with which we prefer to not get too involved with.

4.4 Psychology, Euphemisms and Oxymorons

Chavismo has been creative and prolific producing arguments to defend the Revolution. The language of social sciences, in general, and psychology, in particular, has been recruited for those purposes (Llorens, 2018). A rather distinctive characteristic has been its emphasis on using the language of progressive causes and critical perspectives to downplay its authoritarianism, often using them to deny the abuses committed. As a result, Chavismo has often rendered them empty and meaningless.

For example, in 2016, the government set up a Ministry of Ecological Mining. When asked what exactly "ecological mining" is, the government officials conceded that it is not yet a clear concept (Arconoticias, 2017). This Ministry was inaugurated along with the CAMIMPEG, a national mining company, administered by the military that exploits the Arco Minero (the Mining Arc), a mining belt along the Orinoco River in the Amazon that covers 112,000 km^2. They have made deals with companies from Russia, China, Canada and the Republic of Congo to exploit the area, even though it is considered a protected territory free from commercial exploitation by Venezuelan law that decreed the Amazon National Park in 1973.

Investigative reports confirm how vast amounts of territory are controlled at present by organized crime linked to military officers (López, 2017). Reports calculated 200 ha of Amazonian forest have been lost between 2016 and 2017 due to the unregulated mining of these groups.

In the same vein, the government created in 2013 a Vice-Ministry with the extravagant name of Vice-Ministry of the Popular Power for the Supreme Happiness of the People. The explanation of its duties is rather vague, and it is practically impossible to know anything about what it is actually doing. It follows a trend in a number of countries that, following ideas coming from Positive Psychology, have begun to focus on happiness and its measurement as a governmental goal. As far as one can see in Venezuela, it was created as an act of propaganda. When Chávez arrived in power in 1999 there were 14 ministries. By 2014 the number had increased to 32 ministries and 107 vice-ministries (Infobae, 2014), making it, by 2017, the Latin American country with most ministries.

Much darker has been the euphemisms used to publicly justify the violent state of security commandos who have executed thousands of citizens. The security program launched in 2015 was named "the Operation to Liberate the People." It started off in 2015 with a militarized incursion into a poor neighborhood in Caracas that resulted in the murder of 14 young men and the arrest of almost 200 others (Zubillaga & Hanson, 2018). This program has systematically committed extrajudicial killings, most of which have occurred in poor neighborhoods. In March of 2017, the Attorney General reported that more than 4600 Venezuelans were murdered in 2016 at the hands of government's security forces. In 2017, the NGO Cofavic, accounted an even higher total of 5535 murders committed by security forces (Amnistía Internacional, 2019). After being highly criticized following the mass killing of 11 youngsters who were found in a mass grave without being identified, the government dealt with the issue renaming the program as the "Humanistic Operations to Liberate the People," and calling the mass murder "an isolated case" (Melendez, 2016), even though the appearance of mass graves has become a common affair (Llorens, 2016).

Another example of covering up human rights abuses with the tools of psychology refers to the trial of prominent opposition leader Leopoldo López. During the first day, on February 12, 2014, of what would be months of mass protests, three men were murdered, after which the government representatives blamed the opposition leaders through Twitter of those deaths. But the videotapes collected by news reporters and testimony of one of the victims proved that the national intelligence agency, SEBIN, was the author of all three murders, forcing government to change its version of the events (Boon, 2015). From accusing the opposition of perpetrating the murders, they decided to accuse the opposition leader, Leopoldo López, of planning and instigating the violence that happened on that day, which included a fire that was started in the building of the Attorney General's office.

Since it was demonstrated that López was not present when the fire erupted and when the murders occurred, he was accused of instigating the events based on three speeches that were "analyzed" by a lingüist and an "expert on discourse analysis." Expressions such as "this is a criminal, murdering, drug trafficking state," were taken as proof of his instigation to destroy public property. It is probably the first case of sentencing someone on the basis of a discourse analysis.

López was arrested, his trial dragged on for 19 months, in which the discourse analysis was considered the main bit of proof. He was condemned to serve 13 years and 9 months in jail, of which he served the first three in a military prison. Following the trial, the prosecuting attorney for the state escaped to the United States where he asked for forgiveness stating that the whole case had been a "farse with false evidence" (Neuman & Torres, 2015). The lingüist also later declared that she had been used by the government and that her report in no way constitutes proof against López. Finally, the judge of the trial also escaped the country and confessed to having accepted pressure into sentencing him as guilty (El Nacional, 2017).

4.5 The View from Abroad

Hugo Chávez was undoubtedly a charismatic figure that sparked huge sympathies not only in Venezuela but also across the globe. Chávez had a histrionic humorous character that helped to draw attention to his stunts, like the speech at the United Nations in which he famously began by saying that the devil had been there a day before and that the podium smelled of sulfur alluding to a previous address given by George Bush.[1] His revolutionary rhetoric, that defied traditional colonial powers and broke protocol along with the incredible amounts of income that entered the country, thanks to a spike in the prices of oil, during his first years in office, generated an image of an original voice in international politics, as well as a truly egalitarian president that was transforming the country for good.

Venezuela cannot be fully understood if one does not take oil into account. It is necessary to consider that, when Chávez came into power in 1999, oil was at its historical minimum. But starting in 2003 a huge oil boom began that allowed Venezuela to receive the largest commodity windfall in Latin American history, reaching the amount of one trillion dollars of revenue from 2003 to 2014 (Monaldi,

[1]See at: https://www.youtube.com/watch?v=ele3C0z2I7Y

2019). That allowed for a huge amount of spending money that was used in part on social programs, a lot on international relations and on propaganda. The unprecedented surplus was accompanied by huge amount of corruption and social programs based on hand-outs, but very little investment on infrastructure and development. A year into the downturn of the oil market, Venezuela's economy collapsed and the country has entered a hyperinflation ranked among the highest and longest in history and what has been termed as a prolonged humanitarian crisis by experts (Escobar, 2020).

Yet critical thinkers and social scientists around the world, such as Noam Chomsky, were charmed. He publicly exchanged kudos with Chávez. The latter mentioned that he always carried one of Chomsky's books during his trips and the former praised Chávez for "building a new world" during his celebrated visit to Caracas in 2009. International reporters described Chomsky as being "seduced" by Chávez (El País, 2009).

While international left leaning academia were praising Chávez, in Venezuela things were a little less bright. Many local social scientists who had originally been optimistic had begun to signal out massive corruption, clientelism, authoritarianism and human rights abuses.

Trying to express the terrible risks that the increasingly authoritarian and militarized rule that Chávez represented for Venezuela was, in many social scientific forums, an uphill battle. Inside, Venezuelan universities have had to fight censorship, restrictions to funding, lack of access to public information (Camardiel, Briceño-León, & Ávila, 2012) and, many times as has been mentioned, direct persecution (Kozak, 2018). Universities continue to operate in great part because of many professional's personal commitment to their disciplines, even though economic pressures have put many of them in a state of poverty. Acosta (2018a, 2018b), for example, has chronicled the effects of the economy on university professors of the country's oldest and probably the most prestigious public university, reporting cases of teachers who cannot buy their basic food supplies with their salaries.

Outside Venezuela we faced the condescending look of social scientists who were convinced they knew better than researchers in the country who were most surely part of the privileged elite who only wanted to harm the revolution and resist social change.

Activists from many parts of the world flocked to Venezuela to support Chavismo. However, many of those enthusiasts became disillusioned when they looked at it up close.

Clifton Ross, writer and college professor, who traveled to Venezuela many times since 2004, filmed a flattering documentary called "Venezuela: revolution from the inside out"[2] and co-wrote "Until the Rulers Obey" (Zibechi, Ross, & Rein, 2014). He recalls how he was actively courted, invited to literary festivals and celebrated as part of the international intellectuals that supported Chávez. He had

[2]https://www.youtube.com/watch?v=faDoxJoHGCw

begun to see many of the revolution's failings. But, at first, hesitated to report them, feeling he did not want to disempower the revolution. When speaking to the members of the opposition he found himself agreeing to the observation that Chavistas could only respond to criticism with empty rhetoric.

He began to listen to the other side of the story: "In Caracas, I met with opposition human rights activists, union leaders, and left wing academics for interviews. As the missing pieces of the puzzle began to fall into place, the reality of the Bolivarian catastrophe overwhelmed my resistance" (Ross, 2019).

Kozak argues that the seduction of the Bolivarian rhetoric, along with flagrant cases of buying sympathies with millions of dollars, like in the case of the academics from the spanish political party PODEMOS (Fiallo, 2019), has contributed to closing spaces for the majority of Venezuelan academics who oppose government end up being stereotyped as: "white, lettered, liberals, neo-conservatives, from the right, petty bourgeois, disconnected from popular sectors, 'middle classed'" (2018, p. 117).

Nahon-Serfaty, for example, who has confronted environmentalist movements for keeping silent about Chavismo's destruction of the Amazon with mining contracts (2018), reported that after confronting Chavismo's propaganda machine in a panel at the Public Service Alliance of Canada in Ottawa, a panel that didn't include one Venezuelan but did include various foreign ex-employees of the Venezuelan embassy in Canada. He was accused of being an "imperialist pig" and not having "renounced his white privilege" (2019).

Increasingly, Clifton Ross began to feel that his critical opinions that described Chavismo as a "synoptic delusion—compounded by immense waste, runaway corruption and populist authoritarianism" were risky. Other journalists reporting similar events were jailed and, on his last visit, he was unable to enter Venezuela before the elections, when government unexpectedly closed the border with Colombia during 6 days (Ross, 2013). He increasingly began to feel threatened:

> I had traveled to Venezuela in 2013 to cover the April presidential elections. By the time I returned to the US, I was disillusioned and depressed. I decided I needed to start writing and speaking about what I had seen there. In an article I wrote for the radical magazine *Counterpunch* around that time, I argued that "the so-called 'Bolivarian Revolution is bankrupt: morally, ideologically, and economically,' and I asked what we, as leftist solidarity activists, should do in response. 'Should we continue to make excuses for incompetence, corruption, and irresponsibility and thereby make ourselves accomplices?' I asked. 'Or should we tell the truth?'. (Ross, 2019, para. 2)

It leads to the point of inflection reported by Clifton Ross that occurred while speaking to a Venezuelan reporter who has written extensively about the tragic destruction of Guayana, part of the Mining Arc (Prat, 2012). Prat told him:

> Some of you in the critical, intellectual circles of Europe and the United States seem to think it's fine that in the countries of our Latin America there are arbitrary governments and processes full of abuses that in your countries you wouldn't consider allowing for a minute. No, in your own country you'd militantly reject the same things you seem to feel are perfectly fine to take place down here, far away, where it's exotic and interesting… (2019, para. 18)

Clifton Ross writes that he felt his: "face redden with shame, and I suddenly felt my whole world capsize" (2019, para. 18).

Two relevant consequences for psychology have been that, on one hand, it has been difficult to denounce the abuses reported in the international forum; on the other hand, that critical perspectives, which should serve to hold science accountable, were so misused by Chavismo's rhetoric that they have lost credibility. Inside the country, calls to social science and critical perspectives, like when Maduro states that Chávez was the creator of "twenty-first century feminism," are received with suspicion of being empty words used to justify power (Llorens, 2018).

4.6 Regarding Our Task as Psychologists

Perhaps the painful list of historical events that have led to the misuse of psychology as a weapon of repression and abuse, as well as the moments it has become a target of persecution can help us render visible the risk that clinical practice runs of being deformed to serve authoritarian political projects and not human suffering. It might also help us to open up the debate about the risks of training in a craft that attempts to develop independently from its political circumstances, blind to its contextual conditions.

It is risky because it simplifies the contexts in which suffering takes form and therefore leaves out crucial information that we should be listening to. It is also risky because it leaves our work unprotected, and it does not prepare us to respond to the dilemmas that political circumstances will continue to confront us with. The lack of training and reflection regarding the political dimension makes us vulnerable to manipulation and authoritarian abuse. When it happens, we are not prepared to protect the intimacy of the concrete people we owe ourselves to.

Those of us that have had the honor to work with those that have confronted abuses of power, in the private or the public realm, know the healing potential that a safe place to explore life can offer, a place where we can examine and accompany the experiences of terror, frailty, indignation and rage produced by these circumstances. We also know the liberating potential of having even only a tiny space where we can register the testimonies of struggle that allow us to defend our place in the world. Psychotherapy fosters the existence of the intimate truths that the powers, on occasion, are not willing to acknowledge. That is why I believe there is a huge liberating potential not only for the private lives of the people we work with but also for our collective existence.

Over and over again we have seen how the opening up of intimate, but shared space, where repressed voices can resonate and be heard, can help sustain personal freedom and offer hope to communities. Psychotherapeutic space validates silenced experiences, serves to witness struggles that otherwise might have passed unseen and unheard. It offers support and strength to those that have survived oppression.

Perhaps, along with the list of horrors that we have reviewed in the last two chapters, we should list the incredible amount of efforts psychiatrists and psychologists make around the world to offer a protected space of listening for those that have been persecuted, tortured and oppressed.

It is not surprising that governments around the world that seek to impose their view of the world and control all aspects of life distrust our craft. The effort to defend psychotherapy in times of crisis is not only an effort of professional survival, it is also an effort to defend freedom, to open space for debate and reflection in times of crisis, and protect the value of intimacy.

In George Orwell's (1979) classic dystopia, 1984, the protagonist begins to reflect on his experience under totalitarianism, thanks to two rather fortuitous events. A rather low-ranking public official, who works in the Ministry of Truth, discovers that the camera placed in his apartment to supervise his every breath is slightly tilted to one side, leaving a tiny space where he can put a desk and sit down without being seen. This marvelous discovery leads to the impulse of buying, without giving much thought to it, a pen and a notebook in which to start writing a personal diary. He begins writing without much of a plan, but immediately begins to feel a mix of fear and guilt, along with the desire to continue. The day before, in a obligatory public event in favor of Big Brother, he had run into a workmate with which he exchanged glances and seemed to recognize a shared feeling of rejection to the ideological imposition that they endured. The narrator tells:

> It was as though their two minds had opened and the thoughts were flowing from one into the other through their eyes. 'I am with you,' O'Brien seemed to be saying to him. 'I know precisely what you are feeling. I know all about your contempt, your hatred, your disgust. But don't worry, I am on your side!'. (p. 9)

These two small coincidences, a corner outside the control of external power and an instant of personal resonance with another human being, who shared his dismay, were enough to stir Winston Smith's capacity to take distance, take a step to one side, to reflect on the version of the world he was indoctrinated into, and search for a more personal version.

That is often enough: a small corner where intimacy and personal freedom can open space for personal transformation. In it lies the potential threat of therapy to authoritarianism.

References

Acosta, Y. (2018a). Sufrimiento psicosocial del Siglo XXI: Venezuela y la revolución. *Revista de Investigación Psicológica.* 19. Retrieved from http://www.scielo.org.bo/scielo.php?pid=S2223-30322018000100009&script=sci_arttext. Accessed 23 April 2020.

Acosta, Y. (2018b). Soy una profesora en Venezuela. *Prodavinci*. http://factor.prodavinci.com/profesoraenvenezuela/index.html. Accessed 12 August 2019.

Alzualde, C. (2017, March 15). Personal communication.

Amnistía Internacional. (2019). *Seguridad para la Vida: hacia una reconstrucción de una política pública integral.* Caracas: Amnistía Internacional.

Arconoticias. (2017, October 26). Preguntas (y respuestas) incómodas sobre el Arco Minero de Orinoco. *Arconoticias*. https://arconoticias-info.blogspot.com/2017/10/preguntas-y-respuestas-incomodas-sobre.html. Accessed 20 April 2020.

Ávila, K. (in press). ¿Qué pasó con la reforma policial en Venezuela? In V. Zubillaga, & M. Llorens (Eds). *Dicen que Están Matando Gente en Venezuela: violencia armada y políticas de seguridad ciudadana.* Madrid: Dahbar.

Boon, L. (2015). La investigación que desarmó la historia oficial sobre el 12F. *Runrunes*. http://runrun.es/rr-es-plus/investigacion/186376/la-investigacion-que-desarmo-la-historia-oficial-sobre-el-12f.html. Accessed 17 Februrary 2017.

Buada, G. (2019, May 22). Trabajadores de la salud perseguidos por visibilizar la crisis en Venezuela. *Amnistía Internacional.* https://www.amnistia.org/ve/blog/2019/05/10568/trabajadores-de-la-salud-perseguidos-por-visibilizar-la-crisis-en-venezuela. Accessed 14 March 2020.

Camardiel, A., Briceño-León, R., & Ávila, O. (2012). Los 30 delitos más comunes en la información oficial. In R. Briceño-León, O. Ávila, & A. Camardiel (Eds.), *Violencia e Institucionalidad: informe del Observatorio de Violencia 2012* (pp. 115–121). Caracas: Editorial Alfa.

Casey, N. (2016, October 1). At a loss for meds, Venezuela's mentally ill spiral downward. *The New York Times.* https://www.nytimes.com/2016/10/02/world/americas/venezuela-mental-health-medicine-shortages.html. Accessed 14 March 2020.

Casique, I. (2009). La intelectualidad peligrosa de la revolución bolivariana. *El Puente, 6,* 6–7.

Ciudad CCS. (2016, September 24). Venezolana de Televisión estrena este jueves La Política en el Diván. *Ciudad CCS.* https://web.archive.org/web/20160924212831/http://www.vtv.gob.ve/articulos/2015/10/15/venezolana-de-television-estrena-este-jueves-la-politica-en-el-divan-141.html. Accessed 15 March 2020.

El Nacional. (2004, March 27). Federación Médica Venezolana: defensa institucional de los médicos venezolanos. *El Nacional.* A-5.

El Nacional. (2004, April 26). Federación Médica llevará a Capella a Tribunal Disciplinario. *El Nacional.* B-16.

El Nacional. (2015, October 23). Jorge Rodríguez: Oposición sufre de trastorno antisocial de la personalidad. *El Nacional.* http://www.el-nacional.com/noticias/politica/jorge-rodriguez-oposicion-sufre-trastorno-antisocial-personalidad_37618. Accessed 2 December 2017.

El Nacional. (2017, November 22). Jueza del caso de Leopoldo López huyó del país por miedo al gobierno. *El Nacional.* http://www.el-nacional.com/noticias/politica/jueza-del-caso-leopoldo-lopez-huyo-del-pais-por-miedo-gobierno_212524. Accessed 23 April 2020.

El País. (2009, August 25). "Chávez construye un mundo diferente y posible": el prestigioso intelectual Noam Chomsky se deja seducir por el presidente venezolano en Caracas. *El País.* https://elpais.com/internacional/2009/08/25/actualidad/1251151204_850215.html. Accessed 15 August 2017.

Escobar, M. (2020, March 17). Lo de Venezuela es una Emergencia Continuada. *El Tiempo.* https://www.eltiempo.com/mundo/venezuela/venezuela-susana-raffalli-habla-sobre-informe-del-programa-mundial-de-alimentos-474138. Accessed 23 April 2020.

Fernández, J. (2018, November 17). La mujer que se enfrenta al río. *La Vida de Nos.* http://www.lavidadenos.com/la-mujer-que-se-enfrenta-al-rio/. Accessed 15 August 2019.

Fiallo, M. (2019, April 3). Grabaciones filtradas demuestran cómo el chavismo financia a Podemos. Panam Post. https://es.panampost.com/mamela-fiallo/2019/04/03/grabaciones-filtradas-demuestran-como-el-chavismo-financia-a-podemos/?cn-reloaded=1&__cf_chl_jschl_tk__. Accessed 30 April 2020.

Flores, J. (2017, June 15). Derecha busca con guerra psicológica naturalizar la violencia política. *Ciudad CCS.* https://issuu.com/ciudadccs/docs/ccs_15062017. Accessed 23 April 2020.

Giuliani, F. (2017, July 1). Personal communication.

Goncalves, M., & Gutiérrez, J. (2005). *Análisis del acoso psicológico laboral (mobbing) en despedidos del sector público en Venezuela.* 2003–2005 (Unpublished Thesis). Caracas: Universidad Católica Andrés Bello.
Hanke, P. (2019, November 13). Venezuela's hyperinflation drags on for a near record - 36 months. *Forbes.* https://www.forbes.com/sites/stevehanke/2019/11/13/venezuelas-hyperinflation-drags-on-for-a-near-record36-months/#6f8957676b7b. Accessed 14 March 2020.
Infobae. (2014, July 3). Venezuela es el país con mayor número de ministerios en todo el mundo. *Infobae.* https://www.infobae.com/2014/07/03/1578082-venezuela-es-el-pais-el-mayor-numero-ministerios-todo-el-mundo/. Accessed 19 March 2020.
Kozak, G. (2018). Políticas contra el pensamiento social y humanístico en la Venezuela Revolucionaria. En Chaguaceda, A. y Vives, H. (Eds.). *Las Ciencias Sociales en Contextos Autoritarios: producción académica, censura y represión en los escenarios de post guerra fría* (pp. 116–133). Buenos Aires: CADAL, FHRC y Universidad de Guadalajara.
Krygier, R., & Faiola, A. (2019, November 28). Locked up naked on a soiled matrress: Venezuela's mental health nightmare. *The Washington Post.* https://www.washingtonpost.com/world/the_americas/locked-up-naked-on-a-soiled-mattress-venezuelas-mental-health-nightmare/2019/11/27/e465f16c-0020-11ea-8341-cc3dce52e7de_story.html. Accessed 14 March 2020.
López, E. (2017, September 19). Gang lords rule the Orinoco Mining Arc. *OCCRP.* https://www.occrp.org/en/goldandchaos/gang-lords-rule-the-orinoco-mining-arc. Accessed 20 April 2020.
Llorens, M. (2016, November 28). When mass graves are 'normal', normality isn't. *Caracas Chronicles.* https://www.caracaschronicles.com/2016/11/28/mass-graves-normal-normality-abnormal/. Accessed 19 March 2020.
Llorens, M. (2018). Análisis del discurso para perseguir: la perversión chavista del lenguaje de las ciencias sociales. *Analogías, 16,* 10–27.
Marcano, S. (1987). Autocracia y violencia política en la insitución psicoanalítica. In H. Calello, S. Neuhaus, C. Kohn, S. Marcano, & H. Da Ruos (Eds.), *Terrorismo de Estado y Violencia Psíquica* (pp. 145–170). Caracas: Tropykos.
Melendez, N. (2016, November 27). Cronología/ Los muertos de Barlovento o como la OLP terminó en masacre. *Runrunes.* https://runrun.es/investigacion/288543/cronologia-los-muertos-de-barlovento-o-como-una-olp-termino-en-masacre/. Accessed 23 April 2020.
Monaldi, F. (2019, June 12). The collpase and upcoming rise of Venezuela and its oil industry. *Forbes.* https://www.forbes.com/sites/thebakersinstitute/2019/06/12/the-collapse-and-upcoming-rise-of-venezuela-and-its-oil-industry/#693504c34992. Accessed 20 March 2020.
Nahon-Serfaty, I. (2018). Why global environmentalists are silent on Venezuela's mining crisis. *The Conversation.* https://theconversation.com/why-global-environmentalists-are-silent-on-venezuelas-mining-crisis-98043. Accessed 20 April 2020.
Nahon-Serfaty, I. (2019, April 1). Confronting Maduro's Propaganda Machine in Canada. *Caracas Chronicles.* https://www.caracaschronicles.com/2019/04/01/confronting-maduros-propaganda-machine-in-canada/. Accessed 20 April 2020.
Neuman, W., & Torres, P. (2015, October 25). Venezuelan prosecutor says opposition leader's trial was a farse. *The New York Times.* https://www.nytimes.com/2015/10/26/world/americas/venezuela-human-rights-opposition-leopoldo-lopez.html. Accessed 15 February 2017.
Núñez, M. (2003, September 12). Renuncié a Barrio Adentro porque constaté mala praxis. *El Nacional.* B-16.
Orwell, G. (1979). *1984.* Barcelona: Ediciones Destino.
Paullier, J. (2018, March 27). "Hay una guerra mediática, psicológica casi de linchamiento en contra de Venezuela": Jorge Rodríguez, Ministro de Comunicación. *BBC.* https://www.bbc.com/mundo/noticias-america-latina-43544726. Accessed 23 April 2020.
Pilato, E. (2010, March 10). Franklin Brito es un caso emblemático de la criminalización de la protesta en Venezuela. *USB Noticias.* http://usbnoticias.usb.ve/post/12193. Accessed 15 March 2020.
Prat, D. (2012). *Guayana: el milagro al revés.* Caracas: Alfa.

Reyes, A. (2006, November 2). Más de siete delitos pueden imputarse al ministro de Energía Rafael Ramírez. El Nacional. A-2.

Rodríguez, E. (2005). *La Disociación Psicótica: arma ideológica de la contrarrevolución bolivariana*. Caracas: Ministerio de Comunicación e Información.

Rodríguez, J. (2016, September 30). Jorge Rodríguez, La Política en el Diván. La Psicosis de Henry Ramos Allup. https://www.youtube.com/watch?v=jbcASrSGMpY. Accessed 23 April 2020.

Rodríguez, J. (2017). *La psicosis es el trastorno de la oposición*. http://jorgerodriguez.psuv.org.ve/2016/09/30/campana/la-psicosis-es-el-trastorno-de-la-oposicion/# Wi7x1Lwwc9c. Accessed 2 December 2017.

Rodríguez, P. (2013, August 30). Franklin Brito: a tres años de su muerte. *Prodavinci*. http://historico.prodavinci.com/2013/08/30/actualidad/el-caso-de-franklin-brito-a-tres-anos-de-su-muerte-por-pedro-enrique-rodriguez/. Accessed 15 March 2020.

Rosales, N. (2017, June 12). I Foro Internacional de Psicología insta a construir una cultura de paz en Venezuela. *Gobierno Bolivariano de Venezuela*. Accessed 15 July 2020.

Ross, C. (2013, April 12). Locked out on the Venezuelan border. *Counterpunch*. https://www.counterpunch.org/2013/04/12/locked-out-on-the-venezuelan-border/. Accessed 20 April 2020.

Ross, C. (2019, February 1). The Bolivarian God that failed. *Quillete.com*. https://quillette.com/2019/02/01/the-bolivarian-god-that-failed/. Accessed 20 April 2020.

Sarmiento, M. (2019, July 8). Murió paciente psiquiátrico que tenía pie infectado con gusanos. *Crónica Uno*. https://cronica.uno/murio-paciente-psiquiatrico-que-tenia-pie-infectado-con-gusanos/. Accessed 14 March 2020.

Smilde, D., & Hanson, R. (2014, January 13). Maduro militariza vigilancia policial en Venezuela, de nuevo. *Insight Crime*. https://es.insightcrime.org/noticias/analisis/maduro-militariza-vigilancia-policial-en-venezuela-de-nuevo/. Accessed 23 April 2020.

Torres, S. (2017, June 13). Villegas: solo la verdad puede alcanzar la justicia. *Ciudad CCS*. https://issuu.com/ciudadccs/docs/ccs13062017. Accessed 23 April 2020.

Vásquez, P. (2010). Compassionate Militarization: The Management of a Natural Disaster in Venezuela. In D. Fassin, & M. Pandolfi (Eds.), *Contemporary states of emergency. The politics of military and humanitarian interventions* (pp. 135–149). New York: Zone Books.

Vásquez, P. (2019). Somatic power in the Bolivarian Revolution: Biopolitics and sacrifice in the case of Franklin Brito. *Bulletin of Latin American Research*. https://doi.org/10.1111/blar.12948 . Accessed 20 April 2020.

Venezolana de Televisión. (2010, January 14). Fiscal general: El productor Franklin Brito está incapacitado mentalmente. *VTV*. http://www.vtv.gov.ve/noticias-nacionales/28562. Accessed 15 April 2014.

Zibechi, R., Ross, C., & Rein, M. (2014). *Until the rulers obey: Voices from Latin American social movements*. Michigan: PM Press.

Zubillaga, V., & Hanson, R. (2018). Los operativos militarizados en la era post-Chávez: del punitivismo carcelario a la matanza carcelaria. *Nueva Sociedad*. Noviembre-Diciembre, 278.

Zubillaga, V., & Llorens, M. (in press). Dicen Que Están Matando Gente en Venezuela. Madrid: Dahbar.

Chapter 5
Psychotherapy with Victims and Survivors of Violence

5.1 Psychology's Resistance

Psychology, since its origins, has had difficulty listening to the testimonies of the victims of violence. Clinicians who have documented the effects of violence in the lives of the people they treat have historically had to face the resistance of their colleagues and the rest of the society. The difficulty that psychology had in order to recognize child abuse is a classic example.

Let's recall Freud's early theories on the origin of his patient's symptoms, as they appeared in Studies on Hysteria, in which the main hypothesis was that these women had experienced some sort of sexual abuse. The promptness with which the possibility of sexual abuse is discarded by some clinicians and the reticence for many psychoanalysts to think of the issue makes it relevant to quote Freud directly in Heredity and Etiology of the Neuroses (1896/1976):

> A passive sexual experience before puberty: this, then, is the specific aetiology of hysteria. I will without delay add some factual details and some commentary to the result I have announced, in order to combat the scepticism with which I expect to meet. I have been able to carry out a complete psycho-analysis in thirteen cases of hysteria, three of that number being true combinations of hysteria and obsessional neurosis. (I do not speak of hysteria with obsessions). In none of these cases was an event of the kind defined above missing. It was represented either by a brutal assualt committed by an adult or by a seduction less rapid and less repulsive, but reaching the same conclusion. In seven out of the thirteen cases the intercourse was between children on both sides - sexual relations between a little girl and a boy a little older (most often her brother) who had himself been the victim of an earlier seduction. These relations sometimes continued for years, until the little guilty parties reached puberty; the boy would repeat the same practices with the little girl over and over again and without alteration - practices to which he himself had been subject by some female servant or governess and which on account of their origin were often of a disgusting sort. In a few cases there was a combination of an assault and relations between children or a repetition of a brutal abuse.
>
> The date of this precocious experience varied. In two cases the series started in the little creature's second year; the commonest age in my observation was the fourth or fifth year. It

M. Llorens, *Politically Reflective Psychotherapy*, Latin American Voices,
https://doi.org/10.1007/978-3-030-57792-6_5

> may be somewhat by accident, but I have formed an impression from this that a passive sexual experience occurring only after the age of from eight to ten is no longer able to serve as the foundation of the neurosis …
>
> The precocious event has left an indelible imprint on the history of the case; it is represented in it by a host of symptoms and of special features which could be accounted for in no other way. (p. 376–377)

In Freud's clinical histories on the study of hysteria, recollections of very clear events of sexual abuse are reported. Perhaps the most evident is that of Katharina, a youngster Freud met in the middle of his vacations in a mountain. Here he listens to the story of how an:

> uncle had made sexual advances to her, when she was only fourteen years old. She described how she had once gone with him on an expedition down into the valley in the winter and had spent the night in the inn there. He sat in the bar drinking and playing cards, but she felt sleepy and went up to bed early in the room they were to share on the upper floor. She was not quite asleep when he came up; then she fell asleep again and woke up suddenly 'feeling his body' in the bed. She jumped up and remonstrated with him: 'What are you up to, Uncle? Why don't you stay in your own bed?' He tried to pacify her: 'Go on, you silly girl, keep still. You don't know how nice it is.' …
>
> She went on to tell me of yet other experiences of somewhat later date: how she had once again had to defend herself against him in an inn when he was completely drunk, and similar stories. (1895/1976, p. 115)

There are repeated reports similar to the one that point much more to experiences of threat and anguish on the part of the women and abuse of power by their caretakers, than erotic fantasies. The author's anxiety in reporting these stories is also evident on occasion. For example, in the notes of the appendix added in 1924, Freud explains, regarding Katharina, that:

> I venture after the lapse of so many years to lift the veil of discretion and reveal the fact that Katharina was not the niece but the daughter of the landlady. The girl fell ill, therefore, as a result of sexual attempts on the part of her own father. (p. 120)

The surprising and controversial character of repeated reports of sexual abuse in the lives of these women contributed in great part to Freud's dismissal of his seduction theory (Masson, 1997). In the months following the publication of his "Studies on Hysteria," Freud began to shift his theory and change his hypothesis of sexual abuse to presumed unconscious fantasies that expressed repressed desires. Later studies showed how difficult it was for Freud to deal with these observations at the beginning of his exploration of the unconscious and how he debated these ideas in the midst of his worries about the implications if these findings were true. The letters between Freud and Fliess evidence this, as Masson has controversially chronicled (1997).

These debates have continued in the following hundred years. The ordeal regarding Jeffrey Masson's research on these historical events is revealing. The fact that, after being the Director of the Freud Archives, he was dismissed because of his controversial conclusions in the book "Assault on Truth", is a testament to the difficulty these issues pose to the clinical establishment. Even considering that

Masson was tendentious, overinterpreting Freud's fear and failing to recognize reasonable doubt, direct quotes evidence Freud's reticence to expose clear cases of sexual harassment. The fact that Anna Freud tried to avoid the publication of Masson's book is a terrible stain to psychoanalysis.

Other clinicians like Alice Miller, who were psychoanalytically trained, have also widely reported multiple cases in which analysts have left out clear evidence of situations of sexual abuse in their therapeutic work. She signals out how denial on the part of therapists, because of the emotional impact that incest produces, colludes with ideological beliefs rendering episodes of abuse invisible (1984/1991). This brings us back to a controversy that has been in psychoanalysis from its beginnings, and that Ferenczi presented in 1932 in the XII International Psychoanalytic Congress, with his now classic paper "The Confusion of Tongues," where he criticizes his colleagues for having disregarded for so long the "traumatic factors in the pathogenesis of neurosis" (149, p. 225).

The clinicians who continued during the twentieth century to insist on the importance of traumatic external events to obtain a complete and contextualized comprehension were often relegated to the margins of the scientific debate (Herman, 1997; Masson, 1997; Miller, 1997).

The resistance to recognize the presence of violence against children occurred in other places besides psychology. It wasn't until 1962 that the medical field began to do it, thanks to a pediatrician that began to report injuries found in his consulting room as product of mistreatment rather than accidents. When Henry Kempe published his article in 1948 on the "battered child syndrome," he met with considerable rejection of his ideas from the medical establishment (Wiehe, 1998).

It is relevant to mention these episodes to illustrate the difficulties psychology has had carrying the weight that comes with the recognition of the extension and severity of situations of abuse. On occasions, the impression that these findings produce is they are so terrible that they cannot possibly be true. I underline this fact because I believe that it continues to happen in clinical practice. In spite of all the advances made regarding these issues and that most clinicians are much more aware of them, it is often still the case that the relevance of violence and the difficulties of the contexts in the lives of the people we treat are left out.

Salter (1995) has collected a series of texts from the twentieth century that stated sexual abuse had no negative effects or that it was even potentially beneficial. She considers that psychoanalytic theory, with its emphasis on the intrapsychic, has tended to dismiss the weight of external traumatic experience in the production of clinical symptoms. Other analysts have had similar opinions in different latitudes like Bowlby in UK (Bowlby, 2005) and Giberti in Argentina (2002).

We know how difficult it is to listen to those who have suffered persecution and abuse. Experiences of extreme helplessness disturb our most basic beliefs and our relation to the world. For example, those who listen to the stories of extreme violence can begin to feel more vulnerable, invaded by thoughts of threat and feelings of terror. They can begin to feel impotent faced with the impossibility of stopping some of those situations or frustrated by the time it takes to restore safety and adaptation. Beliefs and faith in humanity can be questioned. Some stories of abuse defy our capacity to imagine if such acts of cruelty are really possible. All this can lead us to downplay the veracity of some reports or dissociate. It is not uncommon for a therapist to have difficulties reconstructing elements of a particularly intense session in which a patient relived some of his traumatic memories. On occasions, therapists can reject their feelings of impotence and vulnerability by blaming the victim of not having done enough, or for having "provoked" the events, which of course is terribly damaging.

These experiences that can happen in the intimacy of the therapeutic relationship can also happen to all of society. Countries struggle with the task of listening to the voices of the victims of human atrocity as well as to sustain the memory of traumatic histories; they tend to silence or forget painful or shameful events or downplay their significance. We have been able to witness recently, for example, how Colombia is in the middle of an intense society-wide struggle to listen to the voices of the victims of its long-armed conflict in which steps have been taken to acknowledge those experiences, while other forces try to dismiss and deny them. When advances to repair the damage, reach agreements and attend to the aftermath have been achieved, other events seem to pull everything back again (Holmes, 2019).

Herman (1997) tells us about the dilemmas of the war veterans in the United States. Once the wars are over, they become uncomfortable reminders of trauma. Those that have struggled to denounce the horrors of history have met with pressure to not dwell on the past and turn the page. Elie Wiesel, in a talk given in a forum on memory and history, titled "In Praise of Memory" (2002), recalled how, after returning from concentration camps people would advise him to forget such a nightmarish experience. He writes: "Forgetting was given as pedagogic and therapeutic advice for youngsters; those youngsters that had turned into old men" (p. 223). In the same manner, our Latin American societies have had enormous difficulties assuming the results of the truth commissions installed after the atrocities committed in dictatorships in Argentina and Chile (Sábato, 1998).

Herman argues that the study of psychological trauma has taken its place in psychology, no thanks to the efforts of the professionals of our discipline, but thanks to the political movements that have struggled to keep those issues alive. She chronicles how three decisive events that opened up space to listen to victims were politically motivated. The first one was when Charcot, in Paris, wanted to prove that hysterical symptoms of the women hospitalized at the Salpetriere were not suffering from spiritual problems and their cure was not religious, but medical. The power struggle between the church and the science was the context that allowed the first reports of trauma and child sexual abuse to surface. The second event was the World Wars, where the marks of combat forced psychiatrists and psychologists to rethink their theories and approaches. The third moment occurs as a result of the feminist movement. In the 60s and 70s, the movement organized women in discussion groups who began to share their personal experiences. These groups evidenced the extent to which abuse and family violence was present in the society. This led to a series of epidemiological studies that confirmed the enormous number of women who reported of being victims of rape and/or child abuse. Herman also shows a collection of researchers who registered the issue but were later relegated and forgotten. Pierre Janet perhaps being the most relevant example. Her words resonate with our experience in Venezuela:

> The systematic study of psychological trauma therefore depends on the support of a political movement. Indeed, whether such study can be pursued or discussed in public is itself a political question. The study of war trauma becomes legitimate only in a context that challenges the sacrifice of young men in war. The study of trauma in sexual and domestic life becomes legitimate only in a context that challenges the subordination of women and children. Advances in the field occur only when they are supported by a political movement powerful enough to legitimate an alliance between investigators and patients and to counteract the ordinary social processes of silencing and denial. In the absence of strong political movements for human rights, the active process of bearing witness inevitably gives way to the active process of forgetting. Repression, dissociation, and denial are phenomena of social as well as individual consciousness. (Herman, 1997, p. 9)

Jorge Semprún, the Spanish writer who was held at the Nazi concentration camp in Buchenwald during the Second World War, was almost 50 years later, able to record his memories of that experience in a beautiful book titled: *Literature or Life*. In it, he details the years after the war and the strategies he used to avoid the suffering caused by the remembrance of the many traumas and losses suffered during captivity. The book is a moving account of a man struggling between his desire to never have to return to the memories of those years and the need to express them in order to free himself from them. Simultaneously, he describes the look of those that know his traumatic past and struggle with their own resistance of having to listen to its horror. From the first instant, when he is freed, he meets the compassionate and horrified look of others. In the midst of his personal struggle to confront his life, Semprún questions a humanity that is struggling with its own difficulties to hear these testimonies. His questions are particularly relevant to those who work as therapists. He wrote:

> But will people hear everything, imagine everything? Will they be able to understand? Will they have the necessary patience, passion, compassion, rigor? I begin to doubt it, in that first moment, that first meeting with men from before, from the outside, emissaries from life - when I see the stunned, almost hostile, and certainly suspicious look in the eyes of the three officers. (Semprún, 1995, p. 26)

5.2 Rendering Family Violence Visible

So it is not until the 70s that the study of the frequency and effects of family violence begins to consolidate. The feminist movement helped evidence the amount of violence in private lives and challenged the public perception about its presence in society. Public manifestations were organized. For example, in 1976 an International Court to prosecute crimes against women was set up in Brussels. In the United States the movement generated judicial reform. Women researchers fought to open up space for these issues in academy. The first large-scale epidemiological studies were done in those years (Horowitz, 1999). The psychiatrist, Salter (1995), shows how the last 40 years produced a growing increase of research in this area.

Even though clinical literature had described signs and symptoms related to the exposure to traumatic events such as "shell shock" and "rape trauma syndrome," it wasn't until 1980 that post-traumatic stress disorder (PTSD) was incorporated into the DSM-III. The creation of the diagnosis influenced the significant increase in trauma research. Studies on prevalence, risk factors, protective factors and treatments multiplied.

Along with the wave of research on PTSD, research on the different situations of abuse in the private domain also increased. At the end of the 70s and the beginning of the 80s, a number of studies on the prevalence of histories of abuse in the childhood of the adult population were done (Haugaard, 2000). These studies found alarming numbers that helped raise awareness. The stats of the National Center on Child Abuse Prevention Research of the National Committee to Prevent Child Abuse (NCPA) reflect the increase of awareness throughout the years. The numbers show that in 1976 there were 10.1 abuse cases reported for every 1000 inhabitants, a rate that increased systematically reaching 47 reports every 1000 inhabitants in 1996 (Wiehe, 1998). In a national victimization study with a sample of 2000 youngsters from 10 to 16 years of age, 15.3% of the girls and 5.9% of the boys reported some type of sexual assault, for a total of 197 youngsters affected. Of those 197 youngsters, only 64% communicated the event to another person. 48% of the sample reported that the abuse was repeated (Boney-McCoy & Finkelhor, 1995). In other countries like Spain, the first studies about incidence of the problem were done toward the end of the 80s (Costa, Morales, & Juste, 1997). The study mentioned that they were probably only beginning to register the "tip of the iceberg" when they found reports of sexual abuse in 1.5% of the population.

Research began to not only evidence the high prevalence of cases but also the harmful effects of those experiences. So, for example, with respect to child abuse, researchers have recollected a very wide series of observations that allow us to understand the effects on wellbeing. Even though the literature at the beginning of the twentieth century surprisingly stated that child sexual abuse did not have emotional consequences for the victims (Bender & Blau, 1937; Weiss, Rogers, Darwin & Dutton, 1955; cited by Salter, 1995), the stories of abuse and a wide array of psychiatric diagnoses like dissociative, anxiety, post-traumatic, affect, substance abuse, eating, psychosomatic, borderline and histrionic personality disorders, along with psychotic episodes have been confirmed to be related (Andrews, Brewin, Rose, & Kirk, 2000; Briere, 1992; Busby, Glenn, Steggel, & Adamson, 1993; Dubner & Motta, 1999; Kernberg, 2001; Pérez de Antelo, 2002; Stone, 1989). Herman adds that many adult survivors of abuse can pass unnoticed during long periods, keeping traumatic memories dissociated until an event precipitates a crisis that can manifest itself in the shape of many different psychiatric categories (1997).

Studies done with psychiatric patients found that up to 57% have been reported being victims of child abuse (Brown & Anderson, 1991). The same authors compared psychiatric diagnoses with the presence of physical or sexual abuse and found that 40% of the sample of 96 patients had a personality disorder diagnosis, 29% of adaptive disorder, 17% alcohol abuse and 11% abuse of another substance, along with lower percentages of major depression, generalized anxiety disorder, PTSD, eating disorders, schizophrenia and sexual disorders.

The research on substance abuse disorders has consistently found a significantly higher rate of abuse in patients than in the rest of the population. A study done with a large sample in Los Angeles found that 45% of sexually abused men had diagnoses of abuse of illegal substances, compared with 8% of a control group. 14% of women had the same diagnosis, as well as 21% who had an alcohol abuse diagnosis, compared to 3 and 4% in the control group (Salter, 1995). Dissociative identity disorder is another important diagnosis that has demonstrated to have previous experiences of sexual abuse in rates from 83 to 95% (Herman, 1997; Kluft, 1991; Putnam, 1989).

When looked at from the perspective of depressive and anxiety-related symptoms, rather than from diagnostic categories, those who suffered abuse present these symptoms more often than the general population and have a younger age of onset (Boney-McCoy & Finkelhor, 1995; Lizardi, Klein, Crosby, Riso, Anderson & Donaldson, 1995). Higher rates of self-injury have also been found (Salter, 1995).

It is relevant to underline how victims of child maltreatment have a higher rate of violent adult relationships. It has been consistently found that victims of sexual abuse in their childhoods have a higher probability to suffer rape in their adult lives as well as higher probabilities of getting into prostitution (van der Kolk, 1989). Studies have found that 41% of abused children present self-harming behaviors such as hitting themselves in the head, biting, cutting or burning themselves. Finally, scientific literature reports that a higher percentage of delinquents with destructive actions toward others had childhood experiences of abuse. For example, a study done with 14 young murderers sentenced to death in the United States showed that 12 of them had been brutally abused and five had been sodomized by family members (van der Kolk, 1989).

What I am trying to bring attention to is how our field dismissed such a significant etiological cause of psychological and social suffering for so many years.

5.3 Interpersonal and Political Violence

Even though the previous section seems to diverge from our main theme, it is useful to explore in order to evidence how it questioned traditional clinical thinking. In the first place, they direct our attention to the weight of external circumstances in the etiology of emotional suffering (Kemper, 1992). In second place, abuse is a direct consequence of oppressive relationships in which the abuser takes advantage of its power to submit the other. This is a key element in the way suffering is later expressed. The comprehension of the symptoms and the treatment needs to include the effects of the experiences of helplessness. This makes the distribution of power in relationships a central factor in the dynamic comprehension and the clinical intervention, which is another way of saying that it places politics at the center of clinical considerations.

Research on trauma, as we have seen, demonstrated the existence of many more cases of family violence than what specialists had recognized. Violence had not been considered a central issue in clinical training. Increasingly it has grown to be considered an urgent theme.

Clinical theory, developed in the medical tradition, tends to search for the root of disorders in individual, internal factors, constitutional predispositions, developmental factors, neurobiological disorders, etc. Even though environmental factors have never been excluded, their analysis has been framed in an individual perspective. For example, Freudian theory of war neurosis considers that traumatic events affect the individual in relation to their psychic constitution and early experiences. The impact of war is in a sense diminished and our exploration is directed toward individual and constitutional elements.

Even learning-based theories like behaviorism, although oriented toward searching for causes in the environment, tended to emphasize the immediate and interpersonal contingencies, much less the cultural and political ones (Malagodi, 1986). Cognitive perspectives, derived from behaviorism, continued to relegate culture until more recently (DiMaggio, 1997). Some behaviorist researchers have even concluded that cultural influences are not relevant in areas such as education (Kauffman, Gardner, & Oswald, 2008).

Medical tradition colludes with the emotional impact that work with victims has on witnesses. The suffering of war veterans, refugees, persecuted political dissidents, victims of rape, of sexual abuse or mistreatment can be so intense and chronic that the reports of those experiences become threatening to others. It has been widely reported how the "just world hypothesis" can operate as a defense against awareness of these events. The just world hypothesis can make observers ask victims, "what did you do to provoke this?". It is difficult for those who have not experienced these events to tolerate the knowledge that terrible acts of cruelty can occur (Bar-On, 1999). All of these elements tend to take our view away from the contextual factors that provoked the violence and direct it to the victim.

Family therapist, White (1995), was acutely critical of theories that point to the internal original of victimization and applied it to his work with women who had suffered violence. He explained how the tendency to psychologize personal experience can be a very conservative position, pathologizing the historical and political factors that lead to abuse, avoiding having to deal with them.

Work with victims of violence began to direct our gaze toward wider contextual factors that had been traditionally left out of clinical theory. For example, inequality, social prejudices and power begin to surface as relevant factors to understand the dynamics of abusive relationships.

Again, the feminist movement played a key role in reviewing and challenging theory. The reflection on the general conditions of inequality that have affected the lives of women in most or all contemporary societies led the discussion toward the historical, political and social factors that have contributed to oppression. In regard to domestic violence, it began to be evidenced that abuse cannot be explained away pointing to a sadistic male or a masochistic woman. The amount of violence did not confirm this reading, and a detailed analysis of each case discarded this hypothesis. Other variables, such as patriarchy and *machismo*, began to evidence their relevance in the construction of unequal intimate relationships that were prone to strategies of domination in which violence is one of those strategies.

The sharpest illustration of the challenge to clinical thinking that I have heard was from a clinician from Costa Rica, Cecilia Claramundt. During an event in Mexico City, where Cecilia was training medical personnel on the management of cases of gender violence, a psychiatrist who was attending stood up to question the workshop arguing that, in his experience, all the women who he had seen that were in a violent relationship hada masochistich element in their personality that explained why they stayed in the relationship. Cecilia calmly answered that if the high prevalence of family violence in Mexico could be explained exclusively by the presence of intrapsychic factors like masochism in women, then it seemed logic to think that the circumstances suffered by the indigenous cultures that had been subjected to centuries of abuse, slavery and violence during Spanish colonial rule, could also be explained by the presence of masochism in those ethnic groups. The reaction of the audience, filled with male Mexican doctors, being told by a female Costa Rican psychologist, that their culture might have been masochistic was the perfect climax for her to conclude: "if we disregard historical, economic, cultural and political factors and only emphasize individual psychological variables, we run the risk of over-simplifying and labeling people who live in oppressive circumstances." An effective clinical treatment of violence must include the social and political dimension in the comprehension and treatment of these cases.

Systemic family theories, although much more active incorporating contextual factors to their formulations, have also been criticized for their management of incest and violence in the family. The systemic logic that locates responsibility in all the members can serve to obscure the power differentials and strategies of control, secrecy and oppression that can be used by abusers, as well as the societal context in which abuse occurs. The responsibility of the aggressor can be blurred behind the comprehension of family dysfunction.

For those that deal with violence, patriarchy, gender stereotypes, economic factors are essential to think of the problem and articulate solutions (Jukes, 1999). The inclusion of the analysis of the distribution of power in relationships introduces the political dimension in clinical considerations and allows a framework that transcends a strictly intrapsychic conception. It does not necessarily imply abandoning considerations of personality, development, individual conflicts of the individual being treated, rather it allows us to connect these dimensions to their place in the social sphere. It allows us to, if we are trying to help someone in an oppressive circumstance (think, for example, slavery), alleviate the symptoms of their suffering, without losing sight of the fact that true help cannot leave out addressing the situation of oppression. It must be considered a central factor sustaining the suffering. Only attending to the individual contributes to naturalize the condition of slavery, render invisible to the social constraints that are producing the suffering, make the person carry all the weight of resolving the problem caused by forces that are not in his or her reach (Pakman, 2004).

Michael White incorporates the writings of Michel Foucault in his therapeutic practice. Foucault helps evidence how practices of power are often obscured in social relations and institutions such as the medical system. White takes from Foucault and considers that power needs to be addressed not only on the macro-social sphere but also in the local, daily social practices that constitute it (1993).

White incorporates this invitation in his therapeutic practice. But we will look at a therapeutic technique in Chapter 7, and let us now look at the transformation these considerations have had on clinical practice.

In the first place, the etiological importance of violence in many diagnosis has led to incorporate the systematic examination of the presence of violence in the lives of many of those that seek help. It has become much more common to have protocols that routinely ask for histories of violence in mental health centers or to consider this experience in the evaluation of people with a number of disorders.

Research has shown how the systematic exploration of the presence of violence in initial evaluations significantly increases the reports of traumatic experiences made by consultants. In a study done in Venezuela, the inclusion of four questions that explored experiences of violence during a triage done at a psychology service increased the rate of detection to 38% of the cases in comparison to the 7% previously reported (Guedes, Stevens, Helzner, & Medina, 2002).

We know that if we do not explore directly the presence of violence it may not be spontaneously reported by clients, even though they might have the desire to share these experiences. The experience of abuse often leaves a trace of shame, guilt and secrecy that counters the need to talk about it.

But crisis interventions have also been developed that allow us to detect high levels of risk and intervene accordingly. Analogous to the detection and handling of suicide risk, we have been able to develop effective strategies to lower risks of injury and death in the case of children, youngsters or adults that are suffering in violent relationships.

Our task here is not to present these clinical tools, but to show how these advances evidence an evolution in our field that has incorporated some basic strategies to our repertoire as an answer to the challenges violence has made. The protocols dealing with violence have incorporated the notion that a person that is in a violent relationship is someone who needs urgent protection, before he or she needs interpretations and insight. The primary clinical function is to help reduce the risk as soon as possible, before one considers the possibility of opening up space to reflect on the person's life.

This leads us to one of the more controversial elements that working with victims has introduced, and it has to do with the therapeutic stance. When a therapist evaluates that there is considerable risk and takes concrete actions to decrease the risk, the therapist is taking a stance with respect to violence. In other words, he or she is not being neutral, is not standing aside letting the actors involved decide exclusively for themselves while he or she listens and offers space for reflection.

The therapist is including his or her voice, offering a perspective and on occasion, doing specific things to stop the abuse. This is seen as problematic in traditional frameworks.

At this point, doing such things when there is a risk of suicide is not considered controversial, yet in many settings (at least in Latin America), doing it when we are dealing with violence is still considered dubious. This is not to say that dealing with suicide or abuse does not entail complex ethical and technical dilemmas, it does. But it underlines how our stance of neutrality has begun to shift.

Therapists who work in this area have been insisting that there is no way of not playing a part in the power relations of the people we work with. Even a passive stance that tries to not take sides influences the course of the events and the distribution of power. When there is a dangerous, unjust situation the therapist's silence contributes to keep that imbalance unaltered and ends up favoring the offender. The therapist becomes a silent witness. If he goes further and interprets the causes of what is happening as individual characteristics of the victim, the explanation helps to understand the imbalance as a natural course of events or as the responsibility of the victim. The silence of doctors, teachers, psychologists and social workers who have had a glimpse of the lives of children and adults subjected to lives of oppression has been considered one of the causes of the maintenance of family violence. The oppressor seeks to silence his or her acts of abuse, and therefore seduces, promotes, threatens, blackmails in order to achieve it. Secrecy becomes one of the tools used by the abuser to maintain control. If a professional opts to keep silence because of his or her belief in "neutrality," he or she contributes to consolidate the silence, leaving the victim more isolated from the social institutions that could offer help.

The Chilean psychiatrist, Jorge Barudy, who has worked with victims of family and political violence writes:

> The existence of offenders and victims does not suffice to explain organized violence; a third party is needed, the others. These are the direct/national or transnational accomplices, as well as the indirect accomplices who, because of fear or not wanting to get involved, support offenders and their instigators …
>
> Those third parties that participate in child abuse are other family members, as well as members of the social network, incapable of offering protection to victims since, to them, the fact that a father or mother can torture, neglect or sexually abuse their children is part of the unthinkable, or they simply don't want to get involved because of fear or, to avoid further trouble or, what is worse, ideological complicity with the perpetrators. Among these third party co-producers of abuse there are still many doctors, psychologists, teachers, judges, social workers, etc. that minimize the existence of violence and/or are incapable of establishing a relation between the signs of suffering and the disorders of children. Some professionals are often prisoners of their theoretical models and their roles and need to be helped to awaken to the existence of this drama. For some it is much more difficult to recognize this drama because they protect an idealized image of parents and family or simply subordinate their ethical reflection to an authoritarian, patriarchal or adultist belief (2000, p. 24).

Even though the quote and this chapter has centered more on interpersonal violence, the idea fits with the abuse perpetrated by authoritarian governments and the silence that many psychologists have kept, either because of fear or not wanting to get involved or the idealization of authoritarian projects as in the case of Venezuela.

In these dilemmas, the influence of modernity in the origin of our science becomes evident. The apolitical ideals of objectivity led twentieth-century thinkers to keep silence, sometimes in front of atrocity. They believed their opinions belonged only to the private sphere and that they had nothing to do with their tasks and vocations. That they could separate the social, economic and political considerations from their practices. They didn't consider that their silence was in itself a political act and that there is no way we can escape history and our contemporary social dilemmas. These types of reasonings, as we have seen, have been detrimental once and again to those who have suffered from political persecution, war, sexual exploitation and oppression.

Finally, the introduction of the analysis of power in interpersonal relations has also opened the door to examine the dynamics of power in the consulting room. The therapeutic relationship places the client in an asymmetrical position that wields less power, in front of a professional that offers expertise, a socially validated voice, with a contract organized around the professional's perspective. Those that have survived child abuse were subjected to adults that were supposed to care for them but used their position to abuse them. Some of these adults on occasion also offered support, affection and comfort, which makes them even more complex and confusing for the victims. The establishment of a therapeutic relationship with a professional that offers privacy, containment, protection in order to talk about our intimate lives, subjects the client to the risk of having their trust betrayed once more or of having to deal with the ambivalence of desiring to receive support while risking being subjected once more to feeling vulnerable in relation to someone who wields more power.

Therapy places the survivor in a potentially dangerous situation. We know that, regretfully, therapists are not exempt from being abusers (Masson, 1997). One study found that 27 of 99 survivors of child sexual abuse had been abused by their therapists, which matches findings by another study that found a revictimization rate of 30% (Penfold, 1998; Salter, 1995).

To complicate the relationship between therapy and politics in Venezuela even more, Edmundo Chirinos, the psychiatrist who was publically Hugo Chavez's personal counselor ever since he came to power and was considered a prominent authority on the president's psychological characteristics—for example, John Lee Anderson begins his article in The New Yorker describing Chávez in 2001, with an interview of Chirinos—murdered a patient in 2008, after she publicly began to speak of the sexual abuse she was enduring in her treatment. The police investigation led to the finding of 1200 pictures of nude patients, taken while they were sedated in his consulting room, as well as blood stains belonging to the murdered 19-year-old woman. He had been raping women patients for years (Pacheco, 2011). Even though he was sentenced to 20 years in prison, he was allowed to serve his sentence in his home instead of prison, for "humanitary" reasons.

The clinical literature has warned about the risks and difficulties of the power of the therapist. We know that Freud quickly caught on to the possibility of influencing the judgement of analysands through the trust and affection that appears in the analytic situation. Freud widely discussed these dilemmas and the need to find ways to protect the analysand's personal liberty while offering support. In Lines of Advance in Psychoanalytic Therapy (1919/1983) he writes about the power of the therapist and suggests caution with respect to the differences of those that come to analysis. Perhaps though, it is naive to believe that his ethnic origin, educational background, social status or gender had no influence in the relationships he established and that, even if he made efforts to not deliberately influence others, his undeniable stamp of his European, intellectual and professional background framed his work.

Other authors have underlined the problematic aspects of the power of the therapist. Jay Haley's The Power Tactics of Jesus Christ (1969) and Guggenbhül-Craig's Power in the Helping Professions (1974) are two classic examples on the subject. Both demonstrate, from different perspectives, that neither abstinence, nor the therapist's best intentions, are enough to secure avoiding manipulation or imposition of the theoretical view of the therapist.

Work with survivors of abuse puts the therapist's power back on the stand. It problematizes it and helps shed light on subtle aspects of the working relationship. Some authors have been able to illustrate how power can be transmitted in culturally subtle ways, sometimes almost imperceptible (Hirigoyen, 1999). The use of silence, the distribution of the furniture in the office, the tone of the communication, the arguments based on culturally validated sources, the professional licenses and academic titles on the wall, the attire, all influence relationships. Sandor Ferenczi wrote in 1933:

> The analytic situation - i.e. the restrained coolness, the professional hypocrisy and - hidden behind it but never revealed - a dislike of the patient which, nevertheless, he felt in all his being - such a situation was not essentially different from that which in his childhood had led to the illness. (1949, p. 133)

If we understand that the consequences of the person who was victimized stem not only from the explicit violence but also from the strategies of power of the abuser, then it is evident that the therapeutic relationship, if it is to be helpful, should serve to help build relationships where differences are not denied or minimized but where they are acknowledged and elaborated, in which he or she can defend his or her quota of participation, draw the lines of the limits he or she desires and negotiate any relevant aspects of the exchange. Psychotherapy should, among other things, help develop trust and autonomy for those that were subjected to totalitarian or arbitrary control. Herman (1997) writes: "No intervention that takes power away from the survivor can possibly foster her recovery, no matter how much it appears to be in her immediate best interest" (p. 133).

The therapist that works with violence therefore does not avoid the issue of power but rather confers it a space to be dealt with. He or she does not try to avoid his or her quota of power or administer it with "neutrality." Rather, he or she acknowledges the power and deals with it transparently inviting clients to give their opinions and negotiate any relevant elements. Swartz (2005), who studied the influence of society's power differentials on the therapeutic relationship in a country with a traumatic past such as South Africa, suggests that many of the problematic aspects of power are transmitted in that which goes unsaid, in silence.

A concrete example of this has to do with the physical distance between the therapist and the client. A therapist aware of distrust or fear in the client can ask if he or she prefers to leave the door open or widen the distance between the chairs in the consulting room until the client feels comfortable. Such a therapist is not only attending to the body language of the client but also actively inviting the person to put these formal aspects of the relationship into words and opening space to negotiate them. This invites the person to develop the notion that they can have some sort of control in relationships, as well as communicating from the start that the specialist is open to listen and negotiate in the collaboration they are about to embark. The therapist is trying to make a conscious and reflexive use of the power the client is turning over. The inclusion of this element in the therapeutic relationship seeks not only to build a space of trust that allows the client to be able to explore their intimate life, but also seeks to foster the (political) capacity of expressing one's own opinions, sharing one's needs and establishing one's limits.

Some authors go even further. Herman (1997) suggests that effective clinical work needs to engage with the political movements that address the inequalities of society that sustain violence in the intimate sphere. Only in connection with political activism can we defend our rights and, following Herman, make it possible to talk about that which has been silenced. This has been the case of those that have worked with victims of torture and persecution of the dictatorships in Chile, Uruguay and Argentina (Hollander, 2010).

In Venezuela, the Unit of Attention to Victims of Gender-Based Violence of the NGO Plafam has built a psychological service for women suffering from violence and, in parallel, developed spaces for political participation that include legal council and lobbying in the National Assembly to favor the development of legislation. They have participated in public protests, in the collaboration, discussion and writing of laws as well as national and international events in the defense of women's rights. Some of the women who entered the program as psychotherapy clients, later became collaborators and activists.

One of the most original initiatives that combine therapeutic action and political activism was developed through the collaboration of the psychiatrist Marius Romme and one of his patients, Patsy Hage (Romme & Escher, 2000). They founded the movement "Hearing Voices" that organizes diagnosed patients with schizophrenia in work groups that try to retake control of their lives. The movement seeks to question the stereotypes that society and institutions have about schizophrenia and how these often contribute to the chronicity of the problem. On the basis of many studies, they have challenged traditional comprehensions of the hallucinatory experience and built an international support network. They have done this through self-help group where patients discuss, without the presence of a professional, how each one has done to deal with their lives and cope with their symptoms. These groups also build support networks with community resources (specialists, hospitals, job opportunities, educational institutions) that multiply the amount of people aware of the issues and are available to offer support. This movement has continued to grow, particularly in Europe and has gradually gained space in the formal mental health network, influencing community-based mental health programs and events such as the "Hearing Voices" conferences developed at the Manchester Metropolitan University (Totton, 2000). The movement has introduced changes in the language with which we understand hallucinatory experience, has developed an international network called INTERVOICE and has empowered voice hearers to take up the roles of researchers, advocates and writers. Their voices that previously were only included as clinical examples have begun to occupy much more space in psychiatric literature as rightful experts on the experience. This demonstrates changes related not only to health issues but also political ones (McCarthy-Jones, 2012).

These initiatives seek—along with offering relief of emotional suffering—to help develop autonomy and self-determination. The therapeutic position here has evolved from a professional who limits his task to alleviating symptoms without awareness of wider societal constrictions, to one that actively helps to foster communities that can challenge, rebuild and influence those societal limitations.

These last examples show instances in which therapy has joined political activism. This does not mean that psychotherapy has to reach this type of activities to be politically reflective. These activities are a possibility that is worth observing, studying and discussing. Yet, there is much that can be done in parallel from the intimate setting of the consulting room to intertwine personal development with the development of a social and political context, adopting a reflective approach that can incorporate these elements.

References

Anderson, J. L. (2001, September 3). The revolutionary: The president of Venezuela has a vision, and Washington has a headache. *The New Yorker*. https://www.newyorker.com/magazine/2001/09/10/the-revolutionary. Accessed 24 April 2020.

Andrews, B., Brewin, S., Rose, S., & Kirk, M. (2000). Predicting PTSD symptoms in victims of violent crime: The role of shame, anger and childhood abuse. *Journal of Abnormal Psychology, 109*(1), 69–73.

Bar-On, D. (1999). *The indescribable and the undiscussable: Reconstructing human discourse after trauma*. Budapest: Central European University Press.

Barudy, J. (2000). *Maltrato infantil Ecología social: prevención y reparación*. Santiago de Chile: Editorial Galdoc.

Boney-McCoy, S., & Finkelhor, D. (1995). Psychosocial sequel of violent victimization in a national youth sample. *Journal of Consulting and Clinical Psychol ogy, 63,* 726–736.

Bowlby, J. (2005). *A secure base: Clinical applications of attachment theory*. London: Routledge.

Briere, J. (1992). Methodological issues in the study of sexual abuse effects. *Journal of Consulting and Clinical Psychology, 60,* 196–203.

Brown, G., & Anderson, B. (1991). Psychiatric morbidity in adult inpatients with childhood histories of sexual and physical abuse. *American Journal of Psy chiatry, 148,* 55–61.

Busby, D., Glenn, E., Steggell, G., & Adamson, D. (1993). Treatment issues for survivors of physical and sexual abuse. *Journal of Marital and Family Therapy, 19,* 377–392.

Costa, M., Morales, J., & Juste, M. (1997). Prevención del abuso sexual infantil. *Psicología en España, 1,* 1014–1018.

DiMaggio, P. (1997). Culture and cognition. *Annual Review of Sociology, 23,* 263–287.

Dubner, A., & Motta, R. (1999). Sexually and physically abused foster care children and posttraumatic stress disorder. *Journal of Consulting and Clinical Psychology, 6,* 367–373.

Ferenczi, S. (1949). The confusion of tongues between the adult and the child - (The language of tenderness and passion). *International Journal of Psycho-Analysis, 30,* 225–230.

Freud, S. (1895/1976). Studies on Hysteria. In J. Strachey (Ed.), *The complete psychological works of Sigmund Freud* (Vol. 1–24). W.W. Norton & Company.

Freud, S. (1896/1976). Heredity and Aeteology of Neurosis. In J. Strachey (Ed.), *The complete psychological works of Sigmund Freud* (Vol. 1–24). W.W. Norton & Company.

Freud, S. (1919/1983). Los caminos de la terapia psicoanalítica. In *Obras Completas*. Madrid: Biblioteca Nueva.

Giberti, E. (2002 July). Los malos tratos y las violencias contra niños y niñas. *Actualidad Psicológica*. Julio.

Guedes, A., Stevens, J., Helzner, J., & Medina, S. (2002). Addressing gender violence in a reproductive and sexual health program in Venezuela. In N. Haberland & C. Meashan (Eds.), *Responding to Cairo: Case studies of changing practice in reproductive health and family planning* (pp. 257–273). NewYork: Population Council.

Guggenbhül Craig, A. (1974). *Poder y destructividad en psicoterapia*. Caracas: Monte Ávila.

Haley, J. (1969). *The power tactics of Jesus Christ and other essays*. Nueva York: Discuss Books.

Haugaard, J. (2000). The challenge of defining child sexual abuse. *American Psychologist, 55,* 1036–1039.

Herman, J. (1997). *Trauma and recovery: The aftermath of violence -from domestic abuse to political terror*. New York: Basic Books.

Hirigoyen, M. (1999). *El acoso moral: el maltrato psicológico en la vida cotidiana*. Barcelona: Paidós.

Hollander, N. (2010). *Uprooted minds: Surviving the politics of terror in the Americas*. New York: Routledge.

Holmes, C. (2019, August 30). Colombia's peace process under stress: 6 essential reads. *The Conversation*. https://theconversation.com/colombias-peace-process-under-stress-6-essential-reads-122696. Accessed 20 March 2020.

Horowitz, M. (1999). *Essential papers on posttraumatic stress disorder*. New York: New York University Press.

Jukes, A. (1999). *Men who batter women*. London: Routledge.

Kahn, S. (1996). *Ferenczi's mutual analysis: A case where the messenger was killed and his treasure buried*. http://pandc.ca/?cat = sigmund_freud&page = ferenczi_mutual_analysis. Accessed 20 June 2009.

Kauffman, J., Gardner, R., & Oswald, D. (2008). Cultural sensitivity in the application of behavior principles to education. *Education and Treatment of Children, 31*, 239–262. https://www.jstor.org/stable/42899976. Accessed 24 April 2020.

Kemper, J. (1992). Brazil: Mental health in social distress? The dialectic between inner psychic and external social reality. *International Forum of Psychoanalysis, 1,* 129–135.

Kernberg, O. (2001). Psicoterapia focalizada en la transferencia. Psicodinámica de pacientes con organización de personalidad borderline: una visión general. *Trópicos: Revista de Psicoanálisis*, IX(1), 73–95.

Kluft, R. (1991). La violencia familiar y el desorden de personalidad múltiple. *Revista Intercontinental de Psicología y Educación, 4,* 29–55.

Lizardi, H., Klein, D., Crosby, P., Riso, L., Anderson, R., & Donaldson, S. (1995). Reports of the childhood home environment in early-onset dysthymia and episodic depression. *Journal of Abnormal Psychology, 104,* 132–139.

Malagodi, E. (1986). On radicalizaing behaviorism: A call for cultural analysis. *The Behavior Analyst, 9,* 1–17.

Masson, J. (1997). *Against therapy*. London: Harper Collins Publisher.

McCarthy-Jones, S. (2012). *Hearing voices: The histories, causes and meanings of audiotory verbal hallucinations*. Cambridge: Cambridge University Press.

Miller, A. (1984/1991). *Though shall not be aware: Society's betrayal of the child*. New York: Meridian.

Miller, A. (1997). *Breaking down the wall of silence*. London: Virago Books.

Pacheco, I. (2011). *Sangre en el Diván: el extraordinario caso del Dr. Chirinos*. Caracas: Random House Mondadori.

Pakman, M. (2004). The epistemology of witnessing: Memory, testimony and ethics in family therapy. *Family Process, 43,* 265–274.

Penfold, S. (1998). *Sexual abuse by health professionals: A personal search for meaning and healing*. Toronto: University of Toronto Press.

Pérez de Antelo, A. (2002). *Estudio del grado y tipo de disociación reportada en niños con maltrato físico y/o abuso sexual a travs de la lista de chequeo de conductas disociativas de Putman (CDC)* (Unpublished Thesis). Caracas: Universidad Católica Andrés Bello.

Putnam, F. (1989). Pierre Janet and modern views of dissociation. *Journal of Traumatic Stress, 2,* 199–223.

Romme, M., & Escher, S. (2000). *Making sense of voices: A guide for mental health professionals working with voice hearers*. London: Mind Publications.

Sábato, E. (1998). *Antes del fin: memorias*. Bogotá: Seix Barral.

Salter, A. (1995). *Transforming trauma: A guide to understanding and treating adult survivors of child sexual abuse*. London: Sage.

Stone, M. (1989). Individual psychotherapy with victims of incest. *Psychiatric Clinics of North America, 12,* 237–255.

Semprún, J. (1995). *La Escritura o la Vida*. Barcelona: Tusquets Editores.

Swartz, S. (2005). "Can de clinical subject speak?" Some thoughts on subaltern psychology. *Theory & Psychology, 15,* 505–525.

Totton, N. (2000). *Psychotherapy and Politics*. London: Sage Publications.

van der Kolk, B. (1989). The compulsion to repeat trauma. *The Psychiatric Clinics of North America: Treatment of Victims of Sexual Abuse, 12,* 389–411.

White, M. (1993). Deconstruction and therapy. In S. Gilligan & R. Price (Eds.), *Therapeutic conversations* (pp. 22–63). New York: W.W. Norton and Company.

White, M. (1995). *Reescribir la vida: entrevistas y ensayos*. Barcelona: Gedisa.

Wiehe, V. (1998). *Understanding family violence: Treating and preventing partner, child, sibling and elder abuse*. London: Sage.

Wiesel, E. (2002). Elogio de la memoria. In *¿Por Qué Recordar?: Foro Internacional Memoria e Historia*. Buenos Aires: Granica.

Chapter 6
Postmodern Bases for a Politically Reflective Psychotherapy

6.1 Latin American Community, Liberation and Clinical Psychology

The challenges to traditional conceptions of psychology in Venezuela began long before the Boliviarian Revolution came to power. As in some of the examples (Chap. 3) regarding Argentina and Uruguay, social and political conflicts began to question the practice of psychology in the 70s in several Latin American countries.

Social psychologists began questioning the application of imported social psychological theories to the issues of Latin America fraught with authoritarian governments, economic crisis and inequality. Researchers considered psychology to be limited in its response to our continent's problems because of its focus on individual functioning and fragmentation of reality. Authors like Montero criticized its false objectivity and neutrality (2004).

Alternatives appeared in different forms. Participative Action Research developed in part by the sociologist Fals Borda in Colombia (Fals-Borda & Anisur, 1991), Critical Pedagogy developed by Freire in Brazil (1970) and Liberation Psychology proposed by Martín-Baró in El Salvador (1986, 1990, 2002) influenced many branches of Latin American social science.

In Venezuela, in particular, Latin American community psychology began to propose a critical and alternative approach to psychological theory and research (Montero, 2003, 2004; Montero & Varas Díaz, 2007). Community psychology thrived through the work of a number of academics of the Universidad Central de Venezuela and produced an epistemological review, a theoretical framework, an array of research tools and intervention approaches that has influenced psychology in Venezuela and extended into the world. Montero and Montenegro (2006) consider it one of the main representatives of critical psychology in Latin America. It considers that positivist perspectives contribute to sustain the status quo instead of helping to transform the structures that produce some of our relevant social and psychological problems. It has helped to question Latin America academy's

M. Llorens, *Politically Reflective Psychotherapy*, Latin American Voices,
https://doi.org/10.1007/978-3-030-57792-6_6

tendency to look abroad instead of stimulating the production of local knowledge and contextualized answers to our problems.

Montero (2003, 2004, 2006) is the most internationalized author, systematizing and publishing a complete framework for Latin American community psychology. In particular, directly relevant to the issues discussed here, she has proposed that a paradigm is made up not only of an epistemological, ontological and anthropological framework, but also of a political and an ethical one. She has challenged social scientists to reflect upon and make explicit the political and ethical commitments of their theories, considering that community psychology springs from the political and ethical position of emphasizing relevant contextual issues, including the voice of those who are studying as valid collaborators in the production of knowledge. That, and its emphasis on those who are most in need is relevant, not only to social but also to clinical psychology, that has to treat many people who suffer from the consequences of oppression.

These debates were the expression of what was called the crisis of social sciences in the 70s. In the meantime the mental health professions were confronting their own dilemmas; for example, critiques from the antipsychiatry movement had repercussions on the clinical settings in Latin America. In Venezuela, the movement influenced deinstitutionalization. An expression of this was the Declaration of Caracas, that in 1990, in a World and Panamerican Health Organization sponsored conference, led to South American countries manifesting their determination to shift the focus from conventional psychiatric attention toward a more community-based, decentralized approach.

But it was probably Ignacio Martín-Baró who first brought the discussions that appeared in Latin American social psychology to clinical issues. He developed them under the term "Liberation Psychology," that has continued to represent a school of thought in Latin American social psychology and has had impact in other latitudes (Montero & Sonn, 2009). His work as a social psychologist in El Salvador during the civil war included very sharp observations on the sufferings of many of those that were displaced because of violence (1984/1993). He argued that if they were observed in classic clinical terms, many of them could have been described as suffering from pathologies. But, in the light of the events of the war, many symptomatic expressions, like frequent paranoid attitudes, could be understood as adaptive responses to grave alterations of the context. If we only looked at the individual we would not be able to attend the causes of suffering, it would be a well meaning but short-sighted and limited approach to help. We needed to think in terms of what he called "psycho-social trauma" understanding it as the suffering reflected on both sides of the dyad, the individual and the social sphere. Effective interventions had to, accordingly, attend to both dimensions. Furthermore, these arguments, that pertained to sufferings emerging as a consequence of war, were relevant for many other issues observed in Latin America, such as mass poverty, state violence and homelessness.

When in the 90s, Venezuela entered into a decade of social conflict and economic crisis, some of the consequences of these problems, which began to appear in our consulting rooms, resonated with the discussions that community psychologists and liberation psychologists had been developing for a couple of decades.

I began working with homeless children on the streets of Caracas in the middle of the 90s, a phenomenon that exploded in Venezuela toward the end of the 80s (Llorens, 2009a, 2009b; Llorens, Alvarado, Hernández, Jaramillo, Romero, & Souto, 2005). I was surprised by the rather orthodox approaches trying to treat many of these youngsters of symptoms such as addictions and conduct disorders without taking into account the very dramatic contexts in which many of them had developed. Many of the existing programs were naive. Program facilitators reported huge amounts of frustration dealing with incredible challenging circumstances and many of the resulting explanations ended up falling into blaming the victims for their ordeals. We began doing research, using qualitative approaches, to understand the lives of these youngsters and were able to register some of the notorious failures that certain programs were having (Hernández, Llorens, & Medina, 1999). We soon found that our focus could not concentrate on the psychological functioning of the children but had to include the institutions that were attempting to "treat" them.

Venezuelan society in general had a strong reaction to these children as they became a symbol of the country's crisis: songs were written, movies were filmed, politicians emphasized them in their speeches and charity programs were created (Glauser, 1999). The construction of who these kids were supposed to be and what the intervention programs had to do with them became part of the problem. Helping them required us to take this context into account.

In 1994, a group of psychologists of the Universidad Católica Andrés Bello led by Juan Carlos Romero organized a psychological unit to provide services to the *barrios* (spontaneous self-built neighborhoods or slums) that had continued to grow in the hills of the valley of Caracas (Campagnaro, 2017; Romero, 2017). The project met with some detractors that were of the opinion that lower economic communities would not be interested in psychological services. But experience quickly proved them wrong. The rapid growth of the service led to the unit becoming a central component of a community center that the university inaugurated in 2000.

Before that, in 1997, based on the many demands that began to arrive from lower income neighboring communities, a postgraduate specialization program on Clinical Community Psychology was created in the same university to develop professionals specially oriented to being able to attend the psychological needs and sufferings of the lower income communities of our city. The study program and the psychology unit of the community center became our base from which to reflect and organize a psychological practice attuned to the needs of our particular context.

The idea was to include a clinical and community perspective that would allow us to develop creative psychological understandings and solutions to the many social problems that were rapidly growing in Venezuela. For that task, we were lucky to be able to receive the support of Maritza Montero who joined a team of mainly clinical psychologists to begin to reflect and develop a clinical community approach. That process consolidated my conviction that community psychology could offer a critical viewpoint from which we could question clinical theory and open new possibilities.

This combination of events resulted in providing fertile ground and creative tension for the development of new ideas. On the one hand, the focus of the psychology service on the needs of lower income communities challenged many of our conventions. The impact of poverty, social exclusion, lack of transportation, no access to justice, deficient public services, stigmatization, etc. proved relevant and came up again and again in the problems of the people we were working with. On the other, the simultaneous presence of clinical and community psychologists in our team provided constant opportunities to contrast viewpoints, comprehensions and approaches to offer solutions.

In the midst of the growth of our team, Hugo Chávez attempted a coup d'etat in 1992 and was later elected president in 1998, leading to an ongoing political struggle. The intense political scenario offered an interesting but defying context for the development of our ideas. The political events became an intense background to our relationship with the communities we worked with.

The challenges that had come to the complete metatheoretical, theoretical and methodological building of social psychology seemed to fit with the challenges our clinical work was facing day in and day out. This experience led us to begin to rethink how we could build effective therapeutic conversations with a population in circumstances that didn't necessarily fit into the schemes of clinical manuals (Llorens, 2003). We began to reflect on our experience assisted by the reviews clinical psychology was confronting in the world to be able to develop effective relationships with the communities that our university worked with (Llorens, 2009a, 2009b).

6.2 Postmodernism and Clinical Psychology

We saw in Chapter 2, how psychotherapy, being a technology that arose from psychiatry and psychology, developed its ideals in the midst of modernism. Each version of psychotherapy imports its epistemological, ontological and notions of what the human subject is from the theories on which they are based. Even though there have been numerous efforts to discuss the underlying conceptions of the different schools of psychotherapy (García de la Hoz, 2000; Kelly, 1966; Rychlak, 1981), it is not frequent for clinical training to take time to examine the bases of these practices. This helps to obscure the assumptions held by each practice and make difficult the possibility of adopting a critical perspective.

It is curious how psychotherapy, considered in many aspects an activity centered on reflection, that seeks to foster conversations that allow people to return to themselves and understand intellectually and affectively, their preferences, desires, conflicts, fears, etc., often has difficulty returning its gaze on itself and reflecting on its own foundations. It is also common that, as the therapist develops and adopts a particular theoretical framework, he or she begins to have even more difficulty identifying the epistemological, ontological, methodological, ethical and political bases of his or her practice.

Alvin Mahrer, who studied the philosophy of science of psychotherapy, considers that many of these fundamental beliefs have been smuggled in clinical language and practice. He also proposes a series of questions to help each practitioner render visible and examine the beliefs under which he or she operates.

Another psychotherapist and philosopher of science, Rychlak (1981, 2000) has developed a review of a large number of personality and psychotherapy theories analyzing the epistemological foundations from which each of the different traditions organize their discourse. As an analytical tool, that helps to illustrate the differences between traditional positivist approaches and phenomenological ones, he proposed what he termed the "lockean model" and the "kantean model." Some of his ideas feed our discussion.

In addition, Anderson (1997) proposed that all psychotherapeutic theories can be studied examining three great categories: the therapist position, the psychotherapeutic process and the psychotherapeutic system. In the first category one analyzes: What is the role of the therapist according to the theory? His or her intention? Responsibility? What does his or her expertise entail? How is the relationship with the client conceptualized?

In the second category one asks: What are the objectives of the relation? How is change expected to happen? What needs to happen to foster change? When has enough change happened? How is what happens in the consulting room transferred to real life? What type of therapeutic questions relevant?

In the last category Anderson considers: Who and what is considered the focus of therapy? How is the membership in the therapeutic relation defined? Is the treatment of the individual or of the family? What relation is there between the therapist, the client and the external context of the therapy? Is the therapist included in the focus of change?

Psychotherapy, originated in modernism, offered a set of answers to these questions. The modern therapist tends to think of himself as striving to be an objective observer that applies the truths of science to "discover" what it is that is happening in the patient. This task of discovery is clearly expressed by Freud's famous analogy of the analyst as an archeologist. The analyst, thus conceived, is a systematic and acute observer that, on the basis of factual evidence, reconstructs the image of what has happened. That is, he or she discovers "real" objects that exist.[1] Psychoanalysis' circular formulation and scientific limitations have been widely established, but that does not mean that Freud didn't think of himself as a representative of the modern tradition, expecting to objectively observe psychological phenomena.

The conception of reality and truth that Freud proposes is clearly in line with the positivist ideal.[2] That was his intention. Therefore the analyst must not be

[1]See, for example, Freud's Construction in Analysis (1937/1983) in which Freud explicitly develops the analogy of the analyst as an archeologist.

[2]Expressed, for example, in Freud's New Introductory Lectures in Psychoanalysis (1933/1983).

influenced by his or her ethnic, socioeconomic or political origins. He or she should be able to transcend his or her gender, religious conceptions and value preferences.

Seen from this perspective, the therapist has a privileged view of psychic phenomena. I have heard analysts defend the idea that they have a clearer picture of what might be going on in the client than the client themselves. Mitchell (1993) quotes known analysts defending a similar position:

> As Charles Brenner (1987, p. 169), one of the staunchest defenders of classical theory in our times, has put it, "Obviously the person that has the best opportunity to understand a patient's conflicts correctly is the patient's analyst" (It is certainly not the patient!) The analyst delivers the truths to the patient, and the latter, if he is able to consider them openly and unresistantly, is transformed by them. (p. 41)

These certainties about truth discovered through psychotherapy have been problematized by numerous developments. The possibility of a psychoanalysis anchored in positivism has been widely debated. In first place, the multiple theoretical perspectives that allow different interpretations and emphases on clinical data require us to doubt about the "veracity" of the therapist's findings. In second place, traditional empirical research hasn't brought a undeniable defense of any one theoretical approach, even though they have helped weed out different hypothesis. In third place, the review of the foundations of modern science has impacted the theories of psychotherapy and invited many to, what has been called by Geertz (1973), the "interpretive turn" in human sciences (Bruner, 1990). In psychoanalysis this has been expressed by authors like Schafer (1992) who states that the traditional Freudian conception of a reality external to the observer is naive and that psychoanalytic theory seems to evidence that we can only access different versions of reality. In this conception of science, Mitchell following Schafer concludes that reality, at least in psychotherapy, is always mediated by narration.

In spite of this, many initial foundational beliefs have continued in our psychological discourse. Neutrality, as a fundamental technical base, being one of the clearest legacies of this modernist conception. The catalan psychoanalyst Coderch (2001) underlines how the emphasis on abstinence, anonymity and objectivity was an attempt to achieve the separation between the observer and the observed. The definition of neutrality taken from the classic text (LaPlanche & Pontalis, 1994) shows the incorporation of this scientific ideal into the development of our field:

> The analyst must be neutral in respect of religious, ethical and social values—that is to say, he must not direct the treatment according to some ideal, and should abstain from counselling the patient; he must be neutral too as regards manifestations of transference (this rule usually being expressed by the maxim, "Do not play the patient's game"). (p. 256)

This "neutrality" leads analysts to not take position regarding ethical, political and social dilemmas in the lives of their clients. Only recently has it begun to be debated how neutrality in dealing with problems of life and death can be a risk toward those living in violence. Also, the possibility of an analyst being a blank slate, not framed in his or her social history, has also been questioned.

Some therapists who do not dare question the idea of neutrality, as in the case of Kernberg (1998, 2004), at least have conceded that when political crisis appear, neutrality seems to be impossible. Based on his observations in Chile during the 70s, faced with the intense political debates of the times of Allende and later Pinochet, he believed neutrality was only possible if the analyst and the analysand shared the same political beliefs. In this situation Kernberg (2004) recommended the preservation of neutrality but in a "non-conventional" way. It is a rather vague resolution that seems to try to defend a traditional neutral stance and a "non-conventional" critique at the same time. The problem appears right where the author believes to have resolved it.

The supposed agreement regarding political beliefs according to Kernberg is a careful avoidance of political conflict that makes it easier to obscure this dimension. The problem is that historical events sometimes put politics on the table and make it impossible to avoid. The neutral position could be dangerous, because it is often a veil of a conservative position that allies itself with the status quo, avoiding critical and alternative perspectives, and therefore, favors those that have more power.

In a discussion of these ideas in a psychiatry service in Venezuela, the director of the service challenged me offering an example of how patients want and expect the therapist to remain neutral. He mentioned that he was treating an active general of the Air Force. The therapy was at times tricky since the patient represented the military elite, highly questioned by much of the country, especially the professional class that the doctor belonged to. So at the beginning of their relationship the general conditioned the therapist asking him to leave any politics outside of the consulting room. Even though the doctor felt that this was an example of the need to, as the patient asked, leave politics outside of therapy, I replied that this petition was probably a significant piece of information about how the general leads his life in various scenarios and is precisely a perfect example of politics in the consulting room. What clearer exercise of power in the transference than a general limiting the therapist from the start on which contents are considered acceptable in therapy and which contents are not? That is not to say that one cannot accept the general's petition to allow him to feel safe and comfortable in therapy, but one can signal that it might be something important to come back to. One, for example, could invite him to explore: Why does he feel the need to leave out part of his life in therapy? How does the general feel thinking that he might be questioned in different contexts? How does it feel to have to leave this out in other relationships? Does it happen often? How is it possible to build trusting and close relationships in such a supervised context? Does it come with a cost? What does the patient fantasize that the doctor thinks of his place in the country's political debate? How does that condition his conversation? Is it something that adds to the vulnerability already inherent of asking for help? I find that it is a wonderful example of how bigger political dilemmas filter into the therapeutic conversation in subtle acts of exchange in the relationship.

Frosh (2007) notes how neutrality can easily turn into a place where the avoidance of any type of judgement becomes complicit silence with dominating ideologies, but also worries how the transformation of neutrality can become naive activism that stems from the simplistic belief of being able to easily distinguish right from wrong, which in the end leads to indoctrination. He resolves this by reinscribing neutrality as the political duty to avoid ideological distortions.

But the "avoidance of ideological distortions" or "clarity" in Frosh's words seems to dismiss the many complex social hierarchies and positionings in a social structure. The clarity that Frosh recommends seems innocent and difficult to imagine from a psychoanalytic or postmodern standpoint in which knowledge is inevitably placed in a particular context and biography. How can an analyst assure that he is observing from a position that allows him to clearly distinguish and avoid "ideological distortions?" Isn't ideology, as proposed by Marxism, specifically the capacity to produce distortion?

Psychology directs our gaze and locates problems and solutions inside of the individual. Ann Kearney quoted by Totton (2000) expresses it in these terms:

> I suggest that counsellors, like everyone else, are political beings with a political ideology… which has direct and indirect consequences for their clients… Counselling is informed by a set (of) political values and beliefs which are part of the dominant political ideology of the society in which counselling is being practiced. (p. 139)

The therapist, whether in silence or intervening, influences the direction of the conversation, underlining or dismissing certain themes and contents. In the words of Coderch, inspired by a postmodern review of psychoanalysis:

> Each of the analyst's interpretations lead the patient's attention towards a particular direction, a direction that is influenced by the analyst's personality and theories. At the same time it discourages other directions that could also be possible. Inevitably, the analyst, when interpreting, invites the patient to see things - his mind, his relations, etc. - in a determined way, even if he does so trying to be very respectful of the client's freedom, and this cannot be considered neutrality. Facing the analysand's communication, as with any other phenomenon, the task of picking one direction instead of another goes against the notion of neutrality, independently of how much we are striving to be neutral. (2001, p. 185)

He also states: "to pursue neutrality in human relationships is to pursue a mirage" (p. 182). Gergen and Warhus (2001) add their opinion about the impossibility of neutrality in any human intervention:

> From the modernist/empiricist standpoint therapy is not a forum for political, ideological or ethical advocacy. The good therapist, like the good medical doctor, should engage in sensitive observation and careful thought, unbiased by his/her particular value investments. Critiques of value neutrality have long been extant. The works of Szasz (1970), Laing (1967) and participants in the critical psychiatry movement have made us acutely conscious of the ways in which well-intentioned therapists can contribute to forces of oppression. Congenial with Foucault's (1979) critique of the 'disciplining' effects of therapeutic practices, more recent analysis have focused on the ways in which various therapies and diagnostic categories contribute to sexism, racism, heterosexism, individualism, class oppression and other divisive biases. From a constructionist standpoint even a posture of non-engagement or 'neutrality' is viewed as ethical and political in its consequences (MacKinnon and Miller, 1987; Taggart, 1985). Whether mindful or not, whether for good or ill, therapeutic work is necessarily a form of social/political activism. Any action within a society is simultaneously creating its future for good or ill by some standard. (2001, p. 103)

Marie Langer, of whom we wrote following her work under Nazism and later under the Argentinian dictatorships, came to a similar conclusion, stating:

> And the analyst's neutrality? We don't believe in it as we did before...We believe that isolating oneself and avoiding the historical social process rather than constituting a neutral attitude is an active way of taking part. (1972, p. 265)

A tension has existed from the beginning of psychotherapeutic practice between the positivist premises that represented the scientific aspirations and an activity that is built around subjectivity and interpretation. Psychotherapy opened the door to listen to the detail of the intimate world of daily life. Freud opened the opportunity to think of ourselves in a novel way, to register the private lives of the women he began to treat, and the proliferation of psychotherapy legitimated the exploration of our inner lives. The challenge of achieving a scientific observation of our subjective lives has been a central issue in many theories. Freud is crossed by the romantic influence of his intellectual milieu that dealt with the depths of inner life and the positivist aspirations of progress through the discovery of the universal laws of nature.

The critical challenges to positivism brought on by phenomenology and existentialism began to invite these dilemmas (May, Angel, & Ellenberger, 1967; Zumbalawe, 1996). Even though some authors proclaimed themselves to be phenomenological such as Rogers (1961), the dilemma remained unresolved.

Meanwhile academic research tended to maintain a critical distance from psychotherapy, considering it less scientific and too subjective to allow objective conclusions. Family therapist, Marcelo Pakman, writes:

> The therapist, contaminated by his original sin of being a social actor committed to the resolution of the demands of his "clients", tried often to copy the researcher in his aspiration to reach a position of "objectivity", that has for such a long time been the guarantee of scientific rigor. In spite of such efforts, "academic research" tends to look at that faithful follower of the objectivist theoretical assumptions with distrust, a follower that arrived at the lab stained with the mud, blood and fire of the clinical trench. Research belonged to the academic world, more objective and impersonal of the basic sciences: intervention, in spite of its ideals, to the incarnated field, more subjective and personal of social practice. (1995, p. 360)

Research on therapeutic practice has concluded that therapists don't necessarily base their reasonings and practice predominantly on the reading of empirical findings as the modern ideal posits. But rather, on experience that produce context-dependent understandings (Polkinghorne, 1992).

Even though practice is greatly informed by context and experience, the ontological and epistemological premises of positivism continue to occupy a central place in many of the studies that are done at present on psychotherapy. The foundational beliefs continue to underlie many clinical arguments and techniques that have not fully made explicit the philosophical premises from which they operate. Postmodern reviews of social sciences have opened up possibilities to propose alternative bases that allow different versions of the objectives and strategies of psychotherapeutic work.

Increasingly, numerous authors have begun to consider psychotherapy as a craft based on language and therefore a perspective (or series of perspectives) dedicated to the construction of interpretative versions of reality. This turn implies seeing theories, not as a map that corresponds photographically with the world, but as a series of symbolic tools that serve to give meaning to experience. The possibility of dealing with simultaneous but parallel interpretative versions of reality, each one with advantages and disadvantages, as well as preferred focal points, has been acknowledged.

To conceive theories from this perspective has brought on a series of relevant changes to the way we understand our place as therapists, as well as the nature of the therapeutic relationship and of the process of change. The analyst passed from being conceived metaphorically as an archeologist, to begin to be considered more of a translator. The image passed from being a discoverer, much like Sherlock Holmes who searches among the free associations left at the scene of the crime to an expert listener that helps, through a two-way dialogue, to develop new perspectives and favors reflection. This perspective does not "discover" the "real" causes of the personality dynamics, but offers tools to explore the past with greater freedom, builds bridges through language to re-apprehend experiences that had not been integrated and build less constrictive options.

In the words of the revisionist of modern approaches to therapy, Gergen writes (1991):

> Finally, consider the therapeutic implications of postmodernism. Traditional practices of therapy, guided by both romanticism and modernism, place the therapist in the role of the expert who goes about assessing the problem of the individual mind, locating repressions, conflict, misconceptions, or cognitive aberrations, and correcting such deficits, through therapy. Under postmodernism, not only is the therapist's expertise in mental matters thrown into jeopardy, but the very reality of a "patient" with a "mind to be known and corrected" loses credibility. Rather, the individual is viewed as a participant in multiple relationships, with "the problem" only a problem because of the way it is constructed in certain of these relations. The challenge to the therapist is thus to facilitate renegotiation of the meaning system within which "the problem" exists. The therapist actively enters dialogue with those who maintain the problem definition, not as a clairvoyant, but as a co-participant in the construction of new realities. (p. 251)

Gergen proposes a postmodern review along with the dissolution of the modern self, a central concept in many clinical theories of the twentieth century, that produced many efforts to "discover" one's self and be more "authentic." All these modes of knowing ourselves imply the belief in a core essential self that is waiting to be discovered. The postmodern view that, as we have seen, proposes access to multiple versions of reality, dilutes the possibility of accessing a definite version of who we are, and proposes that what we can achieve is access to multiple reinterpretations of our lives. Interpretations that are developed through interpersonal exchange with different cultural spaces and different consequences.

The British psychoanalyst, Phillips (2000) expresses it this way:

> The alternative to this is the apparently more absurd and strangely plausible possibility that there is no original text, no essential self (or version of the self); that there are just an unknowable series of translations of translations; preferred versions of ourselves, but not

> true ones. So we need not aim to get closer to our true selves - or try to be better and better at being authentic - so much as be available for translation whenever we suffer and desire. And that we need not only suffer other people's redescriptions of us, but that we can also enjoy some of them, and be interested in the fact that this is what we are doing with each other...
>
> There is no real, privileged, original me to refer back to; but you might ask me what I think of your descriptions of me. I don't, though, have the real, original text in front of me to check your (or my) descriptions against. I am like a country without a map; or a country that is always impressionistically mapped. (p. 144)

As we can see, the conception of what human beings are has suffered a significant modification from this perspective. The person is now seen as a being inserted in a network of relationships, co-constructed through dialogue, with multiple possible interpretations offered by his or her cultural space. Access to reality is inevitably mediated by language, so for us it is multiple and constructed. The therapeutic relationship becomes not the passive relation between an expert and something to be discovered but a meeting of two perspectives, one of them developed through the systematic review of contemporary theories and professional practice and the other, through personal experience in the cultural space he or she has developed. The interpretative process begins to transform into a dialogue and a co-construction. The possibility of reaching an ultimate truth begins to appear like a fantasy. I am fond of George Steiner's expression of these same ideas:

> What all parties must remember is this: the games of meaning cannot be won. No prize of transcendence, no surety, awaits even the most skillful, inspired player... The Tablets of the Law, which Moses broke in a moment of deconstructive perception, cannot be re-assembled (2013, p. 186).

George Kelly was a pioneer incorporating epistemological reviews into the theory of personality and clinical psychology. Larsen and Buss (2005) have considered that Kelly was postmodern before postmodernism became popular. With a heterodox academic formation that included math and theater, he developed his ideas in a certain degree of isolation. This combination allowed him to develop a creative outlook on the problems of personality and therapy. His Theory of Personality (1966) outlined not only a novel approach to these issues but also an epistemological revision. Having reviewed psychoanalysis, behaviorism and humanism, he proposed an analogy with the transformations of so-called, hard science. Using geometry as an example, he proposed that two competing theories could be held alternatively to study human phenomena.

That review led to his proposal of "Constructive Alternativism" an epistemological approach that proposes the possibility of looking at a phenomenon from alternative perspectives. We can observe an event using a set of premises that offer a certain viewpoint and afterwards adopt another set of premises that allow an alternative interpretation. Each theory offers a window from which we can obtain a perspective of the human phenomenon. I can't stand at two windows at the same time, but I can do it alternatively.

Another clinical area that gave impulse to these revisions was the area of family therapy. The opportunity to simultaneously work with different stories that offered different versions and perspectives of a shared reality underlined the existence of alternative constructions of the same events. The therapist, faced with a human group with different viewpoints, cannot aspire to obtain the ultimate version of the truth, but rather to find a way to help these contrasting versions live and grow together. It becomes obvious that it is naive to expect family therapy to end up discovering the definite real version of what is happening. Rather, therapy can "prompt the family to accept the epistemological responsibility for the existence of multiple meanings and become more open to loosening its system of construing and behavior" (Niemeyer, 1993, p. 228).

The critique of gender stereotypes that defended a "natural" way of being a woman or a man, also contributed to the interpretive turn, questioning the existence of a "natural" sexuality and proposing rather that what exists are culturally anchored constructions of what it is to be a woman or a man. The same has happened with psychiatric diagnosis. Pathological labels began to be understood, not as illnesses, real objective entities, external, directly observable, but rather social constructions, influenced by a framework of what we consider a good or deviated life to be.

The debate on the inclusion of a "masochistic personality disorder," discussed during the 80s, is a case in point. The proposal was met with the critiques made by feminist groups that argued that the label was going to obscure the cultural, social, political components responsible for the existence of power asymmetries in relationships and was going to end up blaming the victims of gender violence. An intense debate followed, which led to the change of name to "self defeating personality disorder," establishing as an excluding criteria any finding of physical, sexual or psychological abuse. The diagnosis was included in the appendix of the DSM-III-R as a category under study (Fiester, 1995; Herman, 1997; Widiger, 1995).

In that same direction, to Phillips (2000), the notion of deviation demands a belief in a natural essence of normality that can be clearly identified. He provokingly states that instead of pathology, in some cases, we might be looking at "preferred worlds," clearly alluding to the possibility of alternative versions of what is considered normal or abnormal in different cultures or subcultures.

Psychotherapy echoes the debates of the interpretive turn. Anderson (1997), for example, describes the modifications that psychotherapy suffers under postmodernism. She mentions, among other things, the shift from considering the therapist as a knower who is sure of what he or she knows to one that doesn't know and considers knowledge to be a developing ongoing process; from a therapist that operates from a privileged and private position, to one that is willing to share and reflect on his or her assumptions; form a therapist that holds expert knowledge about how lives should be lived to one who is an expert on the opening up of reflective dialogic space; from a therapeutic relationship between an expert and someone who isn't, to a more collaborative one; from a system of individuals, couples or families to a system of individuals related by language; a psychotherapy that believes in the existence of an essential self, to one that considers that people have relational, multiple and linguistically constructed selves.

Similarly, Coderch (2001) proposes a psychoanalysis that attends to language, considers the self to be multiple rather than unitary and is constructed through language. What the analyst does, in a certain sense, changes only subtly; in another sense, it changes radically. On one hand, the psychotherapist continues, as in the modernist tradition, reading, interpreting from his or her theories the material that the person brings to therapy. On the other, he or she is no longer a neutral observer that expects to reach a "true" interpretation, but one who offers their perspective, seeking to open up space for reflection, new ways of feeling and facing life. Phillips (2000) exemplifies saying that it is a change from a therapist that tells the client what the dream means to one that shares what it made him or her think.

6.3 Contributions to a Politically Reflective Psychotherapy

How do these debates influence the possibility of approaching the political realm in psychotherapy? How does this metatheoretical review help create new tools?

In the first place, it helps us appreciate our scientific apparatus without idealization. We can approach it with a critical perspective, subjecting its proposals to discussion in each of the contexts where it will be applied. The postmodern reflection has helped to reduce the weight of the great narrations of modernity. The political theories that promised to predict the laws of history and drove masses to the systematic murder of many on the base of "science," are now seen with much more skepticism. This, by itself, has political effects, lowering science from a pedestal and inserting it in a social dialogue that forces us to doubt and debate. In the lucid words of the family therapist Pocock:

> Some Roman emperors kept slaves to whisper occasionally in their ear 'You are not a god', in a sometimes vain attempt to prevent the absolute authority of their position from driving them mad. We need the critique that is postmodernism to do the same for our omnipotent and omniscient tendencies. (1995, p. 154)

This cautious approach to scientific discourse transfers to the consulting room. The therapist's interpretation of facts, from this perspective, must be cautious, seen as a perspective, and not the final word. Therefore it allows a dialogue, invites the other to participate in the process and include new perspectives. Thus, it reduces authority of the therapist's voice. Even though the therapist continues to have more control and power in the relation, this power is now more conscious and is subjected to dialogue and negotiation.

The therapist is obliged to review his or her interpretations, not only to make them fit theory, or how influenced they are by one's countertransference, but also to reflect on their social and political placing. The postmodern therapist faces the dissolution of neutrality and is "situated" or "placed" in his or her biography that includes not only personal conflicts but also our economic, political and social context.

This doesn't make our task easier. Now we have to continuously reflect on our assumptions and look for alternative perspectives that help reflect on these conditions. The postmodern therapist is aware that the psychotherapeutic relationship implies the exercise of power and therefore must attend to this dimension. As Totton (2000) has put it:

> Instead of trying hopelessly to eliminate *power* struggle from the therapeutic relationship, we place it dead centre: we highlight the battle between the therapist and client over the definition of reality, bare it to the naked gaze and make it a core theme of our work. This is one style of working with transference. It means, faced with conflicting demands, we do what is best to do in every such situation: we *negotiate*. This negotiation of realities (where 'negotiation' also has the meaning of crossing tricky and dangerous terrain), I would argue, constitutes an authentic and viable psycho-political practice. (p. 147)

From a psychoanalytical perspective, Coderch (2001), assuming a postmodern perspective, also insists on the negotiation of the therapeutic relationship:

> I think that all I have been saying introduces us in the realm of negotiation in the analytic dialogue. The mutuality of recognition brings us to the fact that the patient-analyst relationship is a negotiated one. It is evident that it is negotiated in the external aspects of its setting: the space, days, schedule and the economic commitments. It is also negotiated in respect to the general methodology of the interviews, in respect to what is expected of the patient…
>
> Among others things that are negotiated in the analytic process there is, for example… the emotional climate: is it a warm relationship? Is it cold and distant? Will it follow a medical model or pedagogical one? Authoritarian or tolerant? Will the patient be passive? Will the analyst resist patiently the patient's aggression? Will reciprocity and collaboration predominate or will each try to impose their viewpoints? All of these possibilities are negotiated from the first encounter. (p. 243)

The therapist's position has been transformed. This perspective challenges the therapist to be more reflective, less authoritarian, capable of negotiating the parameters of the relationship and the shared meanings. Some have called this a collaborative position (Anderson, 1997; Strong, 2003). This does not make the therapist equal to any other collaborative process, but does displace him or her from the place of ultimate authority. To impose an interpretation is seen now as an act of authoritarian control. Our expertise resides in the capacity to open up reflective space, to facilitate exploration, to listen with emotional attunement, with the possibility of thinking on the ambiguity of communication not only from theoretical perspectives but also placed in cultural meanings. Gergen & Warhus (2001) argue that the therapist's abilities have to do more with the how than with the what, on how to build a helping relationship.

Jerome Bruner (1990) proposes that this way of doing psychology implies a democratic approach to the conception of power in the craft. This means that the psychologist is prepared to keep an open mind to different perspectives, the ability to negotiate meanings, without losing his or her personal commitments. This challenges us to become aware of how we came to know what we know and as conscious as possible of the values that underlie our perspectives. Finally, this challenges us to have our technique and knowledge audited.

These conclusions suggest that there is not only a diminished emphasis on expert knowledge but also a discovery of the advantages of tolerating and accepting not knowing. Before a psychological reality that admits various interpretations, we have been able to recover the value of doubt and uncertainty. Modern approaches, adept at labeling reality, often seem satisfied with giving suffering a technical name, as if it had "discovered" something. A postmodern approach is skeptical of these discoveries that sometimes seem more like baptisms of faith. It prefers debates where possibilities are explored, languages that work to avoid being fetishized. George Kelly (1980) as well as Wilfred Bion have referred to John Keat's expression of "negative capability" that refers to the ability to live in uncertainty, doubt and mystery without having to despair in search for simplifications; it has to do with the capacity to listen and wait. This wait is necessary to give the emergence of a shared vision an opportunity.

Argentinian writer, Julio Cortázar, wrote something similar when he stated in his labyrinthine novel, Rayuela, "sometimes it helps to give a lot of names to a partial vision, at least it prevents the notion from becoming closed and rigid" (1963/1984, p. 404). The closing down of a notion helps to bring a sense of security and a frame of reference to try to give order to confusing perceptions, but in other cases this closure implies the imposition of a final word and the end of conversation.

A position of not knowing does not intend to discard the psychological knowledge we have acquired through the years. But rather rejects totalizing discourses and actively avoids imposing our interpretation, theoretically colonizing the other. Following Derrida, Anderson (1997) contends that not knowing doesn't mean that we don't know anything, but believe us to never be able to achieve absolute knowledge. One of the postmodern proposals to avoid fetishization is to incorporate contending discourses, the rupture of closed circles of professional thought, favoring a continuous appearance of divergent perspectives that promote challenges to our views. This translates into the active incorporation of people from different cultural backgrounds, different professional trainings, as for example, teams of social and clinical psychologists, along with psychiatrists, lawyers and social workers; or the inclusion of psychologists with different theoretical perspectives; or people from the communities we work with in the discussion of cases, planning of the work, review of institutional policies, service evaluation, etc.

Strong (2002) has borrowed the notion of borders from Jean-Francois Lyotard, suggesting that therapists should seek to actively place themselves in the territory where the conversational territory does not belong to anyone in particular. Clinical case discussion is a good example. Generally, in a traditional setting, they are done among professionals who are inscribed in a particular school of thought or institution, where there are tacit agreements and, very often, established hierarchies that lead to certain interpretations being more easily accepted than others and to having certain figures who hold the right to the last word. The postmodern encounter invites the development of places where professionals have to negotiate their interpretations. Incorporating our clients in these conversations is always a challenging way to open ourselves to new perspectives. They offer opportunities for others to observe us in the construction of interpretations and to build shared visions.

Increasingly, community members and mental health service users have begun to be incorporated into the conversations of professionals. This tendency points to the inclusion of local perspectives, the openness to being questioned, the possibility of negotiating our professional authority and fostering transparency in interventions. Members of a community may feel suspicious about the hidden political agenda of professionals that come to work. Community meetings may help them to get a first-hand perspective about the intentions as well as confront prejudices or simplistic notions that we may hold and not have recognized.

Tom Anderson's development of reflective teams is an example in this direction. He developed the procedure of having the group of professionals that observed a family therapy session, exchange places in the Gessel chamber to discuss the session, so the family can observe this discussion while it takes place. This typical postmodern intervention doesn't invert the power of the therapist, but does make it more public, more transparent, subjects it to debate and shows the family how, even in the group of "experts," different interpretations appear regarding a problem. Those that have participated in this process can attest to the force of these types of procedures to multiply simultaneous readings and build strong alliances between professionals and families. Andersen (1996) describes the reasonings that led to this arrangement:

> In our discussions we began to consider why we left the families during the breaks in the sessions? Why did we hide away our deliberations about the families? Perhaps we should stay with the families and let them see and hear what we did and how we worked with the question? Perhaps, by giving them access to our process, they would more easily find their own answers. At first we did not dare to make our discussions 'public' because we thought that the language we used contained too many 'nasty' words. For example, a team member might say, 'I am glad I am not a member of a family with such a talkative mother!' or 'What is it like to be married to such a stubborn man?' We thought that those words would come into the open easily if we talked in front of the families. In spite of these fears, everything was brought into the open one day in March 1985. On that particular day, a team who had followed the conversation from behind the one-way mirror, proposed to those in the therapeutic conversation (a family and an interviewer) that we talk for a while with them listening to us. We said that we could talk about what we had been thinking while we listened to the talk they had just had. My early fears were not fulfilled. The 'nasty' words did not appear, nor did this conversation require any strong effort from us to avoid 'nasty' words. (p. 57–58)

Some procedures in qualitative research also point toward the search for transparency and negotiation of interpretations (McLeod, 2001). Many qualitative designs routinely include a continuous process of discussion and review of the interpretations developed with the participants that, from this perspective, are not subjects but collaborators. In some approaches, participants are even trained to become co-researchers. As in therapy, it reflects a search for strategies that seek to include local perspectives in the production of knowledge, the emphasis in development of more transparent approaches and the openness to critical voices that open reflective dialogue (Etherington, 2000).

In Venezuela, the social psychologist Alejandro Moreno along with his collaborators (1998, 2002) has pioneered research through his Center of Popular Research (Centro de Investigación Popular) that has trained members of low-income communities to develop a comprehension of what he has termed the "popular Venezuelan family" as well as the gender scripts typical of our culture. His publications always include various co-authors who are members of the communities studied.

Another example is how the psychiatric users movement has opened up possibilities for greater participation in policy design and service provision (Barnes & Bowl, 2001). I was able to attend an Asylum! conference in 2008 designed to include, not only academics and mental health professionals but also service users, family members and activists in an event that sought to open discussions where everyone had equal ground to state their opinions and be heard. The conference sought to actively invite and include perspectives outside the traditional clinical sphere, particularly through the work of the Asylum organization, as well as the Hearing Voices and Paranoia Network.

The speakers were given the instruction to seek to include a wide audience, avoiding overly technical language and the rule of the conference was that any person in the audience could ask the speaker to stop at any moment and explain anything that was not understood by all. I was impacted by the intense and interesting discussions that emerged. Different from more academic-only events, the discussions centered much more on how the issues affect the lives of those to whom services and theories were directed. The lived experience of patients was much more present at that event.

This novel way of conceiving the place of the psychologist allows the inclusion of the social and political dimensions that influence the life of the users of psychology, from inside of the relationship. In this way, the therapist, not only opens up space to talk about the contextual conditions that influence the life of the person, but also invites talk about how it influences the therapeutic relationship. Themes such as gender, ethnic background, social class and cultural contexts are actively addressed.

We have found, in our work with economically deprived communities in Caracas, that many of those that come to therapy don't spontaneously bring their doubts, curiosities, tensions or conflicts that emerge in working with a therapist perceived to be from a different social class. For the therapist meanwhile, it can be particularly difficult to invite others to talk about the perceived social, economic and ethnic differences and privileges. Several authors have analyzed some of the classist tendencies that appear in conventional psychotherapeutic thinking (Altman, 1995; Blackwell, 2002; Cowen, 1983; Pilgrim, 1997; Smith, 2005). Sometimes the difficulty in addressing these issues has to do with the difficulty of imagining what the therapeutic dialogue can do in respect to social problems such as poverty, racism, inequality and exclusion (Kemper, 1992). It sometimes reflects fears of exposing personal prejudices or addressing uncomfortable issues that involve both the therapist and the client. Even when the person's biography evidences the effects of discrimination and injustice in their life, the client and the therapist can act as if those elements weren't present in the consulting room and as if these were abstract issues that are present in the external world and not in the process of trying to build a working alliance. To work from the postmodern perspective implies knowing that alliances need to be forged and not assumed, and that implies hard work, with the hope that in the end this will be liberating for both parts of the relationship. Swartz (2005) proposes that a liberating psychotherapy requires a therapist who is able to listen and explore the silences produced by the legacies of power, as well as a therapist who is able to review his or her clinical privilege. In the next chapter, we will examine how the analysis of privilege can help therapists to become more aware of the history of power in their personal biographies.

Again the problem is not to eliminate the natural asymmetry in the helping relation and social differences but to open possibilities so they can be acknowledged, reflected upon and negotiated if necessary in a collaborative conversation.

We have seen that beliefs anchored in modernity have influenced the answers therapists have traditionally given to the questions of what the place of the therapist is, how we comprehend change and how we understand the therapeutic system. Modifications to that perspective have been suggested, followed by challenges to clinical thinking that have come from critical and postmodern perspectives. Postmodern perspectives have subtracted weight to the expert's omnipotence, opened up space for uncertainty, for multiple interpretations of psychic reality, as well as acknowledged power in the helping relationship and strategies to help critically reflect on our work.

The sum of debates that had been brewing in Latin American community psychology and challenges from inside the field of psychotherapy have seemed to point in similar or complementary directions. These modifications have not been mentioned in reference to any one particular school of psychotherapy, even though we have made reference to Kelly's constructive alternativism and social constructionism which proposed their versions of psychotherapy. I believe that these debates, at a metatheoretical level, are relevant and useful to all clinical approaches independent of their preferred brand of psychotherapy. In the next chapter, we will explore the realm of psychotherapeutic technique and the tools that can help expand our reflective capacity.

References

Altman, N. (1995). *The analyst in the inner city*. Hillsdale: The Analytic Free Press.

Andersen, T. (1996). Reflections on reflecting with families. In K. Gergen, & S. Mcnamee (Eds.), *Therapy as social construction* (pp. 54–68). London: Sage.

Anderson, H. (1997). *Conversation, language and possibilities: A postmodern approach to therapy*. New York: Basic Books.

Barnes, M., & Bowl, R. (2001). *Taking over the asylum: Empowerment and mental health*. London: Palgrave.

Blackwell, D. (2002). Out of their class: Class, colonization and resistance in analytic psychotherapy and group analysis. *Group Analysis, 35*, 367–380.

Bruner, J. (1990). *Acts of meaning*. Cambridge: Harvard University Press.

Campagnaro, S. (2017). Historia del nacimiento de la Unidad de Psicología Clínica Comunitaria "Padre Luis Azagra" del Parque Social. *Analogías del Comportamiento., 15,* 75–78.

Coderch, J. (2001). *La Relación Paciente-Terapeuta: el campo del psicoanálisis y la psicoterapia psicoanalítica*. Bacelona: Paidós.

Cortázar, J. (1963/1984). *Rayuela*. Bogotá: Editorial Oveja Negra.

Cowen, E. (1983). Community mental health and primary prevention. In I. Weiner (Ed.), *Clinical methods in psychology* (pp. 634–695). New York: John Wiley and Sons.

Etherington, K. (2000). *Narrative approaches to working with adult male survivors of child sexual abuse: The client's, the counsellor's and the researcher's story*. London: Jessica Kinglsey Publisher.

Fals-Borda, O., & Anisur, M. (1991). *Action and knowledge: Breaking the monopoly with participative-action research*. Maryland: Rowman & Littlefield.

Fiester, S. (1995). Self-defeating personality disorder. In W. J. Livesley (Ed.), *The DSM-IV personality disorders* (pp. 341–358). New York: The Guilford Press.

Freire, P. (1970). *Pedagogy of the oppressed*. New York: Herder & Herder.

Freud, S. (1933/1983). Nuevas lecciones introductorias al psicoanálisis. In *Obras Completas*. Madrid: Biblioteca Nueva.

Freud, S. (1937/1983). Construcciones en análisis. In *Obras Completas*. Madrid: Biblioteca Nueva.

Frosh, S. (2007). Facing political truths. *Psychotherapy and Politics International, 5,* 29–36.

García de la Hoz, A. (2000). *Teoría Psicoanalítica*. Madrid: Quipú Biblioteca Nueva.

Geertz, C. (1973). *The interpretation of cultures*. New York: Basic Books.

Gergen, K. (1991). *The saturated self: Dilemmas of identity in contemporary life*. United States: Basic Books.

Gergen, K., & Warhus, L. (2001). Therapy as social construction. In K. Gergen (Ed.), *Social construction in context* (pp. 96–114). London: Sage.

Glauser, B. (1999). Definitivamente los 'niños de la calle' están de moda. *Revista Venezolana de Psicología Comunitaria, 1,* 19–27.

Herman, J. (1997). *Trauma and Recovery: The aftermath of violence—from domestic abuse to political terror*. New York: Basic Books.

Hernández, N., Llorens, M., & Medina, S. (1999). Procesos emocionales que surgen en el personal que trabaja con niños con experiencia de vida en la calle. *Revista Venezolana de Psicología Clínica Comunitaria, 1,* 3–22.

Kelly, G. (1966). *Teoría de la Personalidad*. Buenos Aires: Ediciones Troquel.

Kelly, G. (1980). A psychology of the optimal man. In W. Landfield & L. Leitner (Eds.), *Personal construct psychology: Psychotherapy and personality* (pp. 18–35). New York: Wiley.

Kemper, J. (1992). Brazil: Mental health in social distress? The dialectic between inner psychic and external social reality. *International Forum of Psychoanalysis, 1,* 129–135.

Kernberg, O. (1998). *Ideology, conflict and leadership in groups and organizations*. New Haven: Yale University Press.

Kernberg, O. (2004). *Contemporary controversies in theory, techniques, and their applications*. New Haven: Yale University Press.

LaPlanche, J., & Pontalis, J. (1994). *Diccionario de psicoanálisis*. Bogotá: Labor.

Larsen, R., & Buss, D. (2005). *Psicología de la personalidad*. México: McGraw Hill.

Llorens, M. (2003). Buscando conversación: Nuevas maneras de construir conversaciones terapéuticas en nuestras comunidades. *Revista Venezolana de Psicología Clínica Comunitaria, 3,* 141–176.

Llorens, M. (2009a). The search for a politically reflective clinical-community approach. *American Journal of Community Psychology, 43,* 100–110.

Llorens, M. (2009b). Liberation psychology on the street: Working with youngsters who have lived in the streets of Caracas. In M. Montero, & C. Sonn (Eds.), *Psychology of liberation: Theory and applications* (pp. 237–258). New York: Springer.

Llorens, M., Alvarado, C., Hernández, N., Jaramillo, U., Romero, M., & Souto, J. (2005). *Niños con experiencia de vida en la calle: Una aproximación psicológica*. Buenos Aires: Paidós.
Martín-Baró, I. (1984/1993). Guerra y salud mental. *Papeles del Psicólogo*. II, *56*, 27–33.
Martín-Baró, I. (1986). Hacia una psicología de la liberación. *Boletín de Psicología, 22,* 219–231.
Martín-Baró, I. (1990). *Psicología social de la guerra: trauma y terapia*. San Salvador: UCA Editores.
Martín-Baró, I. (2002). *Psicología de la liberación para América Latina*. México: ITESO-Universidad de Guadalajara.
May, R., Angel, E., & Ellenberger, H. (1967). *Existencia: nueva dimensión en psiquiatría y psicología*. Madrid: Editorial Gredos.
McLeod, J. (2001). *Qualitative research in counselling and psychotherapy*. London: Sage Publications.
Mitchell, S. (1993). *Hope and dread in psychoanalysis*. New York: Basic Books.
Montero, M. (2003). *Teoría y Práctica de la Psicología Comunitaria. La tensión entre comunidad y sociedad*. Buenos Aires: Paidós.
Montero, M. (2004). *Introducción a la Psicología Comunitaria. Desarrollo, conceptos, procesos*. Buenos Aires: Paidós.
Montero, M. (2006). *Hacer para Transformar. El método en la psicología comunitaria*. Buenos Aires: Paidós.
Montero, M., & Montenegro, M. (2006). Critical psychology in Venezuela. *Annual review of critical psychology, 5*. www.discourseunit.com/arcp/5. Accessed 15 February 2008.
Montero, M., & Sonn, C. (2009). *Psychology of liberation: Theory and applications*. New York: Springer.
Montero, M., & Varas Díaz, N. (2007). Latin American community psychology: Development, implications and challenges within a social change agenda. In S. Reich, M. Riemer, I. Prilleltensky, & M. Montero (Eds.), *International community psychology: History and theories* (pp. 63–98). Irvine: Springer.
Moreno, A., Brandt, J., Campos, A., Nabarro, R., Pérez, M., Rodríguez, W., et al. (1998). *Historia de vida de Felicia Valera*. Caracas: Fondo Editorial Conicit.
Moreno, A., & Luna, P. (2002). *Buscando padre: historia de vida de Pedro Luis Luna*. Caracas: Universidad de Carabobo y Centro de Investigaciones Populares.
Niemeyer, R. (1993). An appraisal of constructivist psychotherapies. *Journal of Consulting and Clinical Psychology, 61,* 221–234.
Phillips, A. (2000). *Promises, promises*. London: Faber y Faber.
Pilgrim, D. (1997). *Psychotherapy and society*. London: Sage Publications.
Pocock, D. (1995). Searching for a better story: Harnessing modern and post-modern positions in family therapy. *Journal of Family Therapy, 17,* 149–173.
Polkinghorne, D. (1992). Postmodern epistemology of practice. In S. Kvale (Ed.), *Psychology and postmodernism* (pp. 146–165). London: Sage.
Rogers, C. (1961/1989). *On becoming a person: A therapist's view of psychotherapy*. New York: Houghton Mifflin.
Romero, J. (2017). Unidad de Psicología 'Padre Luis Azagra, S.J.'. Principios que la sustentan derivados de su historia. *Analogías del Comportamiento*, *15*, 79–84.
Rychlak, J. (1981). *Introduction to personality and psychotherapy*. Boston: Houghton Mifflin Company.
Rychlak, J. (2000). A psychotherapist's lessons from the philosophy of science. *American Psychologist, 55,* 1126–1132.
Schafer, R. (1992). *Retelling a life: Narration and dialogue in psychoanalysis*. New York: Basic Books.
Smith, L. (2005). Psychotherapy, classism, and the poor: Conspicuous by their absence. *American Psychologist, 60,* 687–696.
Steiner, G. (2013). *Real presences: Is there anything in what we say?*. New York: Open Road.
Strong, T. (2002). Dialogue in therapy's 'borderzone'. *The Journal of Constructivist Psychology, 15,* 245–262. https://doi.org/10.1080/10720530290100479.

Strong, T. (2003). Cinco directrices para terapeutas colaboradores. *Revista Venezolana de Psicología Clínica Comunitaria, 3,* 115–139.
Swartz, S. (2005). "Can de clinical subject speak?" Some thoughts on subaltern psychology. *Theory & Psychology, 15,* 505–525.
Totton, N. (2000). *Psychotherapy and politics.* London: Sage Publications.
Widiger, T. (1995). Deletion of self-defeating and sadistic personality disorders. In W. J. Livesley (Ed.), *The DSM-IV personality disorders* (pp. 335–352). New York: The Guilford Press.
Zumbalawe, J. (1996). El paradigma fenomenológico y las teorías personalistas. In Fierro, (Ed.), *Manual de psicología de la personalidad.* Barcelona: Paidós.

Chapter 7
Psychotherapeutic Technique

7.1 Looking for Conversation

The Universidad Católica Andrés Bello (UCAB) is set in the southwest part of Caracas, neighbor to two very large barrios[1] (Antímano and La Vega) as well as a middle-class neighborhood in front of the university (Montalbán). Like the majority of the marginalized communities in the valley of Caracas, they sit upon the slopes of the mountains, so they can be seen from a distance. Between Antímano and the UCAB there is the river Guaire. The UCAB is a private, Jesuit university and the majority of its population belongs to the middle class, even though up to 30% require some sort of economic support to be able to cost their studies.

A few years ago a new building was built and one of the university's administrative directors, who inspired and gave name to our psychology unit, the educator and priest Luis Azagra told a revealing story about the construction process. The university opened a bidding process and Azagra attended the presentation of the various competing projects. He was surprised to hear that almost all of them, including a number of companies with professionals that had graduated from the university, mentioned that the proposals were designed with the intention of concealing the view of the low-income barrios that sit in front. Azagra shared his amazement and sadness over thinking that those professionals that had graduated at our university hadn't realized that the Jesuit's philosophy was precisely the contrary. The project that won the competition was the one that looked directly toward our social reality. It is a telling anecdote on the difficulties of looking at the traumatic conditions of poverty and social exclusion. A difficulty that underlies many of the political conflicts our country has endured, but probably also, a

[1]Barrios are favelas or slums, made up of mostly self-built housing and lack of many basic services such as electricity or public transportation. As the barrios grow older they tend to become more consolidated and have a heterogeneous population with different levels of poverty. The barrios close to the university are particularly traditional ones, that are more than fifty years old.

M. Llorens, *Politically Reflective Psychotherapy*, Latin American Voices,
https://doi.org/10.1007/978-3-030-57792-6_7

difficulty for many other countries. It is also a powerful metaphor of the spirit of our community center. It is located outside the walls of the university at midpoint between it and our neighboring communities.

Universities can be conceived as safe havens, which is a good thing, but they can turn into escape routes to avoid the harsh aspects of our reality. It is a way of turning our gaze from the unresolved issues of our contexts toward the abstract world of knowledge. This is a huge problem if we believe universities are one of our main resources to produce the talent that can tackle society's most urgent issues.

This coincides with the critiques that have stated that our discipline entrenches itself in its own professional world, avoiding wider social issues and, in consequence, working to consolidate the status quo (Pakman, 1997; Parker, 2007). Smith (2005) in the United States and Harper (1991, 2003) in the United Kingdom agree that our profession suffers significant limitations to attend to people in poverty. Installed in its professional class and cultural conventions, Smith writes how her practice worked fluidly, but, outside of those scenarios, she often felt uncomfortable and ineffective.

The new building was finally built with a direct view to Antímano and the community center has reached 20 years of activity. Along with the expressions of evasion and prejudice there are forces that push toward transformation. The university has helped those forces resonate amid the complex social reality that was aggravated by the very difficult place where Chavismo's growing authoritarianism placed it. Those that struggle for social transformation but resist being co-opted by government propaganda have found themselves between a rock and a hard place.

The psychology unit offered us a platform to engage in the very exciting challenge of trying to offer solutions in an increasingly constricted context. On the way, some therapists were disconcerted, others discouraged. One of them expressed, in one of our studies of our own process:

> It's possible that, since there are so many unmet needs of basic services and goods, in this context one is always dealing with urgency, with crisis, and there is little space left to work on deeper issues… I feel that patients here provoke a great amount of frustration in me, since you don't get to see progress as quickly as you would in other contexts. (Meneses, Pérez, Rodríguez, & Westinner, 2001, p. 24)

Through our postgraduate program we were able to systematize a lot of our own reflections dealing with the questions posed by our task in those circumstances. This allowed us to return to expressions like the last one in which we asked ourselves, what do we mean by deeper? What is the image we have of psychotherapeutic work that makes us think there is something with depth, or that there are things that may be deeper than hunger or a constant feeling of injustice? We began to see that we had the tendency to evaluate psychotherapy with a conventional lens that categorized a specific set of contents as truer or deeper.

Social, educational, cultural and economic differences presented a challenge from the very beginning. It was obvious that they framed the enormous material needs that influenced the emotional sufferings of those that sought our help. We had to develop tools to think, comprehend and intervene by adapting the contributions of psychology to our reality.

7.2 Development of Psychotherapeutic Tools

On one occasion, a psychoanalyst visited our center, curious about the combination of a clinical and community perspective. He concluded that we should be called clinical and community psychologists, attempting to separate the two terms. He assumed that we continued working like clinical psychologists have always done in our consulting rooms and, in parallel, community psychologists did their own thing. The only difference is that we shared the same space. As Maslow once put it "if the only tool you have is a hammer, everything looks like a nail" (1966/2002, p. 15).

That is not how we see our work at all. We believe to, following the premise of critical psychology (Montero & Montenegro, 2006), be using the tension produced by different theoretical perspectives to force us to continually question our thinking and so enliven the debate and reflection in regard to our practice. To share the same offices is not just a spatial arrangement but an attempt to foster discussion and continual revision of our perspectives, to actively have to decipher the questions posed by our context from different points of view. We attempt to follow John Shotter's (2000) invitation to avoid distancing ourselves from our context while getting tangled up in our own languages, setting up even more obstacles, rather than trying to tune into our surroundings, and being "more at home" with the complexities of the human phenomenon. We believe that a clinical psychologist, even in the most traditional of settings, in his or her consulting room, can use community psychology as a reference to transcend the habitual formulation of cases.

In the observation of our colleagues, the need to separate the social from the individual, the personal from the political, appeared over and over again, trying to relegate issues to different compartments. The discomfort reported by studies done with international psychotherapists when dealing with political issues (Samuels, 1993) presented itself in our conversations in the therapeutic milieu. We have attempted to develop therapeutic tools that agree with Totton's (2000) proposal of "reinserting therapy in its historical context… re-imbedding it in its political context, from which it has so carefully separated itself" (p. 12).

Our task is to not only criticize fragmented perspectives but also develop tools that help us achieve this reinsertion, to integrate individual and social dimensions. As Prilleltensky, Prillenteksy and Voorhees have pointed out:

> Unless we manage to convert critique into construction, and deliberation into delivery of new practices, the gap between discourse and action will continue to grow, leaving behind a trail of doubly disaffected practitioners; disaffected with the medical model, and disaffected with critical approaches that fail to suggest convincing alternatives for practice. (2008, p. 105)

In this chapter, I will illustrate some of the tools derived from postmodern reviews and Latin American community psychology in the process of translating clinical psychology. As has been stated previously, these tools do not pretend to create a new psychotherapy but shift and complement perspectives. Even though new technical tools provide us with concrete ways of widening our psychotherapeutic focus, I must stress that the fundamental element necessary to develop a psychotherapeutic approach able to deal with the political dimension is a paradigmatic framework that opens up the possibility to listen to the dilemmas that appear in the consulting room.

7.3 Contextualized Understandings

Our first task is to find a way of listening to the people who seek our help without having to isolate the contextual elements that caused it or at least had influence in producing it. Samuels (1993) recommends not listening to political material only as if it were symbolic or referred to transference. This implies searching for ways of understanding these contextual elements without losing our interest in the individual, the personal and the intimate. Or, in the words of Martí-Baró (1984/1993):

> It is important to underline that we do not pretend to simplify a complex problem like mental health denying its individual roots, and, for the sake of avoiding an individual reductionism incur in a social one. In the end we need to answer the question of why this appeared in this person and not in that one. But we want to emphasize how illuminating it is to change our point of view and see health or mental disorder not as something that emerges from inside out; like the emanation of internal individual functioning, but as the materialization in a person or a group of a humanizing or alienating web of historical relations. (p. 28)

We are therefore looking to be able to think in terms of personal biography, interpersonal relationships, emotional regulation, motivation, conflict and coping mechanisms as well as in terms of culture, shared meanings, conflict, ideals, power, habits, roles and collective fears, etc.

Kelly, who proposed the notion of constructive alternativism (1966), also stated that each theory has its own preferred focus and range. The focus refers to the specific applications that the theory explains best and the range to the area of reality that it covers. In that sense psychotherapeutic formulations can feed off alternative perspectives that can focus on the individual, intimate and interpersonal and on the social and political; interpretations that may not produce a definite, polished, unified enunciation but one that produces creative tension. We are looking for interpretations that can be described as on two levels, the individual and the social, that may sometimes prove complementary, but can also help to open debate.

Even though there has not been sufficient development of the political determinants in clinical practice (Sarason, 1981), there is a list of psychologists and psychiatrists that have been able to systematically observe, not only individual dynamics, but also their link to wider social conditions. In world literature, we find examples such as Fromm (1980) and May (1974), or more recently Marcelo Pakman (2011) and White (1993).

In Venezuela, we have also had very lucid examples such as the work of Vethencourt (2009) or Ephraim (1999, 2001). Vethencourt was a psychiatrist who developed a cultural and historical interpretation of many of his clinical observations. His work influenced that of a local social psychologist, Moreno, et al. (1998,

2002), who developed a very original line of work about the cultural world-view of, what he termed, "the Venezuelan popular family." Ephraim is a pioneer in the adaptation of the Thematic Apperception Test and the Rorschach in the Venezuelan population and his work with anthropologist George De Vos helped him to develop an outlook especially sensitive to cultural differences in therapeutic work.

Again, our first task is to consider the context in the comprehension of the clinical material. In the work of people who have been violently victimized this, as mentioned in Chapter 5, has become an increasingly common practice. The inclusion of Post-Traumatic Stress Disorder as a recognized diagnosis in 1980 opened up a category where external experience is recognized as essential to comprehend the symptoms. Martín-Baró (1984/1993) suggested something similar when mentioning that, in his interviews with peasants displaced by war, he found a multitude of what seemed to be hyperalert, distrustful attitudes and beliefs that seemed paranoid, until he explored in detail the severe circumstances they had gone through that made their very cautious and suspicious styles a comprehensible reaction to a very altered context.

Some of the debates that arise, for example, regarding the use of Borderline Personality Disorder instead of Complex Trauma to describe survivors of child abuse, are discussions of using a label that emphasizes personal functioning over one that tries to place these extreme reactions in relation to a context that caused them.

The resistance of survivors of violent relationships to being diagnosed with a psychiatric label is often, not a rejection of the need to seek psychotherapeutic help, but a rejection of having the problems that they suffered attributed to their individual functioning rather than to the very distorted realities that they had to endure.

Backwell (2005), who has worked with the victims of torture and refugees, gives a similar example, underlining the importance of understanding the political conditions and human rights abuses that produced the suffering rather than using conventional psychiatric diagnosis. Backwell defends the notion that all psychotherapy occurs in a political context, even though in other cases it may be less evident. He goes on to say that if we consider that politically reflective psychotherapy is only for extreme cases, we run the risk of reifying a dichotomy of political and non-political therapy, leaving the medical model intact.

Let us now look at an example extracted from our conversations with training clinicians at our university. It is a case where we have changed several elements but exemplify similar dilemmas that have come up repeatedly in our work.

María is a woman in her late 40s, who asks for help at the psychiatric unit of a public hospital in an impoverished area of Caracas. She is referred by the Gastroenterology Service, reporting anxiety, insomnia, frequent bursts of crying, sadness and the persistent idea that she is suffering from cancer, even though doctors, after several evaluations, have assured her of the contrary. She suffers from chronic gastritis that provokes great pain in her and the feeling that she is not sufficiently cared for by her family or her doctors.

In the first interviews that the clinical psychologist brings to a case discussion, she believes that the patient is suffering from a Major Depressive Disorder and is considering the possibility of some sort of hypochondriac condition. The therapist has transcribed, with permission, parts of the first sessions of her evaluation. In them, the woman talks about a recent visit she made to her birthplace, a small town in the Andes region, after which her symptoms worsened and her feeling of not being properly cared for increased.

M: I feel terrible (cries). This weekend everyone went out and they left me all alone.

Therapist: Tell me, what do you all normally do on weekends?

M. Well, my children go out all day, and I can't tell them to stay at home with me, they are adults now.

T: And what about your husband?

M: He goes out all weekend to bet on horse races… He needs to have his fun and I can't tell him to stay, but I feel bad, where am I going to go?

The psychologist continues to ask about her family situation and the issue of her marriage comes up:

T: Tell me about your childhood and how you met him.

M: My parents lived in a small town and had me working since I was little. Since I was six or seven years old.

T: What were you like back then?

M: Ever since I was little I was a crybaby, when I turned thirteen I ran away from home to live with my older sister.

T: Why did you run away?

M: Because my mother wanted to marry me to a man that was much older than me. He had seen me, liked me and told my mom that he wanted to marry me, but I didn't like him. So I decided to run away, with the help of my older brother.

T: What happened then?

M: My mother got very upset. Finally, she let it pass and after fourteen months I went back home. I was there for a few months until I left again to live with my sister. I prefered to be with her.

…

T: How did you meet your husband?

M: I know him from my hometown.

T: Was he your first boyfriend?

M: No… (lowers her head with embarrassment and says that it is hard to talk about this). At fifteen I had my first boyfriend… but my sister didn't like him. Because he was black.

T: What happened?

M: We broke up because I saw him in a car with another girl. And then I met my husband.

T: How did you meet him?

M: In the town, I was seventeen, my sister didn't like my husband either, so I had to hide to be able to see him. We got married when I was seventeen.

T: Why so young?

M: … (seems embarrassed) I married him because I got pregnant.

T: What did you do?

M: I told my husband that I couldn't tell anything to my sister, because she would have sent me back home to my mother, and there they were going to kill me. So my husband spoke to my mother, explained it all and she told him to take me to his house... My mother didn't meet my children until the second one turned two. She didn't talk to me again until then. My father was more understanding and my sister visited me sometimes....

Then we had to leave to Caracas because my mother-in-law told my husband that there was a job for him in Caracas and that we would be better off there. My husband told me that we had to go. But I didn't want to go.

T: Why?

M: I had struggled to build a home and wasn't going to be able to enjoy it because now we had to go to Caracas. I had a job and he did too and we had our house built. Then my mother-in-law called.

T: Was there no other choice?

M; No, I was married, with two kids, I couldn't do anything. I wasn't about to be left without a husband. I had to go. When we arrived I knew that there was no job waiting for him. Weeks passed and he couldn't find a job. So I found one and began to work cleaning at the hospital. Later I did my course to become a nurse and began to work, first as a substitute. My husband spent nine months unemployed.

On the basis of these initial exchanges, some hypotheses are developed in the case discussion. Tentative psychodynamic interpretations are formulated. Certain lines of inquiry appear related to her demands on her family, her early difficult relationships with her caretakers, perhaps her conflicts relating to aggression and her symptom formation that might be trying to channel her unmet needs, maybe to make others feel impotent, maybe punishing herself for her unsatisfied destructive desires.

These lines of reasoning seem somewhat consistent with the story we are hearing, as well as useful to offer, through the therapeutic relationship, food for thought to try to reorganize and rethink some of the client's affective entanglements. This exploration promises to invite her to re-examine her experiences related to feelings of abandonment, how she deals with her desire to be comforted, her ways of asking or not asking for help which might help her deal differently with her needs and help her understand her suffering a bit more.

But simultaneously, these formulations might help obscure how many of these experiences are also intrinsically linked to poverty and gender. Even though the psychodynamic hypothesis might lead to opening ways to empathize and help her reflect on her emotional world, reflections on what it is to be a woman, her beliefs in regard to her rights and duties and the origins of those beliefs can also open alternative explorations. It seems obvious that the conversation on the terrible restrictions she has faced in her erotic life and autonomy (to choose her partners, to feel entitled to enjoy, even to choose her place of residence) are very relevant. Her life is filled with injustice, the imposition of arbitrary criteria based on racial and sexist prejudices. It's important to highlight that these beliefs don't respond only to a family dynamic, but are set in a shared social setting regarding what a woman's place should be, to the point that María doesn't question them too much, rather internalizes those truths that make her feel embarrassed when questioned by her interviewer. Unquestioned beliefs that have brought a suffering that is unseen and unheard, while she remains tied up, entangled in them.

Waldgrave, who developed what has been called Just Therapy, working with marginalized communities in New Zealand, writes:

> We realised that the problems these families were bringing to us were not the symptoms of family dysfunction, but instead the symptoms of broader structural issues like poverty, patriarchy and racism. (1990, p. 5)

The case presented does not refer to a victim of torture, state violence or exile. Her suffering doesn't openly seem to refer to the political sphere, but it is quite evident how different power relations have played out in her life and are crucial to complete the picture of how she internalized the structures that oppress and repress her. It refers to what, following Foucault, Pakman (2011) has referred to as the micropolitical dimension. The gender scripts that she has internalized undoubtedly contribute to her self-image, her guilt and her shame. We often find that people who have grown in places of deprivation feel ashamed and guilty for the difficulties they suffer, using the same sexist and classist reasonings to evaluate their lives that have limited their growth in the first place. The descriptions that María gives of herself as impure and faulty prevents her from valuing the courage she must have had to be able to run away from home at 13, in order to rebel against a marriage that she didn't desire and the efforts that took to be able to build her home once and again in order to have the family that she desired. What tools does therapeutic dialogue have to help María take a critical distance from the discourses that have subjected her and pushed her further into a place of disadvantage, so as to examine her life from a new perspective and perhaps resist some of these impositions?

7.4 Denaturalization/Rendering Visible

In the discussion with the young psychologist and her exchange with María I asked her what she felt when she mentioned that she had been forced to come to Caracas with her husband. I was curious about her question: "Was there no other choice?" It seemed that maybe, from the therapist's perspective it seemed incredible that she had been forced to quit all the things that she had struggled so much for and hadn't been able to negotiate another option. The psychologist confirmed that she had felt shocked by much of what María was telling about her life and reacted in fashion. The life of the psychologist, as a woman that comes from a central city, with higher economic and cultural capital, as well as access to contemporary gender scripts, is framed in higher expectations of autonomy and self-determination. But, from the perspective of María the decision was clear, there was no other option: "No, I was married, with two children, I couldn't do anything else, I wasn't about to be left without a husband." Part of her requirement to go to Caracas probably came from the notion that to be a woman is to be properly married. In our country, to be a wife and a mother confers a series of responsibilities that are very difficult to question or rebel against, which, on occasion, can even include the obligation to follow your husband to another city. It is clear that the man has more prerogative about the decisions of the destiny of the couple. What is important to note is that it is true for María, even though it leads to suffering, even if she might, in her inner world, feel it to be unjust. But it is a natural thing, "how things are." At the same time, for a therapist, who has been able to grow professionally and had many other opportunities, it seems a bit amazing that María can be tied down by such limiting social pressures.

We have inherited from community psychology the notion of naturalization, which Montero describes as:

> Process through which certain phenomenons or patterns of behavior are considered the way things are in the world, as an essential nature of society. Naturalization is responsible for maintaining a simplification of circumstances in daily life, by including negative aspects that can make life more difficult or by denying the possibility of certain critical and/or harmful aspects (2004, p. 292).

I owe professor Fernando Yurman (2005) the reference to the quote from Jorge Luis Borges that illustrates wonderfully the mechanism of naturalization. In the "Argentine writer and tradition," Borges writes:

> in the Koran, there are no camels; I believe if there were any doubts as to the authenticity of the Koran, this absence of camels would be sufficient to prove it is an Arabian work… Mohammed as an Arab, had no reason to know that camels were especially Arabian; for him they were a part of reality, he had no need to emphasize them (1932 para. 14).

That which has been considered part of the natural order of things does not need to be emphasized and can go unnoticed for the locals. That which is natural is not highlighted in the story. Culture operates this way. We are inscribed in culture in a way that our frames of reference become invisible. For María and her community's culture, some ways of being a woman, that can make life harder and unjust, even unbearable, have been naturalized to the point of going unquestioned. When we begin to identify these assumptions as cultural constructions we open up space to be able to re-examine them, take distance, to see them as historical processes and therefore open possibilities for alternatives, which Montero has called "denaturalization" and is analogous to what feminism has called "rendering visible." It implies the process of taking critical distance from certain notions and beliefs that sustain the "way life is" so they can be stripped of their naturalness. It allows us to signal aspects of reality that had gone by unnoticed.

We have found that it is useful to work to denaturalize patterns of interaction that are painful and whose bases often go unnoticed. In regard to child abuse, for example, for some parents their difficulties with their emotional regulation fit well with notions of authority that have naturalized abuse. They need to question the cultural given as a complement or their emotional growth and acquisition of parenting skills.

Denaturalization relates to what family therapist Michael White has called deconstruction (1993). He has referred to the work of Derrida as an influence to develop therapeutic conversations that help question "truths" that come dissociated from the contexts that produced them. White seeks to: "exoticize the domestic." It helps to look again at that which was considered natural.

The mere act of asking helps to acknowledge that an idea, behavior or feeling is not inevitable, but that it might have other possibilities, even though it may seem like a natural response. Once these issues are placed in their historical context, even more avenues open up to rethink them. The therapist's question, "was there no other option?", opens the first possibility to reconsider. Other similar lines of conversation might be: what would have happened if you had done something else? what would have others said? who would have said what? why? what factors of your upbringing would have made you think that way? do you know any woman who has chosen differently? what happened to her? what did others think of her? why? They help to search for ways of identifying how these gender scripts are sustained in culture.

This is also similar to what feminists have termed "rendering visible" (Burin & Meler, 2000; Espín, 1993; Hague & Mullender, 2005; Skinner, Hester, & Malos, 2005). Rendering visible the structural conditions that have passed unnoticed, or the process of giving voice to those that have been silenced. The defense of citizen rights and therapy have a common ground that can produce powerful collaborations. The recording of personal stories is essential to both activities. Psychotherapy has the potential to offer a forum for private stories that counter not only psychological repression but also social repression. Intimacy can be a privileged place for resistance. Shared stories in psychotherapy offer material that, following human right's researchers, Schafer & Smith (2004) can help register testimonies of abuse, challenge dominant narratives of oppressors through the experience of the protagonists, call on the wider community to react, help share the humanity of those that have been dehumanized, provide empathy and indignation, help strengthen support networks, foster hope, recover evidence and mobilize public opinion and collective action.

The defense of the rights of those who have been abused and the psychotherapeutic processing of those experiences hold hands at this crucial point. Ferenczi (1933/1994) was the first to point out that the violence of sexual abuse is not the only element that leads to disorder. Having to live in a family that acts as if nothing happened is a central part of the suffering and the symptoms. Ferenczi notes:

> the perpetrator behaves as though nothing had happened, and consoles himself with the thought: 'Oh, it is only a child, he does not know anything, he will forget it all.' Not infrequently after such events, the seducer becomes over-moralistic or religious and endeavours to save the soul of the child by severity. (p. 163)

Denial subjects victims to a confusing reality that alternates the experiences of abuse to that of "normal" family life, acting as if nothing happened. Clinical work has confirmed that abusers use denial and try to isolate and keep victims in silence, analogous to oppressive government's efforts to deny atrocity and silence victims of state violence. Like living with an abuser it has been dumbfounding and enraging to hear the many versions of denial Venezuelan government has offered through the years to reject any charge of grave Human Rights abuses including the confirmations made by international observers like the Human Rights Commission of the United Nations led by Michelle Bachelet (2019). The NGO Human Rights Watch's (HRW) report states that:

> Despite the overwhelming evidence of human rights violations, we found no evidence that key high-level officials—including those who knew or should have known about the abuses —have taken any steps to prevent and punish violations. On the contrary, they have often downplayed the abuses or issued implausible blanket denials (HRW, 2017).

Those that experience abuse and oppression are exposed daily to painful situations that pass unnoticed by officials that are supposed to attend to their grievances. There is a long list of newspaper reporters, researchers and doctors who have been threatened and persecuted because they dared to report the stories of abuse committed by government forces (Mackintosh, 2019). But it is even more painful and enraging to have outside witnesses deny your experiences of victimization. In the Drowned and the Saved, Primo Levi begins his reflections on the experiences suffered in the Nazi concentration camp, describing that one of the most common nightmares of survivors was that of going back home and telling family and friends what they had gone through, only to find their account being discredited.

In the case of Venezuela, those that have suffered imprisonment and torture report their rage and surprise when ideological sympathizers speak in admiring terms of Venezuela without mentioning that from 2016 to 2018 we have a register of 16,344 murders committed by state security forces (Ávila, in press). In the midst of the polarization that Chavismo provokes, Venezuelan academics have written of having to continuously deal with Chavismo sympathizers that deny the gravity of government's abuse in academic circles (Llorens, 2019; Kozak, 2018). Psychologist Cristal Palacios, while doing her PhD in Ireland on Peace Psychology, writes about Irish "deniers" of the Venezuelan crisis and wonders: "have they forgotten what it means to live in hell? have they forgotten how it feels to be lectured by outsiders?" (2019).

When a circumstance has become "naturalized," it becomes invisible, unnamable. The pain the situation provokes becomes unnoticeable and therefore unrecognized. This adds isolation to the suffering of the abuse. In the words of family therapists Hardy and Laszloffy (2002):

> It's one thing to lose something that was important to you, but it is far worse when no one in your universe recognizes that you have lost it. The failure to acknowledge another's loss is to deny that person's humanity. Hence, when loss remains unacknowledged, we refer to this as the *dehumanization of loss*, which is the mega-loss. (p. 28)

So one of the first tasks to begin to deal with the sequels of violence, oppression and abuse is to name it, identify it and render it visible (Hirigoyen, 1999). Making power visible plays a therapeutic and political role. Political because it allows us to question power asymmetries and open up space for adjustments to be made, especially if someone is being left in a vulnerable, unjust position. To make it visible helps break the abusers control of the situation, helps the victim link to social support networks, even with others that may have the power to stop the abuse. Therapeutically it helps to reduce the isolation and validate the victim's perception. To name the abuse helps the victim to not have to live in a dissociated reality, having to go on as if there had been no abuse. Feelings of fear, rage, pain and confusion are recognized. This helps to counter the internalization of shame and guilt. It helps to begin to understand what has happened in terms of power.

Not only women are subjugated by stereotyped roles that limit their life options. In our work in communities we constantly find men trapped in rigid roles of masculinity which they feel they are not able to fulfill, in part because of the economic inequalities they suffer. Men in poverty are frequently confronted with expectations based on economic success and professional status that make them feel inferior. The structural conditions that produce lack of access to quality education, to economic resources and to social networks complicate the attainment of status symbols. The resulting poverty and unemployment is often internalized and interpreted as evidence of their personal failure.

In the following fragment of a family session, a man who works at night in a parking lot, tells us how he often doesn't return home after work for two reasons: it's dangerous to enter his neighborhood at that hour and because he is ashamed to return without any money to bring home. It's interesting to note that he doesn't manifest anger about being subjected to the insecurity of his barrio or about receiving a terrible salary that is never enough to take care of his family, but rather shame, and that shame contributes to him drifting away from his wife and kids. He feels he is a bad father because he doesn't have enough money, and as a consequence, abandons them. As if he were not honorable enough to occupy his place as a father, because he is not bringing money home:

Father: Last week I didn't return home because I didn't have any money.

Therapist: Why?

Father: Even if I am left without anything I like to bring something home.

Therapist: You prefer to not see them than have to face them asking for something that you may not have, and have to deal with having to say no?

Father: Exactly, say they need money for the bus and I can't give them anything. I don't like that.

This man was surprised to hear in therapy that his children enjoy and need his presence, even without money. He is surprised to hear that the therapist thinks that there might be other valuable things he can give as a father that are not based on his material production. He begins to think about alternatives and begins to ask himself how he developed this notion of fatherhood. It is a step toward denaturalization. It is possibly, a therapeutic advance, as he begins to hear things his children ask of him from a different perspective. It is also a micropolitical intervention, in the sense that he can begin to take some distance from the societal values and attributions of responsibility through which he has evaluated himself, as he examines the origins of how he came to internalize them.

Therapists like Pakman (2011) and Hardy and Laszloffy (2002) consider that challenging societal ideals in therapy is a form of cultural critique that has transformative potential in the micropolitical sphere. The task of the therapist, rather than that of the educator, is not to seek to change a set of values with another set (seemingly more progressive or just). The task is to open space for reflection, where the person can return to think about one's ideals, beliefs, preferences and dislikes and how they operate in trapping oneself and others in entanglements. Once the conversation has opened space up for this line of reflection, the tools of cultural critique become a useful resource to examine how naturalization operates in daily life.

The examination of popular culture is often a conversation that isn't as threatening as that of personal beliefs. Humor is highly valued in the Venezuelan society, as well as all of Latin America. The exploration of daily jokes or humorous popular characters is a conversation that clients engage without feeling defensive. I have often asked groups that are examining their ideals if they know of any super hero from Latin America? (Llorens, 2006). It is interesting to see how they work through their memory without identifying one. So I stress, might Superman be Colombian? or Aquaman Dominican? which always brings a bit of laughter. It seems ridiculous to think that these super heroes could be Latino. But in the end, one always comes up. A famous Mexican comedy character called the *Chapulín Colorado*, something like the Red Grasshopper, a television character who wore a red cape and a big heart on his chest and did all he could to help others but often failed miserably. But he was charming and funny, and you ended up loving him nevertheless. *Chapulín Colorado* has helped me ask Latinos why we have difficulty seeing ourselves in the place of the super ideal, and it is easier to see ourselves as a heart warming, humorous type of hero, who tries and fails, but has a joke in the end in order to recover some dignity.

The review of popular songs is similar. Every generation can quote a lyric from a popular song that justifies gender violence. When the conversation opens up I ask if they can recall one. There is a famous traditional Cuban song that was heard over all of Latin America that sings: "María Cristina wants to govern me, and I play along. Cause I don't want people saying that María Cristina wants to govern me.[2]" It is a song that many relate to and can help us think aloud if the man is worried about being governed by his wife or about hearing others make fun of him because he is governed, and why that may be so. The song's history has been forgotten but is a jewel, to open up reflection on the origins of our machismo. The song was created in the nineteenth century in Spain during the rule of María Cristina de Borbón precisely mocking the fact of being ruled by a woman.

Havel (1987/1991), in a precious essay about the struggle to resist governmental repression, tells of a friend that was incarcerated for political reasons in former Czechoslovakia subjected to Soviet domination. His friend was suffering from

[2]"María Cristina me quiere gobernar/y yo le sigo, le sigo la corriente/porque no quiero que diga la gente/que María Cristina me quiere gobernar." Ñico Saquito.

asthma during his arrest, and his life was endangered as a result. Trying to find support for his friend he writes to a North American newspaper. But the answer that he receives is to write back if his friend dies. Havel continues writing that all of his country was suffering from asthma, a condition that was chronic but not dramatic enough to merit the attention from the international community:

> we are unworthy of attention because we have no stories, and no death. We have only asthma. And why should anyone be interested in listening to our cough? One can't go on writing forever about how hard it is to breathe. (p. 178)

The struggle to resist power's efforts to suffocate our voices is also the struggle of many of those that have suffered oppression in the domestic and the public sphere.

7.5 Validating and Containing

We can find therapeutic manuals that deal with the effects of torture, exile and political persecution, after people have survived. But there aren't many papers on what to do if you are working with someone who is currently being threatened. How does one deal with someone who is in imminent danger of being unjustly imprisoned by the state?

A similar case appears when working with people in extreme poverty. We have more information about what to do with someone who has survived extreme circumstances of deprivation and injustice. But what does therapy look like when the person is in that situation during the process of asking for help?

Therapists often reasonably worry, when working with underprivileged populations or victims of oppression, about what to do with material situations that cannot be easily resolved from the consulting room. Shouldn't one refer the person to a center that can deal with their extreme deprivation, before beginning therapy? Isn't their hunger more important or imminent than their emotional issues? Isn't it necessary to resolve the hunger before one can think of one's emotional issues? All these are valid questions that need to be addressed. But the fact is, that sometimes you can't call the police when you are in a dictatorship. Sometimes there are no government offices able to help clients extremely deprived when a country is in a deep institutional crisis. That poses very difficult questions for psychotherapy.

In my experience, even patients suffering from extreme deprivation, or threatened by governmental persecution, actively seek and appreciate a place where they can receive support and deal with despair, in order to recover the capacity to think about their situation. Therapy can be a place to contain anxiety and begin to think of ways to organize one's resources under extreme circumstances to be able to work out strategies to survive. As in crisis intervention, extreme circumstances tend to overwhelm the person's psychological resources, and containment is a first step toward recovering some control over one's life. There is, of course, no novelty in proposing the use of Bion's (1962) containment or Winnicott's holding environment (1960) in therapy. Yet, I believe it is not often thought of as a useful tool when dealing with extreme circumstances like political persecution. And yet, it probably is a key tool to help people survive.

The anxiety provoked by these situations, added to the fact that they can pose novel questions to a therapist, sometimes lead to the despair of the consulting team. If there is no network in place, no institutional or material support available, which is often the case in Venezuela, the therapist becomes the place where, once despair is contained, resources can begin to be identified, strengths recovered and plans organized. Where one can begin to think.

On one occasion, a family therapist, that visited our center to conduct training sessions, was working with a family we were already acquainted with, because one of the children was receiving support from the educational psychology team. The family comprised a grandmother, two grandchildren and a mother, who lived in the same house, but had not come to the session. They had begun therapy because the mother was a drug abuser and disappeared for days at a time, leaving the grandmother overwhelmed with the responsibilities of working to bring home money and taking care of the preadolescent boy and girl.

The grandmother was talking about the terrible stress and physical exhaustion that she was suffering, saying how worried she was about the children staying out in the street when she was out working but having few possibilities to be able to supervise them because of their dire circumstances. She expressed despair of not being able to hold things together, while her daughter had seemed to have given up and the children ran around in the consulting room, incapable of sitting down.

The therapist, flustered, suggested that they would benefit from having some recreational time together to be able to alleviate the stress they were suffering, maybe go to a public park where they could spend some time during the weekend. When the therapist said this, the grandmother breathed deeply and her body seemed to sink into the chair. Defeated she answered: “yes we should do that,” and stared silently toward the floor. At the same time the boy, who has running around the room, begin playing with the curtains while shouting: “there’s no money, no money!”

The school psychologist who was listening to the session from the other side of the one-way mirror told us that the family didn’t have enough money to even pay for the bus to come to the center for the therapeutic sessions. They relied on a neighbor that gave them a ride. You might not have guessed it by how neatly dressed each one was. The grandmother obviously took extra care to present their best face before the therapist. To go to a public park is a much more expensive trip than one could imagine if one has not had experience with extreme poverty.

The therapist had made a well intended but decontextualized suggestion. From his class perspective, anyone can afford to go to a public park. But the fact is that the grandmother would have to find a way to get transportation all the way to the public park. One of the greatest obstacles of living in the barrios in Caracas is that these self-built neighborhoods are far from the formal city and therefore lack many public services, including a strong public transportation system. But the grandmother would also, at least, like to have some water and snacks for the trip. What seems incredibly simple from the therapist's perspective is probably much more onerous than one can imagine. In any case, the grandmother didn't explain that his suggestion was difficult, she just sank her shoulders and breathed deeply as if feeling incapable of fulfilling a very simple expectation.

From behind the one-way mirror we called into the session and suggested that the therapeutic team ask the family how it was able, with all the incredible difficulties and scarceness they suffered, to come weekly to our therapeutic sessions. The grandmother's posture changed, sitting upright once more and began to share all of the efforts that implied, not only asking for a ride to the center but also asking for borrowed shoes so her oldest grandchild could come looking more "presentable."

Work with those that live in extreme inequality or under oppressive regimes has shown us that the internalization of that experience often leads to feelings of shame and guilt. Before any theory blames them for failing to beat the odds and thrive under such circumstances, they have already thought that they are probably not doing enough. And surely they suspect that many around them judge them with that lens.

To come to a therapist, who probably belongs to a professional class, has a different economic and cultural status, is often a challenge for a family who is living in poverty and has much less access to any of those resources. If it is a public hospital or a low-cost health center as ours, the family probably doesn't get to pick who it is they want to be seen by, and would have had to wait for a spot to open to be able to receive attention. All these elements weigh in on the power differences in the relationship. The cultural stigmatization of poverty and the difficulties of access contribute to a client not challenging a therapist that doesn't understand the gravity of their situation instead of sinking their shoulders and feeling, once again, that no one understands their plight or that they are not doing enough.

If one goes to a private therapist that one pays out of one's salary and the therapist suggests that, because one is suffering stress, one should consider going to Paris over the weekend, one would probably confront the therapist explaining that a plane ticket to Paris is completely preposterous and implausible. The key element here is that, if one has been on the short end of power for a long time, it is much more difficult to challenge it. Many of the subtle unfair ways that the structure imposes inequality go unseen and unnoticed. Even well-meaning attempts to help may add insult to injury. Again, it is in silence that many of these issues reside.

A politically reflective therapist must make efforts to comprehend the context in which the clients that come to therapy reside, must have made efforts to reflect on his or her own background and the many differences it may have with those that seek help and must also be especially aware of the uncomfortable silences that come up in therapy, identifying when some of them spring from cultural dissonance that the client may not feel comfortable pointing out.

While studying with the critical psychologist Ian Parker, I heard him repeat something that has been enlightening: "common sense is filled with ideology." Every time a therapist speaks from common sense, we must take a step back and examine the beliefs that underlie it. When a therapist suggests something commonsensical and silence results, we are possibly dealing with a silence that has to do with cultural and/or material dissonance.

All this introduction helps to point out that we must be able to witness and validate the struggle and feelings arising from those struggles. For example, we know that survivors of child abuse often deal with large amounts of rage. So much rage that those around them often become tired or frustrated of having to deal with it. Terr (1990), in her work with abused children, states that the amounts of rage in survivors must never be underestimated.

This is a crucial task that may be more difficult than one initially imagines. Because, on the one hand, it may be difficult to tolerate such intense emotions in the consulting room. On the other, it is hard to share the rage, the fear, the despair that accompanies being in extreme situations, especially if the therapist doesn't have many more tools than the therapeutic relationship to protect the person. But a powerful task of therapy is the possibility of holding or containing these extreme emotions so as to open space to begin to share them and examine them with someone else. If the person can begin to feel that those feelings are valid, rather than an expression of some personal flaw, they can begin to rethink their personal image and self-worth. They can identify their strengths and think of themselves as actively struggling to resist, in spite of the odds.

Hardy (2006) is great at capturing the power differentials that come up in therapy between the therapist and the client and helping therapists acknowledge these differences, to be able to help surface the societal issues that underlie the helping relationship. When these are identified and acknowledged, the client can begin to talk about issues and, Hardy concludes, that dehumanization is countered, opening up the possibility of rehumanizing loss. A therapist that tolerates the despair of being in an extreme and incredibly unfair situation is able to show empathy and helps identify the acts of resistance that the person has been able to develop, can help validate the person's feelings and help think about how to organize one's own resources more effectively.

In 2004, people took to the streets, in one of the many waves of protests against Chavismo. Protests arose when government delayed and placed all kinds of obstacles to accept the constitutional right of asking for a referendum to revoke the president's term. An article appeared in the health section of a prominent newspaper titled "clean yourself of hate," with a picture of people protesting on the street. The article was authored by Vanessa Davies, who soon became a prominent governmental figure, later named the director of the state television channel. At that time she hadn't publicly identified herself with government but was writing to discredit protests through her post in the health section of the paper. The article was full of medical considerations on the risks of prolonged rage, and suggestions of relaxation techniques. It almost seemed to be sarcastic, but it didn't pretend to be, consulting with "specialists" on emotional disorders, that went along with the question on the problems that arose with prolonged anger, blind to the context of the collective indignation that was protesting for their confiscated rights. The message was: "don't protest, don't scream, don't feel abused by power, that is dangerous for your health. Relax, go to therapy. You are the one that is the problem."

The article turned out to be very useful, when I returned to meetings with psychologists and psychiatrists who felt that government was disavowing citizen's rights. Seeing themselves in the shoes of the protesters, they were able to acknowledge how health considerations without considering the context from where suffering emerges, risks blaming the victim and discrediting valid rage.

Anger management can easily go against efforts to validate the pain of being oppressed. The objective is not to mitigate rage, but to offer relief and help the person recover control of one's life and face challenges more effectively without harming others. Under oppression, rage can be a powerful source to push people in that direction. There is a significant difference between rage and violence. We can stop violence. But we can validate rage and work to channel it. Critical psychologist, Erica Burman, wrote: "to be distressed in an unjust and oppressive society is more politically healthy condition than to be happy" (2000, p. 52).

7.6 Problematization

The tools that are being mentioned are closely related. After rendering visible the structures that imprison life, and validating the feelings arising from these circumstances, we will try to open up reflection through problematization. Montero (2004, 2006) has developed the concept, taken from the work of Freire (1970). She defines it as: "The critical analysis of life circumstances and the role one plays in them that questions the usual explanations and considerations about these circumstances" (2004, p. 293).

Arribas-Ayllon and Walkerdine propose another useful definition, from the field of discourse analysis. They have defined it as processes where: "discursive objects and practices are made 'problematic' and therefore visible and knowable. They often form at the intersection of different discourses and expose knowledge/power relations" (2008, p. 99).

Problematization seeks to generate a process in which:

> … worn out answers, usual explanations, clichés stop providing ordinary answers and produce a mobilization of consciousness faced with the absence of the overused explanations, contradictions that are evidenced or the absence of solid grounds (Montero, 2006, p. 230).

The explanations Montero gives of the problematization process in the community have many analogies with a reflective psychotherapeutic process. She underlines that the relationship is indispensable for the process to occur. She mentions the following conditions to favor it: the ability to listen, dialogue, openness to doubt, emphasis on a bidirectional exchange free from preconceptions, reflective capacity, respect, critical thinking, reflection of concrete real-life circumstances, emphasis on transformation and the capacity to tolerate silence (2006).

Problematization resists simplistic formulas and slogans referred to what a good life is and helps people identify the sources of those conceptions, the discourses that constitute them. This perspective recognizes how ideals and evaluative frameworks influence life and help us take a step back and realize that they are not absolute or inevitable.

Often, when people seem stuck in an inevitable course of action or interpretation of an event, we ask if there isn't any family member or known acquaintance that might have chosen another way of resolving the situation or thinks differently about the issue. It is a simple question that sometimes opens up conversation of different perspectives as well as why and how some people have been able to see things differently.

In Venezuela, one of the causes of the terribly high murder rates we suffer are the codes of honor based, among other things, on masculine stereotypes that call for revenge when one of your group has been insulted or injured by a rival group (Zubillaga, 2005). In one of the low-income barrios with which we have developed a close relationship and worked with for more than a decade, a long-standing feud between two neighboring communities had led to a series of murders between the groups of youngsters, which in one of the communities was constituted as a gang (Zubillaga, Llorens, Núñez, & Souto, 2015). The local community activists and the priest had worked tirelessly for many years to position the idea of dialogue and alternative means of conflict resolution. They had organized religious groups that empowered community activists among many of the mothers of the youngsters involved in the violence. We had worked as therapists with many family members of the victims. But a significant change did not occur until an extraordinary event happened. A teenage boy was murdered after a particularly violent confrontation in which the gang of one sector invaded the other to seek revenge for a slight suffered. After hours of a violent siege, they found the boy they were looking for and executed him.

The mother of the child, along with her neighbors, awoke in the morning with the murdered body of her son. In the midst of her pain she confronted the other mothers that accompanied her and pleaded with them to tell their children that she did not want any revenge regarding the murder of her son. She wanted to see her remaining son live, and the only way that could happen was if the chain of violence was stopped. She didn't ask for revenge, and wanted the other mothers to help her talk to the other sector and ask for a truce. Her courageous plea, in such a dramatic moment, challenged everyone to think and commit to a very different course of action than had been occurring, in which each family grieved their murdered family members in private and fed the grudge against the neighboring sector that contributed to the cycle of never-ending violence. The empowerment that the community interventions in favor of negotiation had been developing finally opened up an effective course of action through this alternative reaction to traumatic loss that this mother was able to propose. A very moving and effective process of community negotiation began, which we have been able to chronicle (Zubillaga, Llorens, Núñez & Souto, 2015). The mothers began a series of conversations in both sectors that led to a community-wide negotiation that included the gang and the youngsters on both sides.

This evidences that alternative possibilities to what seemed an inevitable cultural response to such a traumatic experience such as violent loss are possible. Of course, this wasn't a therapist that problematized the logic of the cycles of violence but, even more powerful, one of the community's own members. Family therapist White (1995) explores what he calls exceptional circumstances, occasions when things didn't fit the usual interpretation or logic of events. These exceptions help problematize automatic explanations to behavior and open up space for alternative interpretations.

He is particularly lucid formulating questions that help question naturalized explanations that constrict life. He invites therapists to locate the usual attributions that are used and then ask questions such as: how were you recruited to defend that opinion? In which circles are these ideas more strongly held? Do all those that belong to those circles agree with those opinions? What do you think would happen if you disagree with them in their presence? What type of pressure to conform would you receive? What consequences would you have to face were you to choose a different path?

These questions help locate specific sources of the judgements people use to interpret their lives, as well as the power mechanisms that hold them in place. And, by asking if everyone agrees, the possibility of alternative options may open up. It is often useful to contrast different perspectives and ask clients to explore advantages and disadvantages of each one. This way, you don't need to defend or condemn any option but open up space to reflect on the consequences of different ways of thinking.

The exploration of language is also useful to denaturalize and problematize cultural conceptions. It is no coincidence that discourse analysis seems analogous to some of these strategies, as they spring from the same critical sources. Language holds the historical origins of our value frameworks. As violence has extended its influence into popular culture, we find that its language has permeated the slang youngsters use. In our work, we sometimes stop at these slang words to open up conversation with youth about the meanings and origins that they are often unaware of. In the 90s the word "*cartelúo*" became popular to label something of special value. It is a word that comes from the drug world, referring to a man with a bigger "cartel," which in the underground meant, the man who had committed more murders (Duque & Múñoz, 1995). More recently the word "pran" became popular. The pran is the leader of the gang in control of the jail and is an acronym for "Preso, Rematado, Asesino, Nato," something like a consummate innate imprisoned murderer. To reflect on why youth culture uses these expressions to signify value and why we continually import words from the gang culture is often a useful way to problematize the sources of constructions of masculinity and ideals.

Maritza Montero shared an example of problematization with children that is very illustrative. She mentioned how when one asks young children in Venezuela to draw a house it is common for the houses to appear with chimneys, which is curious because in our tropical country there are no winters, and therefore, no chimneys. But it is a wonderful example of how even our depiction of the world is incorporated through stereotyped images that are influenced by the dominant culture.

Many teachers, when illustrating how to draw houses, draw a stereotyped triangle-shaped roof with a chimney that has nothing to do with the local architecture. In groups where she found this, Montero has challenged the children pointing to the smoke coming out of the chimneys. "Is the house on fire?" she asks. What is this thing the smoke is coming out of? What is it for? Do houses always have that? Let's go to the window and see the houses of our city? Do you see any chimneys? How is it that you learned to draw houses with chimneys? It is a thought-provoking conversation with youngsters that helps take a step back and reflect on how we often interiorize our representations of life without reflection.

Sports also serves as an alternative framework with youngsters that are reflecting on the frameworks that lead to certain courses of action. Again in reference to stereotyped scripts of masculinity that often pressure kids to respond to violence with more violence, their participation in sports is sometimes a useful resource to question what might be a more effective course of action. How do figures of your sport respond when insulted on the pitch? Do they all respond the same? Are there different alternatives and what consequences might each one have? What would responding bravely or maturely look like in this context? Is corresponding violence with violence the bravest course of action when one has been hit unfairly on the pitch?

Pakman (1997, 2011) invites us to consider psychotherapy a practice of social criticism that helps people examine the weight of the political discourses that underlie their personal ideals. The work he develops with Latin American youngsters in the United States seems analogous to much of our work in Venezuela. He writes how it is worth noting that many of the youngsters who present antisocial behavior often defend the ideals of the society they believe to be rebelling against. We often find deprived youngsters, avid to obtain the status symbols that belong to the world they have been systematically excluded from. Pakman mentions how, when conducting reflective conversations, the youngsters are often surprised to find how they defend the very same values they say they are rebelling against.

7.7 The Therapeutic Position

Probably the most controversial issue has to do with the proposal that the therapist is inevitably politically, historically, socially and ethically situated and that these elements influence the therapeutic relationship, whether we are aware or not of the weight of our cultural baggage.

The postmodern critique invites us to reflect on the social context of every theoretical and technical tool, to be able to subject it to continuous critical review and a wider dialogue. Therefore it invites the therapist to reflect on the origins of his or her practice. It also requires one to open oneself to the feedback of those we work with.

The fundamental axis of the therapist's positioning has to do with ethics. Even those therapists that defend the concept of neutrality have an ethical position. In other words, we can understand neutrality to be an effort to defend the rights of others to their free will and freedom of thought, a deep acceptance toward the right of others to conduct their lives as they see fit as well as a belief that our point of view is not relevant and, in the worst cases can lead us to an unethical attempt to recruit others into our own perspective.

But, what we are saying, is that that position is not ethically neutral. It is, of course, a point of view. It is not politically neutral because it influences how I make decisions in the therapeutic relationship. The political and ethical are not dimensions I can take or leave out of human relationships, they are intrinsic to all.

Clinical training is weary of ethical discussions because time has shown how that can turn into moralist indoctrination. Prilleltensky (1997) has signaled out how traditional psychology tends to avoid conversations on ethics because of fear of falling into dogmatic, fanatical and authoritarian positions.

The philosopher and psychoanalyst Guyomard (1999) chronicles the discussions of ethics in psychoanalysis and illustrates how Freud, influenced by the scientific thought of his time, attempted to distance himself from ethical positionings. In a letter to a Protestant pastor named Pfister who had published a text titled "Psychoanalysis in the Service of Education" Freud writes: "I grant you; ethics are remote from me, and you are a minister of religion, I do not break my head very much about good and evil" (Freud, 1964, p. 61). Freud places ethics as part of the repressive instance. Freud in particular, like psychology in general, has contributed to the transformation of many moralist cultural assumptions that limited human expression. It is not surprising that we may fear that ethical positioning can lead to dogmatic imposition or new versions of entrapment. A reflective therapist must avoid turning his or her practice into indoctrination, a new way of robbing clients of their freedom. Previous therapists that developed a political stance tended to drift into activism, turning therapy into political indoctrination (Pakman, 2011) where therapist try to model or influence political correctness. This is a relevant risk to watch out for. But avoiding dogmatic positions does not mean that there is no underlying ethical stance. As Guyomard has stated, the rejection of choosing for the client is, of course, an ethical position.

To avoid the issue, stating that one is not interested in ethics doesn't resolve the problem and only leaves the ethical fundamentals unexamined. Prilleltensky (1997) points to how many problems such as minimizing the clients autonomy, stigmatization using labels, underestimating the importance of social injustice, for example, are done by well-intentioned therapists that think they are doing the best for clients, but have not reflected on the ethical dimension of their technique. The examination of our ethical bases does not assure an ethical practice, but is a step toward that direction.

Prilleltensky proposes that all therapists should make explicit and articulate what their vision of a good individual and collective life is, and the actions needed to advance toward that goal. The psychoanalyst Phillips (2000) says it a little differently when he suggests that therapists should answer the question of what the world would look like if they could cure everyone with their theory. It is a challenge that helps identify the underlying ideals.

Lacan offers a variant to this discussion. His formulation contrasts with Freud's modern position. He recognizes that all human action implies an ethical stance. He dedicates one of his seminars to the issue (1988). There Lacan searches for a measure with which to orient his judgement (Guyomard, 1999), and concludes that measuring stick is desire. The search for desire is the "search for the subject's truth" (Lander, 2004, p. 397). That means the subject discovers and dares to act according to his or her intimate desires. Faced with human action, Lacan proposes we ask ourselves "Have you acted with conformity to the desire that inhabits you?" (1988, p. 362).

From this perspective, the analyst is ethical as long as he or she doesn't contaminate the analysand's desire with his or her own, doesn't offer answers, doesn't present him or herself as expert that has "answers" to the intimate world of the other, but contributes to ask questions that help others continue on their search. This perspective lowers the analyst from the pedestal of expertise. But it continues to suffer from circularity, in the sense that it pretends to not be influencing the analysand with any prior ethical system but clearly is defending personal liberty as a value on which the relationship is built. For example, according to Venezuelan analyst, Lander (2004), the highest truth is the subject's own truth and family and social ideals are impostures. Seen from a social constructionist perspective the word imposture is suspect. Imposture alludes to a reality that is less authentic than another one, to a fake. But to consider one's discourse an imposture is a posture in itself. Is the analyst's bet in favor of the individual, not the central aspect of his or her "desire" or ideal? Is that version of psychoanalysis not constructed upon and belong to a set of societal discourses also?

I think we can agree that psychotherapy is much better when the therapist leaves his or her pedagogical impulses aside and dedicates his or herself to listen with openness and acceptance. In general terms, the search for personal liberty, free from neurotic constraints that often impoverish life, is one of therapy's main functions. But sometimes, when discourses become too homogeneous and institutions close in on themselves naturalizing an intellectual hierarchy, turning habits into dogmas, the adventure of free thought is curtailed. The thought that certain prescriptions can assure the royal road to meaning is a common danger in psychological theory. This has happened often in therapeutic circles. Phillips points out that:

> when psychoanalysts spend too much time with each other, they start believing in psychoanalysis. They begin to talk knowingly, like members of a religious cult. It is as if they have understood something. They forget, in other words, that they are only telling stories about stories; and that all stories are subject to an unknowable multiplicity of interpretations. The map becomes the ground beneath their feet; and maps are always a smaller ground. (Phillips, 1995, p. xvi–xvii)

The dilemma that ethical positionings bring is the challenge of identifying which values we adhere to. Some of these dilemmas seem easy in abstract terms, but in their application, should we stop the person who comes depressed to therapy from losing control and threaten their children every weekend? Should we intervene to lower risks even though the therapeutic relationship will be affected? When do we call the police? Even subtler dilemmas arise daily in therapy. I believe it is useful for therapists to identify these dilemmas and open discussion with their colleagues on a regular basis. Prilleltensky (1997) suggests that identifying one's value system does not substitute, but rather invites to embark on a continuous process of reflection on one's possible omissions and contradictions. The reflective process in itself is perhaps more important than the end result.

Prilleltensky suggests a series of useful strategies to reflect on the ethical frameworks of the practice of psychology (1997, 2001; Nelson & Prilleltensky, 2005). He identifies four sources of an ethical perspective. The first one is called vision and refers to the ideals of what one considers a good life, individually and collectively, to be. The second one is contextual, which looks toward the state of affairs in the context one happens to be at, which implies requesting the opinion of those that we work with and their subjective experience. The third source refers to needs and tries to identify which are unmet in a certain population, as well as the main causes of suffering. Finally, the fourth source refers to action, and the consideration of the feasibility of change, and the practical considerations on the possibilities of real transformation. The first source provides us with vision, the second one with the understanding of the underlying social forces, the third one with the desires of the people we work with and the fourth one with the strategic framework.

Following these recommendations and rescuing the influences of different schools of thought in psychology, Prilleltensky proposes values that, in his opinion, complement and feed intervention. They are autonomy/liberty, health/wellness, personal growth, social justice, respect to human diversity and collaboration/democratic participation (1997, 2001).

I tend to prefer the use of the Universal Declaration of Human Rights as a solid reference to build a professional ethical stance (Kinderman, 2007). I believe psychotherapy is a modality of activism in favor of human rights, an activism that deals with the intimate sphere. Not free from dilemmas, yet this text is still as wide a consensus as we have reached as humanity in the area of shared values. I consider that the human rights doctrine is a useful guide to reflect on therapeutic work. Authors in public health have argued in favor of the evolution of bioethics based on human rights rather than medical conceptions (Marks, 2001). It is interesting to note that the International Psychoanalytical Association (IPA) included human rights in its code of ethics elaborated in 1998, as well as the revised version of 2015 stating that "a psychoanalyst must not participate in or facilitate the violation of any individual's basic human rights, as defined by the UN Declaration of Human Rights" (IPA, 2015).

Other authors consider psychotherapy to be a modality of activism in favor of human rights. Backwell (2005) quotes various professionals in different contexts that share this opinion such as Davidson who worked with Holocaust survivors; Robert Lifton, who worked with survivors of Hiroshima and Vietnam War veterans; Cienfuegos and Monelli who worked with victims of political repression in Chile and Kordon, Edelmano, Lagos, Nicoletti and Bozzolo who did likewise in Argentina. He also mentions the Medical Foundation for the Care of Victims of

Torture to which he belongs that emphasizes psychotherapist's commitment to human rights. Lykes (2000, 2001) also defends the psychological work framed as human rights activism, although she adds a few key critical considerations: the need to keep the ethical discussion open and not conform to a set of closed and set principles, as well as the need to consider the application of those general principles in specific contexts.

To state that human rights is an ethical framework is to say a lot and very little at the same time. It says a lot in the sense that it takes therapy away from the medical model to a wider terrain. It is saying little in the sense that it does not liberate us from the many dilemmas that regularly appear in the consulting room. The therapist inevitably has to face, guided by his studies, experience, self-reflection, supervision and colleagues the many human questions that appear each day. The postmodern perspective only invites one to include oneself on the shared and ongoing process of that conversation.

The many ethical dilemmas of our time are constantly appearing in therapy. The dilemmas in relation to sexual rights, racism, sexism, political polarization are often a source of psychotherapeutic conversations. On occasions, those who bring these issues to therapy want to know my opinion. I think there is no one easy response to these petitions. On occasions, these petitions can be marked by desires clearly inserted in the transferential relationship: the desire to challenge or please the therapist, the desire to forge an alliance, the desire to get to know him or her better or to use it as a way to avoid dealing with more painful or conflicting issues through rationalization, etc. But often, people who bring these dilemmas want to know how safe it is to expand on their personal debates, their contradictions and their fears. Some of those that have been victimized need a safe ethical setting where they can dare to express their thoughts and issues without the risk of being used or put down.

In the midst of a polarized political scenario, some clients have asked about my political opinions. It often leads me to ponder on why the person asks that. Fantasies of the therapist's political ideas can be a fertile ground for therapeutic exploration. From an orthodox perspective, abstinence and neutrality recommend silence or the exploration of the client's fantasies. In my opinion, abstinence can be an option that may prove useful as long as one doesn't believe that it allows us to be neutral, and that unanswered questions do not communicate things through silence or non-verbal gestures; or that the geography of our consulting room, or our taste in decoration or clothing do not communicate something of our social status. Often, the question seeks to explore how safe it is to share political issues that are charged with passion relating to the clients personal and family history. If the setting is not safe, people may tend to keep that portion of their thoughts to themselves and outside of the therapeutic conversation.

I do not think it is useful to respond in abstract if a therapist should share their political position in therapy in general. I think it is an answer that must be given in the specific context of each dialogue. But I do think that an ethical position is a useful tool to effectively resolve this situation. To share the values which sustain the therapy and the notion that these values are central to guide the work that is being done is useful. To share that one has a position (even if it is abstinence) and that our position is inevitably partial, incomplete and open to discussion is useful for opening up conversation about the dilemmas that we all face, questions that may be appearing in the lives of all. To position oneself in favor of the patient's rights, independent of what political opinion one might have in a polarized context also establishes that one works with the defense of the client's welfare as a priority, and that one condemns any abuse of their rights they may have suffered. This may seem like an obvious condition. But from what we saw in Chapter 3, this has not always been the case in the history of psychotherapy.

During the first interviews, while I am evaluating, I invite the person to express any doubt or question about the therapeutic process. In the midst of our many political crises the question of what my thoughts on the situation are has come up occasionally. I think it is a valid concern. I tend to express that I believe that what is happening politically is very relevant and that I hope that the therapeutic space will allow us to think of it. I believe that is a good moment to share the ethical framework that guides my approach. If someone has been persecuted, this framework is generally a necessity to be able to feel safe enough to share this experience. If that isn't the case, the expression of working in favor of the patient's rights is normally a clear answer that inspires trust in the therapeutic space. I often also explore the motivations to ask about those issues, so as to know about the person's story related to the political and to express permission to share this dimension of life. I also ask the person after the first session how comfortable he or she felt, in order to establish how free the person feels to share her thoughts.

In December 2003, right in the midst of the highest points of polarization, a year after a national strike and a coup that had ousted Chávez for three days from office, our psychology unit, through the work of three of our psychologists, had been conducting group sessions in one of our neighboring communities. The group had begun to build trust and various women had begun to share silenced aspects of their lives, in which stories of extreme violence appeared. One of the members shared that as a small child she had been sold by her father to another man and had to escape to be able to return home. The background of the group was the intense political controversy that was going on in the country. Veiled allusions to issues about social status appeared on occasion, such as idealizations about "educational status" and the "good taste" of the therapists or expressions of distrust, or of the incapacity to understand some aspects of the group member's lives because the therapists weren't "from that part of the city," or of not being able to fully understand the trials of poverty and inequality.

In the last session of the year, the therapists gave out a Christmas card as a small token of appreciation to the women. The card had been designed using a drawing by one of the children that assisted the center and expressed an image of national reconciliation. Or so we thought. The picture was of two groups walking toward the center of the picture, the title of "Chavistas" and "opposition" appeared in the title and the people walking were drawn as expressing desires for peace. We naively thought that the postcard expressed hope and was balanced. Our naivete consisted in thinking that the card could be read as coming from a neutral place and not that we, because we belonged to a university community center, were already placed, in our audience's mind as a representative of a particular social class. In the midst of polarization, that rigidly imposes "us-them" labels, our university had been pushed into the opposition in people's minds, even though we had members with different political affiliations.

Even though the members of the group hadn't brought the political tensions explicitly to the group sessions, the political background inevitably tinged the work. All of them thanked the small gesture of the Christmas card, but when one of the women got home, her husband, who was a militant Chavista, was offended and said (according to the woman who later told us this) that we were trying to "brainwash" and indoctrinate her. This led to her abandoning the group, which didn't give the therapists the opportunity to open discussions on the anxieties and worries surrounding these issues.

From a modern perspective, the mistake was of giving postcard that had a political statement. We had not followed Freud's suggestions of acting like a "surgeon" that imposes silence to all his or her affections. We contaminated a process that is thought of as ideologically aseptic.

But I tend to think that not talking about those issues at that time would not have resolved the problem, and just left it as a therapeutic taboo. The group members don't bring it up and the therapist acts as if it is of no importance. Coderch (2001) quotes a marvelous example of this way of avoiding party politics in the psychoanalytic setting:

> A telling quote of what I have been expressing refers to the known North American psychoanalyst R. Greenson (1967). A patient, sympathizer of the Republican Party, shared that he had discovered that he, Greenson, was a Democrat. When the analyst asked him to say why he thought this was so, the patient said that every time he said something hostile about the Democratic Party, Greenson would ask about his associations and ended up giving him an interpretation. But when he said something against the Republican Party, Greenson would stay silent, as if in agreement. Also, when he said something nasty about Roosevelt, he asked him who Roosevelt reminded him of, as if assuming that these thoughts had to come from an infantile experience. Greenson, surprised, had to accept his patient's impressions about a situation that had passed unnoticed to him up to now. (p. 58)

The postmodern perspective frees the therapist from having to speak from an all-knowing expertise, that floats in the pure air of objectivity and instead, invites both participants to deal with the challenges of personal difference. This does not make our task easier, and it doesn't free it from the muddy terrain where the risk of indoctrination continues to appear. But it makes it more honest and places the therapeutic dialogue as a conversation of two people with different histories that are trying to build a professional bridge to be able to reflect on beliefs, attitudes and feelings. This bridge is sustained by the efforts (mainly of the therapist, but not exclusively) to open space for shared reflection, in spite of the dilemmas and fears that arise.

Our reflection afterwards made us question if it was a mistake to have given out the Christmas card, even though the work group was not in an orthodox psychotherapy group setting. My opinion is that, more than the card, the avoidance of opening up the conversation to explore the impressions, thoughts, feelings around the political dilemmas of the time, that appeared indirectly, was the main mistake that, had it been addressed, might have prevented the patient abandoning the group. Because of the tension of the circumstances, the psychologists and the group members preferred to leave out their questions, fantasies, doubts about the political issues that surrounded the group's work and the psychologist-group member's relationships. The card seemed to express the anxieties and desires that operated (at least in the psychologist's minds) without having dealt with them in the group. The imagined differences, and the Christmas setting, appeared in the card as a desire to save those differences, without having to attend to the feelings evoked by those circumstances.

To work from this perspective does not mean that the therapist has a profound, illustrated or definite position with respect to so many political conflicting issues, such as, for example, abortion, human cloning, globalization, the death penalty or even the political destiny of one's community. What the therapist is ready to do, is to look for ways in which these dilemmas are acknowledged and brought to the therapeutic conversation, as well as actively looking out for how these issues relate to the life and interpersonal relationships of those who we work for. The therapist's position is not an objective of the therapeutic process, and may not appear in great many of them. It may not be relevant in many cases. But what is relevant is the therapist's awareness of this dimension and his or her disposition to address it honestly, without trying to avoid the anxiety of this process behind a technical positioning, as if he or she was beyond good and evil. This helps deconstruct the power that sustains the expert position.

In one sense, this agrees with what many of the Latin American therapists that worked with political victims have said about the dangers of neutrality (Hollander, 2010). But perhaps the novelty of examining these same issues in the Venezuelan context is that the therapists that wrote about these issues under the military dictatorships of Argentina, Chile and Uruguay, for example, could place themselves with relatively more ease, in a certain political position, because those authoritarian governments were so clearly abusive. In Venezuela, before Chavismo completely imploded and unmasked its military dictatorship, the polarized political tension allowed for a lot of ambiguity and difficulty in listening to abuse that sprang from different sources. The socioeconomic inequalities many Chavistas grieved about were as relevant as the political persecutions others were suffering. There was (I speak in the past, because I believe this is not so much the case in 2020) a lot of space for controversy and placing oneself on the side of human rights was not always perfectly clear cut. These types of polarized settings are not all that different from the controversies that have emerged in the Trump era in the United States as well as current political tensions in other latitudes such as Spain.

A modern therapist considers him or herself an objective observer that recollects data, avoids the muddy terrain of politics, is an expert on what is healthy and what is not and, therefore, has a strong opinion on what is the proper way to live. In contrast, a politically reflective therapist assumes a position that invites collaboration between people with different perspectives in which his or her expertise resides in the capacity to establish dialogue and reflection and in which the therapist can position him or herself in the place of not knowing, considering knowledge to be dialogic and constantly evolving.

This way of framing therapy allows for a therapist that can take the risk of examining his or her own prejudices and confronting them with the opinion of those he or she works with. Many of the questions that arose working through the political dilemmas in Venezuela were new, and we did not have prefabricated answers, we still don't have definitive ones.

7.8 Training Politically Reflective Therapists

One of clinical training's strengths is that, through supervision and psychotherapy, we are constantly invited to observe and reflect on our own personal issues that influences our work. Therapists tend to be aware of their personal anxieties, conflicts and personal histories that often come up in work with others. Our interpersonal relationships, attachment and coping styles, family histories are common issues discussed in training. Issues that have to do with our gender, ethnic background and sexual preferences are also commonly discussed and reflected on.

A critical examination of our political preferences, our family's political identifications and power issues does not come up as frequently in training discussions (Dudley, 2017). Avissar goes further, considering that the structure of training fosters submissiveness and is conducive to clinical psychologist's passive approach toward politics (2016). Opening up classrooms and supervisions to reflect on this dimension is usually a powerful tool to take advantage of the diversity of backgrounds that all groups bring. A therapist mindful of the challenges of dealing with cultural diversity and political issues is a therapist mindful of the fact that we all have blind spots. That socialization is a process that leads us to assume certain notions in order to interpret our world in a particular time and place. The process of surprising oneself not having considered another's interpretation of what one thought to be obvious is a useful experience.

In particular, I have, along with discussing the themes that have been presented in this book, used a couple of strategies that I find useful for helping therapists develop a politically reflective capacity. Supervision and classrooms are great places to discuss one's family's history regarding political and social issues. Have political events influenced it? Has the family experienced immigration, discrimination, poverty, war? How have historical events influenced the family? Have political positions been homogeneous or diverse in the family? How has the family dealt with difference and conflicting perspectives? Is politics something passionately discussed or avoided? Have there been politically active family members? How are they considered in family lore? Have there been transformations throughout the generations on issues that deal with gender, sexual preferences, ethnic background, religion? Have there been pioneers or rebels that have dared to challenge family positions on these issues? How has that played out? Are there family members that are considered heroes for their political actions? Are there socioeconomic differences among the family members? How are these differences dealt with? How are current political controversies talked about at the family table?

These are just some of the questions that can help open up interesting and enriching conversations among classmates. To be able to explore one's family political history, and also to be able to hear that of others, is always engaging, and students tend to participate with enthusiasm. It opens up the possibility of exploring how these issues influence each other's outlook on life and reactions to these issues in the consulting room. The space to identify contradictions, blind spots, passionately held truths or doubts, opens up.

A second strategy that has been very powerful stems from the work of Peggy McIntosh, a feminist, who, based on her paper titled White Privilege (1989), has influenced a variety of educational settings. The paper, oriented toward race, helps elicit discussion and reflection on the issues of privilege and disadvantage. It challenges us to examine the ways we have been privileged and the difficulties acknowledging it. I particularly appreciate the way she signals the subtle ways privilege operates in daily life. She writes that it is "an invisible weightless knapsack of special provisions, maps, passports, codebooks, visas, clothes, tools and blank checks" (p. 31). The introduction of the analysis of privilege allows us to reflect on the concept of power. Following Foucault, I find it useful to illustrate how many of these positions of privilege fluctuate, are not static, but complex and contradictory. One can find oneself in a place of privilege in a certain role in the morning at the university and yet be faced with oppression when one walks out on the street. The complexity and invisibility of power are two notions that are useful to help clinicians begin to identify power dynamics in their lives.

The notion of analysis of white privilege has been incorporated into clinical training (Ancis and Szymanski, 2001) and I expand the notion inviting students to explore other expressions of privilege such as male privilege or socioeconomic privilege, or other examples that they can identify, as well as experiences of disadvantage. I often ask them to identify a way in which they have been privileged or disadvantaged, and explore how it influenced an aspect of their life and later share it with their classmates. This exercise throughout the years has always been enlightening as the answers never cease to surprise me, offering aspects of experience one often fails to see, even if one has special interest in these issues. Sharing these reflections is a powerful way of confronting us, not only with our personal histories but also with our blind spots toward other's perspectives.

One very simple example has been useful. Many of the students in the clinical community program coursed their pre-graduate studies in the same university. On a couple of occasions, in reference to McIntosh's article, students that came from different universities pointed out how those of us that had been there longer referred to places on the campus, events or known figures as if everyone shared the same references, leaving others out of the conversation. Sometimes they asked for clarifications but sometimes they just went along as if they knew what we were talking about. It is a very simple yet wonderful example of how we often have blind spots in regard to shared meanings and how exclusion can operate in subtle ways. It is a non-threatening example that helps us to acknowledge how, even trained psychotherapists have blind spots and the incorporation of different perspectives helps raise our awareness of them.

Given the very complex era young Venezuelans have grown in, this exercise has allowed me to get to know some of the very challenging lives my students and their families have led, and how their ability to grow professionally often springs from a combination of strengths that have allowed them to overcome terrible disadvantages. I find that these generations that have lived their whole lives in the midst of crisis and instability are much more open than the older ones to explore and incorporate this dimension into their professional repertoire.

7.9 Conclusions

The tools presented here incorporate developments that come from feminism, social constructionism and Latin American community psychology to widen the scope of therapeutic conversation. They pose fundamental questions on the issue of power relations and our theories of knowledge that underlie psychotherapy. If I were to summarize what I believe to be the biggest contribution of working from a politically reflective perspective, it would be that of a therapist that has greater awareness of how power influences the lives of the people he or she works with, as well as the psychotherapeutic relationship, and a therapist whose task is to problematize, to use questions as a tool to incite reflection, not only for the client, but also for the therapist.

References

Ancis, J., & Szymanski, D. (2001). Awareness of white privilege in white counselling trainees. *The Counselling Psychologist, 29,* 548–569.

Arribas-Ayllon, M., & Walkerdine, V. (2008). Foucaldian discourse analysis. In C. Willing & W. Stainton-Rogers (Eds.), *The sage handbook of qualitative research in psyhology* (pp. 91–108). Los Angeles: Sage.

Avissar, N. (2016). *Psychotherapy, society and politics: From theory to practice.* Palgrave MacMillan.

Ávila, K. (in press). Dan más balas de las que reciben. In V. Zubillaga, & M. Llorens (Eds.), *Dicen que Están Matando Gente: Violencia armada y políticas de seguridad ciudadana en Venezuela.* Madrid: Dahbar.

Bion, W. (1962). *Learning from experience.* London: Karnac Books.

Backwell, D. (2005). Psychotherapy, politics and trauma: Working with survivors of torture and organized violence. *Group Analysis, 38,* 307–323.

Borges, J. L. (1932). *El Escritor Argentino y la Tradición.* https://bibliotecaignoria.blogspot.com/2018/06/jorge-luis-borges-el-escritor-argentino.html. Accessed April 27, 2020.

Burin, M., & Meler, I. (2000). *Varones: género y subjetividad masculina.* Buenos Aires: Paidós.

Burman, E. (2000). Method, measurement and madness. In L. Holzman & J. Morss (Eds.), *Postmodern psychologies, societal practice and political life* (pp. 48–78). New York: Routledge.

Coderch, J. (2001). *La Relación Paciente-Terapeuta: el campo del psicoanálisis y la psicoterapia psicoanalítica.* Bacelona: Paidós.

Dudley, J. (2017). Clinical psychology training in Neoliberal times. *Psychology Forum, 298,* 46–56.

Duque, J., & Muñoz, B. (1995). *La Ley de la Calle*. Caracas: Fundarte/Alcaldía de Caracas.

Ephraim, D. (1999). Culturally relevant research and practice with the comprehensive Rorschach System. In R. Dana (Ed.), *Handbook of crosscultural and multicultural personality assessment* (pp. 303–328). Mahwah NJ: Lawrence Erlbaum Associates Inc.

Ephraim, D. (2001). Evaluación del trauma psicológico a través del método Rorschach: violencia contra la mujer y trauma complejo en refugiadas latinoamericanas. *Revista Venezolana de Psicología Clínica Comunitaria, 2,* 153–167.

Espín, O. (1993). Giving voice to silence: The psychologist as witness. *American Psychologist, 48,* 408–414.

Ferenczi, S. (1949). The confusion of tongues between the adult and the child—(The language of tenderness and passion). *International Journal of Psycho-Analysis, 30,* 225–230.

Freire, P. (1970). *Pedagogy of the Oppressed.* New York, NY: Seabury Press.

Freud, S. (1964). *Psychoanalysis and faith: The letters of Sigmund Freud and Oskar Pfister*. New York: Basic Books.

Fromm, E. (1980). *El Miedo a la libertad.* Barcelona: Paidós.

Guyomard, P. (1999). *El deseo de Ética*. Buenos Aires: Paidós.

Hague, G., & Mullender, E. (2005). Listening to women's voices: The participation of domestic violence survivors in services. In T. Skinner, M. Hester, & E. M. Malos (Eds.), *Researching gender violence: Feminist methodology in action* (pp. 146–166). Devon: Willam Publishing.

Hardy, K., & Laszloffy, T. (2002). *Teens who hurt: Clinical interventions to break the cycle of adolescent violence*. New York: The Guilford Press.

Hardy, K. (2006). Espacio para respirar. *Revista Venezolana de Psicología Clínica Comunitaria, 6,* 129–143.

Harper, D. (1991). The role of psychology in the analysis of poverty: Some suggestions. *Psychology and Developing Societies, 3,* 193–201.

Harper, D. (2003). Poverty and discourse. In S. Carr & T. Sloan (Eds.), *Poverty & psychology: From global perspective to local practice* (pp. 185–203). New York: Kluwer-Plenum.

Havel, V. (1987/1991). *Open letters: Selected writings, 1965–1990.* New York: Vintage Books.

Hirigoyen, M. (1999). *El acoso moral: el maltrato psicológico en la vida cotidiana*. Barcelona: Paidós.

Hollander, N. (2010). *Uprooted minds: Surviving the politics of terror in the Americas*. New York: Routledge.

Human Rights Office of the High Commissioner of the United Nations. (July 4, 2019). *UN Human Rights report on Venezuela urges immediate measures to halt and remedy grave rights violations.* https://www.ohchr.org/en/NewsEvents/Pages/DisplayNews.aspx?NewsID=24788&LangID=E. Accessed March 24, 2020.

Human Rights Watch (November 29, 2017). *Crackdown on Dissent. Brutality, torture and political persecution in Venezuela*. https://www.hrw.org/report/2017/11/29/crackdown-dissent/brutality-torture-and-political-persecution-venezuela. Accessed April 5, 2020.

International Psychoanalytic Association. (2015). *Ethics Code.* https://www.ipa.world/ipa/en/IPA1/Procedural_Code/Ethics_code_new.aspx. Accessed April 10, 2020.

Kelly, G. (1966). *Teoría de la Personalidad.* Buenos Aires: Ediciones Troquel.

Kinderman, P. (2007). Human rights and applied psychology. *Journal of Community and Applied Social Psychology, 17,* 218–228.

Kozak, G. (2018). Políticas contra el pensamiento social y humanístico en la Venezuela Revolucionaria. In A. Chaguaceda, & H. Vives (Eds.), *Las Ciencias Sociales en Contextos Autoritarios: producción académica, censura y represión en los escenarios de post guerra fría* (pp. 116–133). Buenos Aires: CADAL, FHRC y Universidad de Guadalajara.

Lacan, J. (1988). *El Seminario, Libro 7 La Ética del psicoanálisis*. Buenos Aires: Paidós.

Lander, R. (2004). *Experiencia subjetiva y lógica del otro*. Caracas: Editorial Psicoanalítica.

Levi, P. (1989). *Los Hundidos y los Salvados*. Barcelona: El Aleph.

Llorens, M. (2006). El Chapulín Colorado y la Psicología del Deporte: Herramientas narrativas en el trabajo con el fútbol venezolano. *Revista de Psicología del Deporte*, 15.

Llorens, M. (May 3, 2019). 'Peace Privilege' also means disgust for someone else's suffering. *Caracas Chronicles*. https://www.caracaschronicles.com/2019/05/03/peace-privilege-also-means-disgust-for-someone-elses-suffering/ Accessed April 4, 2020.

Llorens, M., Souto, J., Zapata, M., Alzualde, C., Escorcia, L., Armas, M., García, K., & González, R. (in press). Militarización de la Mente: violencia crónica y el impacto en la convivencia de las comunidades. In V. Zubillaga, & M. Llorens (Eds.), *Dicen que Están Matando Gente: Violencia armada y políticas de seguridad ciudadana en Venezuela*. Madrid: Dahbar.

Lykes, M. B. (2000). Possible contributions of a psychology of liberation: Whither health and Human Rights. *Journal of Health Psychology, 5,* 383–397.

Lykes, M. B. (2001). Human Rights violations as structural violence. In D. Christie, R. Wagner, & D. DuNann (Eds.), *Peace, conflict and violence: Peace psychol ogy for the 21st century* (pp. 158–168). Nueva Jersey: Prentice Hall.

Maslow, A. (1966/2002). *Psychology of Science: A reconnaissance.*

Mackintosh, E. (March 7, 2019). US journalist reportedly detained in Venezuela is realeased. *CNN*. https://edition.cnn.com/2019/03/06/americas/venezuela-us-journalist-detained-intl/index.html. Accessed April 4, 2020.

Marks, S. (2001). Johanthn Mann's legacy to the 21st century: The Human Rights imperative for public health. *Journal of Law, Medicine and Ethics, 29,* 131–138.

Martín-Baró, I. (1984/1993). Guerra y salud mental. *Papeles del Psicólogo*. II, 56, 27–33.

May, R. (1974). *Fuentes de la violencia* Buenos Aires: Emecé Editores.

McIntosh, P. (July/August 1989). White privilege: Unpacking the invisible backpack. *Peace and Freedom*, 31–36.

Meneses, M., Pérez, A., Rodríguez, P., & Westinner, M. (2001). *Detección de necesidades en la comunidad de Antímano en relación con el Parque Social Padre Manuel Aguirre, SJ.* Unpublished paper. Caracas: Universidad Católica Andrés Bello.

Montero, M. (2004). *Introducción a la psicología comunitaria: desarrollo, conceptos y procesos*. Buenos Aires: Paidós.

Montero, M. (2006). *Hacer para transformar: el método en la psicología comunitaria*. Buenos Aires: Paidós.

Montero, M., & Montenegro, M. (2006). Critical psychology in Venezuela. *Annual Review of Critical Psychology, 5.* www.discourseunit.com/arcp/5. Accessed February 15, 2008.

Moreno, A., Brandt, J., Campos, A., Nabarro, R., Pérez, M., Rodríguez, W., et al. (1998). *Historia de vida de Felicia Valera*. Caracas: Fondo Editorial Conicit.

Moreno, A., & Luna, P. (2002). *Buscando padre: historia de vida de Pedro Luis Luna*. Caracas: Universidad de Carabobo y Centro de Investigaciones Populares.

Nelson, G., & Prilleltensky, I. (2005). *Community psychology: In pursuit of liberation and wellbeing*. New York: Palgrave Macmillan.

Pakman, M. (1997). *Construcciones de la experiencia humana, Volumen II*. Barcelona: Gedisa.

Pakman, M. (2011). *Palabras que Permanecen, Palabras por Venir: micropolítica y poética en psicoterapia*. Barcelona: Gedisa.

Palacios, C. (April 26, 2019). The Trap of the 'Peace Privilege'. *Caracas Chronicles*. https://www.caracaschronicles.com/2019/04/26/the-trap-of-peace-privilege/. Accessed April 4, 2020.

Parker, I. (2007). *Revolution in psychology: Alienation to Emancipation*. Londres: Pluto Press.

Phillips, A. (1995). *Terrors and experts*. Cambridge: Harvard University Press.

Phillips, A. (2000). *Promises, promises*. London: Faber y Faber.

Prilleltensky, I. (1997). Values, assumptions, and practices: Assessing the moral implications of psychological discourse and action. *American Psychologist, 47,* 517–535.

Prilleltensky, I. (2001). Value-based praxis in community psychology: Moving toward social justice and social action. *American Journal of Community Psychology, 29,* 747–778.

Prilleltensky, I., Prilleltensky, O., & Voorhes, C. (2008). Psychopolitical validity in the helping professions: Applications to research, interventions, case conceptualizations and therapy. In D. Cohen & S. Timimi (Eds.), *Liberatory psychiatry: Towards a new psychiatry* (pp. 105–130). Cambridge: Cambridge University Press.

Samuels, A. (1993). *The political psyche.* London: Routledge.

Sarason, S. (1981). An asocial psychology and a misdirected clinical psychology. *American Psychologist, 38,* 827–836.

Schafer, K., & Smith, S. (2004). *Human rights and narrated lives: The ethics of recognition.* New York: Palgrave Macmillan.

Skinner, T., Hester, M., & Malos, E. (2005). *Researching gender violence: Feminist methodology in action.* Devon: Willan Publishing.

Shotter, J. (2000). From within our lives together: Wittgenstein, Bakhtin, Voloshinov and the shift to a participatory stance in understanding. In L. Holzman & J. Morss (Eds.), *Postmodern psychologies, societal practice and political life* (pp. 100–129). New York: Routledge.

Smith, L. (2005). Psychotherapy, classism, and the poor: Conspicuous by their absence. *American Psychologist, 60,* 687–696.

Terr, L. (1990). *Too scared to cry: How trauma affects children and ultimately us all.* New York: Basic Books.

Totton, N. (2000). *Psychotherapy and politics.* London: Sage Publications.

Vethencourt, J. (2009). Criminología, violencia y delincuencia. *Heterotopía, 41,* 77–100.

Waldgrave, C. (1990). Just therapy. *Dulwich Center Newsletter, 1,* 5–46.

White, M. (1993). Deconstruction and therapy. In S. Gilligan & R. Price (Eds.), *Therapeutic conversations* (pp. 22–63). New York: W.W. Norton and Company.

White, M. (1995). *Reescribir la vida: entrevistas y ensayos.* Barcelona: Gedisa.

Winnicott, D. (1960). The theory of the parent-child relationship. *International Journal of Psychoanalysis, 41,* 585–595.

Yurman, F. (2005). *Crónica del Anhelo: ensayos sobre literatura, cultura y psicoa nálisis.* Caracas: Monte Ávila.

Zubillaga, V. (2005). La carrera moral del hombre de respeto y armas: historia de vida de jóvenes y violencia en Caracas. *Revista Venezolana de Psicología Clínica Comunitaria,* 5.

Zubillaga, V., Llorens, M., Núñez, G., & Souto, J. (2015). *Violencia Armada y Acuerdos Comunitarios de Convivencia en una Comunidad Carqueña: una larga marcha por la paz.* Caracas: Equinoccio.

Chapter 8
Clinical Examples

On one occasion, during a supervision, with a team that worked with victims of violence, a case was presented of a woman whose political activism was a very central aspect of her identity, yet, the therapist, who had effectively explored other relevant areas, had not made a single question about her political activities or beliefs. It was 2006 and the confrontation in Venezuela was again very tense. When I asked the therapist why she hadn't asked about the political dimension of this woman's life, she quickly replied: "Because it's like religion, one doesn't talk about those things." We were all surprised by her answer, even the therapist who had seemed to give a knee-jerk response. She explained that she felt that areas of personal fundamental beliefs were not open to discussion. It is a contradictory thought, considering that therapy often begins with the invitation to share whatever appears in one's mind without censoring anything. But the historical events had filtered into our intimate life and people had begun to limit their interactions in the public sphere to avoid unnecessary confrontations and controversy. Just like irreconcilable religious positions, politics began to feel as something that was not possible to resolve and was best avoided.

This is an isolated example of how many psychological spaces began to be censored overt or covertly. A group of students that were conducting part of their training in the public psychiatric hospital were asked to exclude any political content in their clinical notes even regarding delusions that they had recorded. In the psychiatric service of the Military Hospital patients and doctors self-censored themselves to avoid complications. In some university classes professors explicitly asked students to leave any political discussion outside of the classroom in order to avoid irreconcilable differences. Politics became a terrain too emotionally charged to tolerate.

I don't think that this is always a mistake. Perhaps there are places in which a restriction can allow some activities to develop without unnecessary interference. But I would like to think that psychotherapy and university classrooms are some of the places where we should try to deal and reflect on our dilemmas regarding our coexistence, where we should strive to talk about crucial societal issues. Politics

M. Llorens, *Politically Reflective Psychotherapy*, Latin American Voices,
https://doi.org/10.1007/978-3-030-57792-6_8

barges in anyway. We should make efforts to include it ethically and (hopefully) in a way that furthers our comprehension on these matters.

8.1 Crisis Intervention

A contextualized comprehension is necessary from the initial phases of psychotherapy. During social and political upheaval this becomes obvious. One source of cases that arrived at our center during the beginning of this century were Colombian refugees that had been displaced by war.

Incredible amounts of anxiety, sadness, hyperalertness, suicidal ideation, feelings of vulnerability, intrusive thoughts, intrusive remembrance of traumatic episodes, rage against aggressors and against the world in general, confusion, hopelessness and a host of other posttraumatic symptomatology were expressed by a number of those refugees that had been able to reach Caracas, fleeing from their homes. A middle-aged man reported of not having been able to sleep more than two hours each day for over a year. He was visibly exhausted but he told us that each time he began to fall asleep, a terrible fear of losing sight of and not being able to take care of his wife and children woke him up again. This even after arriving in the neighboring country miles away from where the traumatic events took place. He was unable to feel safe anymore.

The amounts of anxiety that he expressed made us decide to have two therapists join in as a team to attend to his case. We felt we needed to act as a team in order to tolerate the intensity of this man's suffering and sustain the capacity to think. This man seemed to be very paranoid. He felt that he was being watched, did not want to leave his residence to come to therapy, felt that people related to his aggressors might be living in the street where he arrived and thought that he had caught a glimpse of them. All of this miles away from Colombia. The observations on war refugees made by Martín-Baró in El Salvador came to mind and how some of the people he talked to sometimes seemed to be psychotic (1984/1993). But that, after listening to the gravity of their experiences, these reactions seemed to be much more comprehensible. Herman (1997) has pointed out that we should avoid underestimating the evaluation of danger made by those that have survived violence, since it is hard, as observers to imagine situations of terror.

We made an effort to understand the context from which he was fleeing talking to the NGOs that were working with Colombian war refugees. They confirmed that there was real risk that this man's aggressors could locate him in Caracas. There were reported episodes of aggression against Colombian refugees inside Venezuela. On top of this, during the weeks that he was in therapy, Rodrigo Granda, one of the main representatives of the FARC (Colombian Armed Revolutionary Forces) was kidnapped by paramilitaries on the streets of Caracas and taken back to Colombia. Part of the Colombian war was being waged inside of Venezuela, as difficult to believe as it was. When one hasn't been in hell, it is hard to fathom that hell can be waiting at the corner. These events allowed us to comprehend this man's evaluation of risk and the fact that the line between paranoia and threat was not as easy to establish as we first thought.

His near death experiences had left a deep mark of fragility and terror. He deeply needed to feel safe again, but was extremely cautious about letting his guard down. Even in the therapeutic relationship. During my studies at the Trauma Service at the Tavistock Clinic in London where many refugees are received, I saw the frequency with which the therapeutic relationship is marked by the fact that refugees have often survived experiences of extreme vulnerability and the therapist represents a new world, and possibly the most constant representative of the host country in which their legal status is in the process of being established. The difference between the role of the therapist and the representatives of the legal systems are not necessarily as clear cut for the client as they are for the therapist, and the relationship carries the extreme experience of vulnerability that comes from not knowing if one is to be legally accepted in the country or sent back. The transference, in a sense, is not only toward the therapist or the center but also to all of the host country.

As any crisis intervention, it is crucial to establish a minimal sense of security as well as help recover control of one's life. In the case of those that had to flee their countries because of violence, this implies the recovery of their basic rights. It is clear in these cases that the comprehension of the social, political and legal context where the person has come from and in which he or she is at is crucial to offer help (Siddiqui, Ismail & Allen, 2007).

8.2 Psychotherapy with Those Affected by Political Crisis

In December 2002, the Venezuelan Confederation of Workers, the organization that groups the worker's syndicates in the country, along with the syndicate of the oil workers (Unapetrol) called for a general strike against the government. The tensions had exploded in April of that year. The oil workers had been staging protests rejecting the government takeover of the company that had traditionally been able to maintain certain independence from the influence and political manipulation of the governing party. The following years, the dramatic destruction of the oil production apparatus of Venezuela as well as the massive corruption of the government collaborators that took over the company—that has included accusations around the world of bribes hovering over two billion dollars—would prove those protests to have been right in rejecting the takeover (BBC News, 2018; Monaldi, 2016).

On April 8, during his weekly show on live television Hugo Chávez publicly fired the main executives, histrionically blowing a whistle, calling their names out and shouting "¡pa fuera!" (you're out!). This gesture exacerbated tensions and mutlitudinary marches immediately erupted in Caracas conducted by the opposition. The climax came on April 11 when a mass of protesters marched to the presidential office called Miraflores. The protest ended in an armed confrontation that led to the murder of 21 citizens and the supposed resignation of Chávez. This led to the unconstitutional proclamation of an interim president and the illegal dissolution of the National Assembly. Chavismo denounced a coup and popular protests in favor of Chávez arrived at Miraflores. Three days later Chávez returned to power and was reinstituted as the president. The events of those days and murders of those citizens have still not been cleared up. A Truth Commission accorded upon by both political sectors, following a negotiation table set up by the Carter Center, never investigated the events (Martínez Meucci, 2016).

The national strike or oil strike (as it is called depending on the political interpretation of the events) led to the paralyzation of the country's oil company (PDVSA) which in turn led to the paralyzation of the country because of lack of gasoline. Government responded by firing 21,000 employees accusing them of unjustifiably abandoning their jobs, labeling them "terrorists."

Daniela was one of those that was fired. An organizational psychologist and a middle range executive in the company, she had labored in PDVSA for 11 years when she decided to join the strike. She was clearly against the government and sternly opposed to the efforts to infiltrate the company. After being fired, she committed herself to organizations of ex-employees that were working in the defense of their labor rights. In particular, Daniela reported how, after being fired, she militantly assisted the marches and organized workshops in different communities trying to explain to the general population the insides of the state-owned company and the risks it was facing.

Her participation in the movement was marked by political persecution that government led against all ex-employees. The settlement that she was owed for being fired was never paid, she lost all the benefits that she was legally entitled to. For example, she was impeded from paying off her home loan, legally losing it. But the most terrifying experience was an assault in which her house was broken into and vandalized without anything being robbed, which left her and her family with the feeling that it was a threat rather than an attempted robbery. Finally, her political rights were confiscated. During the Referendum to revoke Chavez's term, a number of legal signed petitions were rejected alleging that the signatures could not be validated. In the final recollection, Daniela's signature suspiciously disappeared from the final count, effectively losing any possibility of exercising her electoral right. She denounced these events publicly, appearing in newspaper reports that are not quoted to protect her identity.

Daniela arrived at my consulting room on August of 2004 reporting: "I never thought that a political event could affect my life to this extreme." When we began treatment she was visibly depressed. She had endured very high levels of anxiety during a year that manifested itself as recurrent nightmares, hyperalertness, hyperreactivity, panic attacks and an episode where she had fainted. The chronic anxiety had given way to a depression in which the main symptom was anhedonia: she reported having lost the capacity to enjoy anything, even family activities which she previously loved. What finally led her to ask for help was the decision to skip a family meeting that in the past had been very meaningful. Even though she had found work again she reported disinterest in it, in part because she felt that it distracted her attention from the urgent need to attend to the political events that continued to be unresolved, but also because she felt it was a betrayal to her previous work colleagues. She expressed fear that parts of her life had been hopelessly lost in the process and that she had been left damaged without repair. This gave her profound grief.

As a psychologist, Daniela had knowledge about psychological processes as well as the capacity to reflect on herself that came from previous psychotherapies she had been in. She was surprised to find that her issues had centered on her family relationships and attachments in the past and now she was profoundly affected by issues that were of another dimension: politics.

It is interesting that we are surprised by the impact politics can have on our lives. Political stability leads us to take for granted how access to services, rule of law, economic welfare, equality and liberty have profound impacts on our lives. But Daniela and I had the initial challenge of understanding her suffering in reference to the political situation in itself without hurrying to refer to personality dynamics, attachments, emotional regulation, etc. All our theoretical baggage tends to look toward individual aspects of suffering leaving the social dimension in the background.

It is not to say that individual elements are not relevant to understand how suffering is expressed but rather that referring mainly to those aspects obscures the harassment that she was subjected to and the importance of the traumatic circumstances she was experiencing. Daniela felt alienated because the rest of the country, her fellow psychologists, other members of her children's school, those she had casual conversations with, had gone on with their lives, leaving behind the traumatic events of 2002. Well-meaning friends often suggested that she should turn the page, and not think about the political situation. These comments contributed to her feeling damaged and having been left devastated by her experience; guilty of not being able to let go of her pain over the loss of her job of which she had felt proud, her home and her professional projects. Even worse, her feeling of threat had not ended. She repeated "what happened to me can happen to you tomorrow" to loved ones that often dismissed her worries as exaggerated. She doubted whether they were right and she was paranoid or whether her worries of the country slipping into authoritarianism were founded.

In therapy I didn't pretend to have a definite answer to these questions. But they made me think of the reports of war veterans and victims of persecution around the world. These reports evidence the rejection that sometimes appears in their social networks, serving as reminders of collective traumatic episodes that most want to forget. For those that have gone through events of social confrontation, war, collective chaos, mass murders, we know how terrifying those episodes can be. People who have been traumatized by these events can become uncomfortable reminders of intense pain. Venezuelans have experienced the desire to forget, striving to return as quickly as possible to some sense of normality. Judith Herman quotes a Vietnam Veteran who reported:

> Family and friends wondered why we were so angry. What are you crying about? they would ask. Why are you so ill-tempered and disaffected. Our fathers and grandfathers had gone off to war, done their duty, come home and got on with it. What made our generation so different? As it turns out, nothing. No difference at all. When old soldiers from "good"

> wars are dragged from behind the curtain of myth and sentiment and brought into the light, they too seem to smolder with choler and alienation.... So we were angry. Our anger was old, atavistic. We were angry as all civilized men who have ever been sent to make murder in the name of virtue were angry (Norman, p. 27, cited by Herman, 1997).

Even though Daniela, of course, had not been in combat nor suffered shellshock, her experience was similar to those feelings of alienation. She also felt intense feelings of solidarity, support and comfort when she met with her ex-coworkers who had gone on strike along with her and had endured public accusations and political persecution. Something of the complex experience of vulnerability and solidarity made them empathize among them as well as feel that others did not completely care about their grief. I believe that the suffering of Daniela is better understood from the perspective of a traumatic experience. The impact of terror produced by human abuse and the dynamics of power involved have to do with her feelings.

The strategies of domination and control used in abusive relations have been widely recorded and described under political persecution (Amnesty International, 1973); psychological warfare (Martín-Baró, 1990); domestic abuse (Herman, 1997) and mobbing (Hirigoyen, 1999). Government used harassment to quiet protests and Daniela suffered its emotional consequences. For a while, this was a contentious interpretation. I based my outlook on government's public declarations on the issue and research that began to collect evidence of widespread abuse in the public sector (Goncalves, Gutiérrez & Rodríguez, 2009). Repeated reports of threats, intimidation, suspension of work benefits, public shaming, social isolation, indirect firings and all types of coercion were recorded. With the passing of time it became evident that these strategies were systematic and widespread (Carvajal, 2018). Eventually the International Labor Organization (Organización Internacional del Trabajo, 2005) has clearly confirmed that the case constituted a gross abuse of worker's rights.

Framing it as abuse and in terms of power allowed us to examine some of Daniela's reactions in that light, showing how some of the emotional consequences had to do with her feelings of injustice, the humiliation of being publicly shamed on television, the impotence of having to deal with an authoritarian and arbitrary power and the fear of the continued threat. So part of our work had to do with understanding her feelings in the web of complex political events that had occurred, and with validating her feelings of having been trampled on by an abusive power. Among other things, Daniela suffered from what we have characterized as the dehumanization of her loss, given that the wider social context didn't validate her grievances. The non-recognition of her loss had complicated her mourning process.

One of the most complicated aspects was her rage. It had become hard for her family and friends to tolerate her indignation and constant anger. She was constantly invited to let go of her rage without the acknowledgement of the injustice of what she had experienced. The recording of her testimony countered some of this experience of dehumanization and allowed us to begin to identify and put words to her losses which included not only tangible ones, but also more abstract losses as the sense of meaning she had in relation to her work, pride in contributing to the country's most important industry, but also the loss of trust in the public sector. She felt that her honest efforts to contribute to the country had been turned, by the use of propaganda and political confrontation, into a target. To be able to name and identify these aspects of her traumatic experience helped her organize some of her suffering and process her losses. Her experience led to a profound examination of her personal beliefs and to a stronger commitment toward politics. She began to participate in study groups, read and dedicate herself to various movements. As her mourning process advanced she was able to re-evaluate her life with more serenity. In many ways, she began to question many of her previous thoughts on politics, even questioning the limited perspective she previously had on the dynamics that led to Venezuela's political crisis. We talked about her internal debates on distributive justice in Venezuela's history that Chavismo challenged and with which some of the abuses she suffered were justified. Psychotherapy sought to incorporate these questions in order to open space for different perspectives. Talking about these issues allowed her to reflect on the political storm that shook her life and, in a sense, was a profound process of problematization. To name the injustices that she suffered opened up space to reflect on the complexities of many of these issues.

On one occasion she came to therapy reporting feeling very depressed. She had received an email from a former colleague that had been one of the political leaders of 2002, sharing that he had been diagnosed with cancer. It came along with the news that two other coworkers had died in the previous months from heart attacks. She began to weep and hyperventilate feeling that she was suffocating and began to yell: "They're killing us damn it, they're killing us! It's like what I felt when I fainted. My body couldn't take it anymore." The news of the sickness of her friend brought back feelings of vulnerability that she had gone through. She was confronted again with persecutory anxieties from which she could not defend herself. The reappearance of anxiety led her to seek psychiatric help to complement our therapy.

But the psychiatric session followed the medical model. In it, a list of symptoms and a short story of her suffering was recorded. Daniela felt that the doctor, and her husband who was invited to enter the session, directed the conversation. They concluded that she suffered from a General Anxiety Disorder, imposing a pathologized and limited reading of her experience. Neurological examinations were administered that she went along with, leading to no particular finding. In psychotherapy she mentioned that the psychiatric consultation had felt uncomfortable and had brought back the fantasy of being irreparably damaged. The physiological interpretation obscured the historical dimension, resulting in a version of disability instead of one of survival. Even considering that the diagnosis fit (medication effectively reduced some of her suffering), the comprehension centered on the individual left all explanation of the causes on her shoulders. It left her feeling, not a person who had bravely faced unjust and threatening situations, but a person with a psychiatric ailment. The political and social formulation was left out.

When I asked Daniela to read and comment on this rendition of our work she added a relevant consideration that allows us to understand the process. She felt it is important to underline that her convictions had also been part of her recovery. It is relevant because it emphasizes the active role she had in the process and because it implies a re-reading of everything she endured, as a process that she survived and allowed her to strengthen her convictions and personal commitments.

I believe that a politically reflective psychotherapy allowed us to frame and ponder upon the social and political dimensions that led us to understand her experience more completely, to the possibility of validating many of her emotions of indignation, terror, rage and solidarity and finally, to recognize the trampled rights which were a central part of her suffering.

8.3 Torture Survivors

Pedro came to therapy referred by his wife's therapist in 2001, right before the political tensions had begun to erupt. He came because of marital conflict and a successful cancer treatment he had finished recently. He was interested in the work from the beginning, among other things because he had been in a long psychoanalytic treatment 20 years back.

He was in his 60s and his life was a quite amazing story of personal transformation in which political events of the country had impacted it at different moments. He was born in an extremely poor household. His father had abandoned him and his mother when he was very young. They moved in with his mother's new couple who ended up beating him and his mother repeatedly. He often recalled his mother's insistence, asking him to behave in order to not infuriate his stepfather. At seven years of age his mother passed away, which he believed to be a result of the violence she suffered.

Pedro ended up in his grandmother's house, who wasn't pleased about his arrival. He endured the worst years of poverty and mistreatment there. To describe their poverty he mentioned not having been able to use underwear or toothpaste until he became a teenager. They lived in a small town and his life was dedicated to small household chores and trying to bear his grandmother's frustrations.

He was able to go to school without receiving much support, but there he found a place to grow. He remembered how the learning process and his classmates fascinated him. He describes himself as an angry, impulsive, young rebel without a cause. In his home, his grandmother imposed unfair punishments, while his only forms of protest were indirect. When she asked him to do a task outside of the house, he would escape for hours, leaving his grandmother waiting. He never confronted her, his situation was too precarious.

In his adolescence his interest in politics began. Representatives of the left were linked to Pedro's town and developed activities for youngsters there. He began to collaborate in sports events. He found a niche where he could feel useful and accepted. He began to share his experiences of injustice in a group that offered hopes of transformation. He was recruited into a political party that was soon outlawed by the ruling government in the 60s, which was a decade of confrontation of the government with the radical left. His party went underground.

The second part of his life began then, in which he began to develop intellectually and to nurture a strong commitment with the members of his party and its project. He didn't talk much about that time in his life, but did comment that he learned discipline and how to organize his life then. The severe discipline his grandmother had imposed shifted toward this new purpose. His personal severity helped him to survive in hiding, although he was caught and imprisoned on three occasions. In jail he was held in awful conditions suffered beatings, had little food, little human contact and was subjected to sensory deprivation.

After ten years of political militancy he finally decided to leave the party and change the course of his life. He enrolled in a public university and began a life as a professional. He established a romantic relationship with a party member that lasted after they left the party. They had three children. The separation led to him to psychoanalysis in the 70s. He was as disciplined in his treatment as he had been in other aspects of his life. He felt that the treatment had helped him to understand himself.

From all these experiences a man with many strengths developed. He had a clear vision of what he wanted from his life and the confidence that came from knowing he had survived very difficult circumstances. His discipline had helped him keep many of the painful experiences he had endured under strict control. His psychological functioning was based on a very rational, constricted, style which, for example, included never having remembered any dreams in his life. He said he was puzzled by music and poetry which he didn't understand. He also wondered if he really had ever been in love with any of his partners.

We began to work about 15 years after he had finished his psychoanalytic treatment. He talked about his second marriage in which he was in the process of separating, of his children with whom he had a strong attachment, and about his past. He recalled his psychoanalysis with great fondness. In the initial stages of our work it was the only thing of which he talked about with deep emotion. The thought of his analyst brought him to tears. He said he cried because he had felt supported by her as well as because he was proud to have been able to dedicate himself to such a challenging process.

Soon things outside the consulting room began to become more tense. The events of 2002 brought politics into every corner of the country. Polarization took over the nation. Those events moved Pedro profoundly and they were an important part of his present thoughts. Even though he was not active in politics anymore, he had the feeling that his past efforts were reflected, many years later, in Chavismo and they had somehow been able to fulfill some of the things he had struggled for. But he was very hesitant about expanding on these issues in therapy, he only insinuated many of his ideas.

My consulting room was located on the east side of Caracas, in a middle-class sector of the city, that at that moment represented part of Chavez's hardest opposition. This was an inevitable fact that framed our exchange. Pedro came often to therapy with a newspaper published by a Chavista ideologue, folded under his arm, and began various sessions with the same joke: "I don't know if I can walk here in Chacao with this newspaper. It might be dangerous." I shared my interpretation that maybe he was asking himself if it was dangerous to talk about politics in the consulting room or that he may want my permission to expand on his feelings on these issues. On another occasion he mentioned that he felt that psychology had an important part to play in the political process. He said: "It seems like I came here to defend the government, as if I had to convince you of something, but I know that your work has nothing to do with agreeing or not with me. I know there is absolute liberty here to say what I want." He basically expressed his desire to share his thoughts and gave himself his own answer, insisting on his freedom. Politics framed our conversation. I began to cautiously supervise my interventions in case they were charged with my own feelings. I mentioned that he might be worried about sharing political ideas that had been a dangerous aspect of his life at one point. But none of these approximations seemed to open up conversation. He always answered that he felt fine and that he knew he could talk about all he wanted. My feeling was that he tiptoed around issues he was feeling very strongly about.

I debated and discussed in my supervisions whether or not I should insist on trying to invite him to talk more openly about these issues. I was ambivalent about it making our relationship more difficult or maybe making him carry worries that were only mine. I knew that our relationship was important to him, since he was in the process of separating from his second wife. It was as though we both appreciated our relationship and moved respectfully and with extreme caution to avoid complicating it. On one occasion, that he again began to make indirect references to politics, I asked him: "You seem curious about my opinion. Do you want to know what I think about these issues?". Even though it was a simple question, it introduced the possibility of him asking me about my thoughts and about the place where he wanted me to be as a therapist. He fell silent for a couple of minutes and finally answered: "No, I think I prefer not to know."

His answer gave us an interesting starting place that allowed us to explore his anxieties around our differences as well as related to feeling closer to me or knowing me more personally. He worried that that could open up an emotional dimension to our relationship which he preferred to imagine as very intellectual, where he felt less threatened. But his answer helped me feel that we had been able to include the political dimension a bit more. He had the opportunity to think and reconsider how it was that he wanted us to work in regard to our circumstances. This gave us more space to move and the political aspects of his life began appearing more in depth.

A few weeks later he began the session with enthusiasm: "Well, I'm going to start with politics today. I listened to Chavez's visit to the UN. I was very excited to listen to him. I am moved sharing this with you…." A few weeks later he began to recall his first steps in politics, his youth and the experience of his underground militancy. I felt that we had made progress as he talked about the intense training in silence that his political work imposed as he made a few comments about how these things were probably not relevant to therapy. His political work had imposed a silence that was now somehow re-enacted in the consulting room. Silence had been a life and death matter. Sometimes it seemed that he still felt it that way.

It was then that our work was shaken by external events. A district attorney who had been handling all of the political cases was murdered. A bomb exploded in his van as he was getting in. The news of the murder shook the country, it was the first political murder in almost two decades. There were some arrests and a young man that was stopped by the police, regarding the case, opened fire and was shot dead. The young man was the son of a political representative of the opposition. Various figures were accused of the murder of the attorney, but the case soon became muddled and is still, almost 20 years later, unresolved. The events made me feel anxious and brought the frequent idea that it was very difficult to know what was happening in the country.

Pedro came to therapy after the first suspects had been arrested and began the session saying: "I am very happy with the way things are turning out. I am very happy about the arrests regarding the attorney's case. I am glad they arrested Poleo (a news reporter of the opposition). After she talked so much against the government, I am glad that she is locked up. She will probably flee to the U.S., but that will be good too." I kept silence but felt more anxious than I had previously felt when he brought on these issues. I didn't see the arrests as clearly as Pedro, but it wasn't an issue that I had a strong position about. He continued to talk about the case and later went on to talk about his second son's upcoming marriage and some recent medical exams that had come out fine.

A huge amount of anxiety appeared again in his expression. I associated both contents and asked him: "When you went underground or when you were imprisoned, did you ever fear for your life?". Pedro went silent, staring at me, seemingly surprised. Then he said: "Yes, many times… but what I most feared was being tortured. Because I was afraid to break under torture and betray my comrades." He began to weep profusely. The memories of those experiences came back. It was interesting that what he was most moved about was the fear of betrayal. This terrorized him more than his own welfare.

"I was jailed three times and the hardest moments were the first days when they tried to get you to talk. You had to resist under immense pressure. After that, the hard part was the idleness and the hunger. I remember once that I was in a cell smaller than this room, there wasn't a window or a picture I could look at." He looked around, at the paintings on the walls of the consulting room as he said this, and then continued, "I remember that once they gave me a newspaper to read and I devoured it from the first to the last page. But I always worried about giving away a comrade. I never did, but in part, that was what led me to retire. Not wanting to have to go through that risk again." He wept once more with a depth that he hadn't been able to until then.

Pedro, of course, was reliving the sensory deprivation he had been subjected to. It is interesting to note the comparison he makes between the cell he was jailed in and the size of the consulting room, as well as the reference to pictures, while looking around at the images on my walls. Again, not even walls are "neutral," they carry colors and express many comforting or menacing things.

Politics had entered the consulting room, not only as the current events but also in relation to his life, and the traumatic events that had been sealed. I think the murder of the district attorney brought back feelings of threat, vulnerability, indignation and injustice. We had talked about his experiences of political persecution, but the visceral reliving of torture had not been accessed until this event. The reliving of these feelings opened much space to be able to think about his life in relation to what was happening in the country. He reported relief after the session and we were able explore his desires and fears regarding the current events with more freedom.

8.4 Politics at Home

The previous two cases have explicit political events affecting their lives. But all lives are influenced by the political dimension. The point is not that we should be politically reflective in explicitly political cases. This would be a sort of patch that would leave psychotherapy intact. On the contrary, these cases allow us to see clearly and think on the political dimension, and the weight of it in our relationships.

The distribution of power in the public sphere interacts with the distribution of power in our intimate lives and everyone deals with these tensions. The case of María will allow us to think about them. She came to therapy while in her college years. She studied languages and was referred by a psychotherapist with which she had eight sessions in a service of an NGO. But had to close the treatment because it was the maximum number of sessions the center offered. María wanted to continue to explore certain issues and was not happy about having to change therapist and much less of me being a man.

She was the third sister of a family that had suffered considerable abuse from her father. The father had come from a very poor family and had had to go to work in the streets at a very young age. Her mother had also been brought up in poverty but in a home that was much more stable, although very traditional. She had been brought up to marry a virgin and later to stay married no matter what. She endured physical and emotional abuse in her marriage along with a host of subtle controls of her activities and relationships. María reported that, as the smallest of the three sisters, she had suffered a little less physical abuse, but did face very strict prohibitions and was subjected to the ever-changing rules and emotional outbursts of her father. She felt a mix of fear and anger against him, which often came along with guilt. This contributed to developing a very constricted emotional style, constant rumination of vengeance, guilt, large memory lapses of her childhood, difficulties concentrating and short-term memory loss, as well as a diminished sense of self-worth that included feeling completely different from others as well as the painful idea that everything inevitably was going to end up miserably.

Her mother had tried to shelter her from her father's abuse, on occasion making up stories so her father would give her permission to go study somewhere. She saw great intellectual potential in María and had supported her as she advanced in school, and worked hard in order to provide her with the minimum study materials she needed. María had distinguished herself at times, but always felt that she didn't do enough, as a consequence of her severe self-criticism. She also struggled because of her distractions and what seemed spouts of dissociation in stressful moments in class.

During the last two years of high school, her mother enrolled her in a prestigious private school, thinking that it would help her get into a university. The mother had been able to pay the tuition with great effort. They both shared the dream of being able to access better things through her studies. But the project suffered a setback. María came from a rigid household that had made her obedient and submissive. In her new school she had to face classmates that were a little older than her and that came from more privileged backgrounds. She began to be bullied by her classmates. She endured daily insults. Her good grades didn't help and she was attacked by a girl that insisted that no matter what, she wouldn't belong there. The situation became unbearable for María who felt impotent to challenge the bullies. She had learned to endure in silence and did not imagine that authority could or would intervene to stop the abuse. She asked her mother to let her quit school and failed that grade, which led to more questions about her self-worth and the possibility of overcoming her difficult circumstances.

A few years later, after having successfully obtained her college degree she worried about the lack of advancement in her professional development. She reported feeling shy in job interviews and afraid that frustration might lock her in her home again. She was also ambivalent about becoming financially independent and moving out and leaving her mother alone with her dad.

In a session she began to describe the subtle power struggles between her mother and father. He was a fervent Chavista and turned Chavez's frequent speeches on loud at the house. Her mother was identified with the opposition and surreptitiously lowered the radio and television volume every time he wasn't paying attention. In the midst of these events María was invited to a job interview in a state institution. The opportunity was attractive as she was offered the post of teaching adults and the pay was relatively good. But in the session that followed her job interview, she talked about feeling doubts and disappointment. In a group interview with other candidates, the coordinator had expressed that it was "obvious" that anyone selected had to be a government sympathizer and that anyone who wasn't had to abstain from applying for the job. María had kept silent. She wanted the job and knew that the same thing was happening in many other places. She decided to keep quiet as she had always done at home, lowering the volume of an arbitrary imposition.

It is clear that the abuse endured in her home intertwined with the collective environment. The social dynamics re-edited private dilemmas. In the first case, in high school, re-enacting the experiences of discrimination and exclusion, in the other, through government coercion.

To not include the power dynamics in her life would be to exclude a huge part of the onset of her sufferings. María's reactions to bullying at school as well as political abuse cannot be reduced to personal dynamics, they must be explicitly explored so as to identify how disadvantage has played out in her interpretation of her life and of herself. Exploring them allowed us to unearth feelings of rage that authority of any kind provokes in her. To identify her rage and feelings of being abused allowed us to reflect on the present and on the past at the same time.

María had been in therapy for more than a year when this happened and she was able to identify the parallels between her work experience and some of the things she suffered at home. She was able to clearly identify her discomfort and anger. She allowed herself to complain about the institution, which was uncommon for her. Validating her frustration and indignation allowed us to talk about the present and past feelings she often dissociated from.

But in the end, it was not my place to decide what she had to do in regard to her job situation. There was a real need to find work. She was in the terrible dilemma of subjecting herself to an arbitrary authority in order to get a job or rebel and remain unemployed. The therapeutic space sought to discuss the issues and allow for the dilemma to be fully explored. What do you think would happen if you told the coordinator what you really think? How would you feel about yourself afterwards? What would you feel if you quietly accepted the job? What consequences would each option have? What other options are there to this dilemma?

When I asked María to read these paragraphs about our work together to see how she felt represented she wrote this:

> What I can truthfully say, at least in my case, about how I think psychotherapy helped me or how I've been able to advance in my emotional life, is that I feel that it is much harder for me to adapt now or accept situations that I do not agree with. It is almost impossible for me to do that now. I lasted very little in that job, since it became impossible for me to act against my beliefs. My dad passed away in those days and I became very distracted and it became impossible for me to teach the students things that I didn't believe in or agree with. I later found work in another government institution where I worked for almost one year. Either because of the long hours that it entailed or having to deal with high governmental figures (mayors, deputies, ministers, etc.) I didn't feel well there either. I was forced to attend government marches and vocally support the government. That year was too much. I felt very bad with myself. When I quit I felt very relieved. I was exhausted.
>
> Now I still haven't found my place professionally, and fear that I never will, but I clearly know where I don't want to be. I know I cannot accept certain things. Unfortunately I have been able to advance very much in certain areas of my life, having found a wonderful partner and a relationship that is healthy and beautiful. I am expecting a baby and feel that I can offer my children a stable and healthy household. I have a good relationship with my mom, my brothers and have great friends. My husband and I are good friends and we have learned to trust each other. I feel very happy with him. Even though we have problems sometimes, we find ways of resolving them without mistreating each other.
>
> I think therapy helped me to identify when I am not comfortable with something and put a stop to people or situations that I do not agree with. I protect my inner peace now as a priority. I think that once you become aware of what you like and what you don't, what bothers you and what is right, it is difficult to go back and accept intolerable situations.

The sad occurrence of political abuse in her life made her confront her feelings and reactions in relation to authoritarianism. It challenged her to use her strength to resolve it. My task was to accompany, witness and help her to reflect along the way. An important part of her growth has been the struggle to identify and gain confidence in her capacity to resist injustice.

8.5 Final Comments

The cases presented in the chapter were all included in the first edition of the book. As time passed and the political, economic and social situation continued to deteriorate, my work, along with that of the community center to which I belonged, evolved toward the continuous integration of individual and social aspects of our approach, and the cases that sought help increasingly were affected in one way or another by the country's ongoing crisis. Cases in which politics is a central aspect have multiplied: from political prisoners, tortured protesters, family members of executed youngsters, fearful activists, to refugees that have fled the country and solicited our services through the internet.

We have developed close collaborations with human rights groups such as the Human Rights Center of our university and Amnesty International; we set up an NGO, REACIN (the Network of Activists and Researchers for Coexistence) to address many of these issues. I developed strong alliances with political and community activists (Llorens & Caro, 2016). We began to receive many victims of political persecution. During the protests of 2014 more than 4000 citizens were arrested and during the protests of 2017 there were over 5000 arrests (Llorens, 2018). Many of the arrested protesters were university students to whom we had multiple ties. We began to receive victims that had been incarcerated in all types of terrible conditions, subjected to torture, threats, overcrowded prisons, kangaroo courts as well as harassment by government's armed groups employed to intimidate protesters.

Meanwhile, security forces increased their lethality and Nicolás Maduro organized an ex-termination group named the FAES (Fuerzas de Acciones Especial), which led the government execution from 2016 to 2019 of more than 16,000 citizens (Zubillaga & Llorens, in press). As a result, we had an exponential multiplication of family members who have needed emotional support (Sánchez & Guzmán, 2018; Sánchez, in press).

These cases were complex, as they suffered from very extreme circumstances, but the debate in our field, on where therapists should stand, toned down as it became obvious that we had to stand against government's abuse.

Through the years we developed a host of interventions that transcend the psychotherapeutic setting, in which we continue to develop community psychology interventions, human rights activism and the public denunciation of government abuse along with more traditional clinical work (Llorens, 2016; Zubillaga, Llorens, Souto & Núñez, 2013).

These projects aren't directly relevant to the theme of this book, but what is relevant is that in our work with the mothers of young men murdered by state forces we found, over and over again, that many of the women suffered terribly and were grateful for our support, but emphasized that they wanted justice and not emotional relief. On occasion they expressed that they wanted to hold on to their rage to be able to continue to confront the state apparatus. The political dimension of their suffering being much more relevant to them than their emotional suffering (Sánchez, in press). We have had to explain to well-meaning psychologists that, faced with their ills, we must not automatically send them to therapy, but rather analyze along with them what it is that they feel they want to do with their pain.

References

Amnesty International (1973). *Report on Torture*. London: Duckworth.

BBC News (September 14, 2018). Venezuelan ex-officials charged in Andorra over a $2.3 billion graft scheme. *BBC News*. https://www.bbc.com/news/world-latin-america-45507588. Accessed April 18, 2020.

Carvajal, L. (2018). *Noventa Miradas sobre el Chavismo: En lo económico, social, gerencial, político, jurídico e ideológico*. Caracas: AB ediciones.

Goncalves, M., Gutiérrez, J. & Rodríguez, P. (2009). Cuando el acoso se convierte en política: análisis del acoso laboral en despedidos del sector público entre 2003- 2005. *Revista Venezolana de Psicología Clínica Comunitaria. 9*, 31–56.

Herman, J. (1997). *Trauma and recovery: The aftermath of violence—From domestic abuse to political terror*. New York: Basic Books.

Hirigoyen, M. (1999). *El acoso moral: el maltrato psicológico en la vida cotidiana*. Barcelona: Paidós.

Llorens, M. (2016). Where mass graves are normal, normality isn't. *Caracas Chronicles*. https://www.caracaschronicles.com/2016/11/28/mass-graves-normal-normality-abnormal/. Accessed April 27, 2020.

Llorens, M. (2018). Dolor País: versión Venezuela. *Nueva Sociedad*. N274.

Llorens, M., & Caro, G. (2016). *Los Hombres Libres Nunca Tendrán Prisión: conversaciones con Gilber Caro*. Caracas: Libros Marcados.

Martín-Baró, I. (1984/1993). Guerra y salud mental. *Papeles del Psicólogo*. II, 56, 27–33.

Martín-Baró, I. (1990). *Psicología Social de la Guerra*. San Salvador: UCA Editores.

Martínez Meucci, M. (2016). *Apaciguamiento: el Referéndum Revocatorio y la consolidación de la Revolución Bolivariana*. Caracas: Alfa.

Monaldi, F. (October 26, 2016). ¿Qué le enseña el colapso petrolero venezolano a América Latina. *The New York Times*. https://www.nytimes.com/es/2016/10/26/espanol/opinion/que-le-ensena-el-colapso-petrolero-venezolano-a-america-latina.html. Accessed April 18, 2020.

Organización Internacional del Trabajo (OIT). (2005). Caso 2249. Informe 337. http://white.oit.org.pe/sindi/casos/ven/ven200502.html. Accessed June 20, 2009.

Sánchez, F. (in press). Violencia y subjetividad: experiencias de madres cuyos hijos fueron ejecutados extrajudicialmente por operativos en Caracas, Venezuela. In Zubillaga & Llorens (Eds), *Dicen Que Están Matando Gente en Venezuela: Violencia armada y políticas de seguridad ciudadana*. Madrid: Dahbar.

Sánchez, F., & Guzmán, J. (2018). Duelo, trauma e identidad: una aproximación narrativa a las víctimas secundarias de la violencia delincuencial en Caracas. *Analogías del Comportamiento, 16*, 44–61.

Siddiqui, N., Ismail, S., & Allen, M. (2007). *Safe to return? Pakistani women, domestic violence and access to refugee protection—A report of a transnational research Project conducted in the UK and Pakistan*. Manchester: South Manchester Law Centre in Partnership with Manchester Metropolitan University.

Zubillaga, V., Llorens, M., Souto, J., & Núñez, G. (2013). *Violencia Armada y Acuerdos Comunitarios de Convivencia: pistas para la acción*. Caracas: Amnistía Internacional.

Zubillaga, V., & Llorens, M. (in press). Dicen Que Están Matando Gente en Venezuela: Violencia armada y políticas de seguridad ciudadana. Madrid: Dahbar.

Chapter 9
Psychotherapy, Politics and Intimacy: Making the Unconscious Conscious and the Invisible Visible

I have tried to show how psychotherapy, as any other human relationship, is inevitably framed socially and politically; as well as the incredible mess psychotherapy can get into when it tries to disavow the powers that surround it. Finally, we have tried to explore ways in which a psychotherapy, developed from a post-modern stance, can attend to this dimension, the variations this brings to our understandings and the strategies that can be added to the therapist's toolbox. Parting from these considerations, I will try to explore the limitations and strengths that a politically reflective psychotherapy has as a place for resistance.

In his autobiography, The Story of My Experiments with Truth, Gandhi (1949) begins discussing the close relation of his intimate preoccupations and his political projects. He seems to have to justify, or at least explain, how he was able to develop a personal—in his case, spiritual—process along with his political activity, as if it were strange to find them on the same page. As has happened in the history of psychotherapy, it seems that Gandhi faced the idea that there was something suspect of dealing with both spheres at the same time.

But, can the psychotherapeutic exploration, inherently associated with the intimate aspects of life, be called upon to resist political oppression? Does it have anything to offer, besides relief, reflection and contention?

The feminist movement, as has been stated repeatedly, has pioneered the task of illuminating how political dynamics frame intimate life. It has also shown the role of insight in empowering and resisting oppressive structures such as patriarchy.

The review of life under oppression helps bring light to the strategies used to understand the potential and limitations of psychotherapy. Again, the small but relevant material of therapeutic work under dictatorships is a useful guide (Chaps. 3 and 4). Different authors have commented on how, faced with strict vigilance, citizens and psychotherapists tended to separate private life from public life, a dissociation that protected the individual from scrutiny (Conolly, 2006; Harmatta, 1992; Schreuder, 2001; Šebek, 1996).

It is interesting to explore the similarities between the strategies described by these therapists that used their professional work as a refuge for them and their clients and psychological resistance described in other scenarios. Taylor, Gilligan

M. Llorens, *Politically Reflective Psychotherapy*, Latin American Voices,
https://doi.org/10.1007/978-3-030-57792-6_9

and Sullivan (1995) proposed a series of very interesting links and nuances between the processes of dissociation and political resistance through their work with excluded adolescent girls in the United States. They distinguish public resistance (overt) from covert resistance. The first refers to the public confrontation of practices and institutions that oppress and the second one to the process of going underground with feelings and thoughts. Aware of the costs of public confrontation, the girls in the study often acted as if they agreed, while privately resisting. In the interviews they had with young women on the many ways that culture supervises, controls and oppresses the development of women, they identified the frequent use of dissociation of potentially dangerous feelings and thoughts, but also the common use of a conscious and deliberate administration of social conventions to protect themselves from social impositions (Gilligan, Lyons, & Hammer, 1990; Taylor, Gilligan, & Sullivan, 1995).

A wonderful example of this is offered by Schilt (2003) who studied girl's self-edited magazines or zines. She reflects, along with the young girls she interviews, about the social pressures they suffer and the strategies used to resist them. She finds that the creation of these fanzines and the distribution among their friends helps not only to explore their inner world but also as a forum where they question many of the cultural pressures to conform that they face and also as a medium through which many of them begin to have initial contact with feminist references and cultural critique. Schilt finds a territory where the intimate and the effort to deal with developmental tasks converge with political issues and the distribution of power. She takes the categories proposed by Taylor, Gilligan and Sullivan further and proposes that some forms of resistance are, at the same time, public and private, which she calls c/overt resistance. These studies re-examine developmental psychology in a new light and allow us to evidence its political dimension.

A safe place where I can reflect and share my intimate world can be necessary, not only for psychological development but also as a forum for the development of political awareness. Resistance to oppression in interpersonal relationships and the political terrain find here a place to meet. Again, the work of Vaclav Havel has been useful to think about the interpersonal conditions needed to nurture and strengthen political resistance. The reflections about his political work often bring to mind the psychotherapeutic setting. In "Stories and Totalitarianism" (1978/1992), he describes the many covert ways that society used to resist constraints. He mentions that totalitarianism imposed its interpretation of events, stripping history of its meaning. Events and locations lost its idiosyncrasies and disappeared in the generic official rendering. He mentions, as an example, that only in prison was he asked repeatedly what part of Prague was he from. He calls prison and similar settings cracks, places where specific history resists the dominant narrative. He wrote:

> While I was in prison, I realized again and again how much more present, compared with life outside, the story was. Almost every prisoner had a life story that was unique and shocking, or moving. As I listened to those different stories, I suddenly found myself in something like a pre-totalitarian world, or in the world of literature. Whatever else I may have thought of my fellow prisoners' colorful narratives, they were not documents of totalitarian nihilization. On the contrary, they testified to the rebelliousness with which human uniqueness resists its own nihilization, and the stubbornness, with which it holds to

> its own and is willing to ignore this negative pressure. Regardless of whatever crime or misfortune was predominant in any given story, the faces in that world were specific and personal. When I got back from prison, I wrote somewhere that in a cell of twenty-four people you can probably encounter more real stories than in a high-rise development of several thousand. People truly afflicted with asthma -those colorless, servile, homogenized, herdlike citizens of the totalitarian state- are not found in large numbers in prison. Instead, prison tends to be a gathering place for people who stand out in one way or another, the unclassifiable misfits, real individuals with all sorts of obsessions, people who are unable to conform (Havel, 1978/1992, p. 191).

The political task consists of giving life to and sustaining these alternative stories, which is much of what a politically reflective psychotherapy can offer. The psychotherapeutic setting can be a safe place where it is permitted to articulate and share the personal story that defies imposition, and that which can conquer repression (not only the personal but also the external one). The therapeutic space can serve as a resonance box to record the abuse that was denied, to humanize loss, to recover silenced voices, to recognize feelings of indignation over injustices suffered, which are all political tasks. Other authors have commented something similar in regard to therapy and the reconstruction of the testimonies of survivors of abuse and of refugees (Blackwell, 2005; Cienfuegos & Monelli, 1983; Martín-Baró, 1990).

Let us explore one last example. In a beautiful book titled "Reading Lolita in Tehran," Nafisi (2003) tells about her experiences as a university professor during the arrival of the Islamic Revolution in Iran. She chronicles her personal trajectory from her initial hopes to the quick disappointment caused by the abuse toward women that she personally endured and how, in the process of protecting herself, decided to retire to her private life and seek refuge in literature. As a university teacher and a specialist on English literature, she suffered constant persecution that increasingly restricted her freedom. She finally decided to set up a study group at her home with young women interested in reflecting on their lives through books. Curiously, but not by chance, Nabokov's Lolita became the main guide for their reflections on life under a dictatorship. The tale of Humbert, the pedophile protagonist of the novel, helped bring light to the subtle mechanisms through which patriarchal culture justifies itself and operates. But along with the reflective work, the seminar served as a forum where the women who participated were able to take distance from the vigilant gaze and begin to talk, laugh, make ironic comments, transgress and share their personal experiences. A place where their personal histories were unpacked and recovered. They built, taking from Virginia Woolf, a "room of their own." That which had been kept secretly could now become visible in the presence of other witnesses and that strengthened their rejection of authority. The place of testimony and audience, of course, is essential. Nafisi writes:

> Here and now in that other world that cropped up so many times in our discussions, I sit and reimagine myself and my students, my girls as I came to call them, reading Lolita in a deceptively sunny room in Tehran. But to steal the words from Humbert, the poet/criminal of Lolita, I need you, the reader, to imagine us, for we won't really exist if you don't. Against the tyranny of time and politics, imagine us the way we sometimes didn't dare to imagine ourselves: in our most private and secret moments, in the most extraordinarily

> ordinary instances of life, listening to music, falling in love, walking down the shady streets or reading Lolita in Tehran. And then imagine us again with all this confiscated, driven underground, taken away from us (2003, p. 21).

I find those words powerfully personal and political and moving. The presence of the listener is invoked to sustain personal resistance, but also as a witness to denounce injustice. Taylor, Gilligan and Sullivan (1995) came to the conclusion that the presence of adult women available to listen was one of the keys that allowed the young women they interviewed to resist without having to dissociate. Intimacy appears again beautifully as a political act. Psychotherapy, looking at these examples, is a privileged scenario to develop this modality of resistance (or what community psychologists have called empowerment). Psychotherapy then is not only a place that offers holding, relief, articulates and recovers personal meaning and establishes connection, but it is also simultaneously a place where these events have a political parallel, since they offer security, distance from dominant imposed narratives, helps construct testimonies, gives voice to those that have been silenced, questions authority and where connections with wider political issues that cause suffering can be established. All which are akin to what Pakman has termed the "micropolitical tasks" of psychotherapy (2011). In summary, we are not only making the unconscious conscious, but also rendering visible the invisible.

9.1 Final Critiques

Although I propose therapy be framed in a social and not a medical model and although I believe that we can do a lot to enhance our liberating possibilities, I do not think this resolves the ethical and political challenges of our craft. I think we are true to these issues if we leave dilemmas open to debate and to a constant never ending reflection.

In the first place, as has been mentioned, a psychotherapy conducted from this perspective is not that different from traditional perspectives. It incorporates new tools but does not necessarily change our practice that much. I believe, that it is essential that we include the reflection of our social and political place in society. The review of our personal history should not limit itself to our interpersonal relationships, but also to our community, family and historical background.

Some critiques of psychotherapy have come to the conclusion that our activity is inevitably condemned to reproduce the power imbalances of society which constantly risks the appearance of abuse (Masson, 1997). But the critiques that warn how psychology and psychotherapy can appropriate and therefore neutralize political struggles are even more relevant (Jacoby, 1997; Parker, 2007). Jacoby, for example, has chronicled the history of many political movements of the seventies that turned to the personal sphere and psychology to try to understand the social ties that interfered with resistance. These efforts on many occasions led to political activists retiring from their activism, fleeing toward the "psychological" or private sphere. To think of a psychotherapy that attends to the political is not to believe that it can substitute collective action. If the actions of resistance cultivated in the protected spaces described earlier remain limited to those scenarios, they will probably never change the institutions and structures that sustain oppression. Psychotherapy is only one tool among others to resist abuse and transform society.

Attending to the political dimension runs the risk of reifying a dichotomy between the personal and the political, reinstalling the conceptual walls that we have been trying to bring down. To conduct political psychotherapy is not to "open space for the political" or "discuss political issues in sessions," but to recognize that life and the therapeutic relationship are inevitably immersed in power relations. It is to understand that our task is contextualized, conscious of the webs of power in which it is held in place.

Psychotherapy, very easily can be turned into a place where uncomfortable rebels are sent to be "understood," "pacified" and "cured." With ease it can turn into a place where social issues are individualized and victims blamed for their sufferings. Only the continuous ethical review of our practice can avoid that, in the name of compassion, a practice that is supposedly progressive is turned into a polished weapon of oppression. I believe it is our duty to keep a watchful eye and a rebellious spirit in order to protect our craft and resist oppression.

References

Blackwell, D. (2005). Psychotherapy, politics and trauma: Working with survivors of torture and organized violence. *Group Analysis, 38,* 307–323.

Cienfuegos, A., & Monelli, C. (1983). The testimony of political repression as a therapeutic instrument. *American Journal of Orthopsychiatry, 53,* 43–51.

Connolly, A. (2006). Through the iron curtain: Analytical space in post-Soviet Russia. *Journal of Analytical Psychology, 51,* 173–189.

Gandhi, M. (1949). *Autobiography: The story of my experiments with truth.* London: Jonathan Cape.

Gilligan, C., Lyons, N., & Hammer, T. (1990). *Making Connections: The relational worlds of adolescent girls at Emma Willard School* Cambridge: Harvard University Press.

Harmatta, J. (1992). Psychic liberation under political tyranny. *International Forum of Psychoanalysis., 1,* 135–139.

Havel, V. (1978/1992). *Open letters: Selected writings 1965–1990.* New York: Vintage Books.

Jacoby, R. (1997). *Social Amnesia: A critique of contemporary psychology.* New Brunswick: Transaction Publishers.

Martín-Baró, I. (1990). *Psicología Social de la Guerra.* San Salvador: UCA Editores.

Masson, J. (1997). *Against Therapy.* London: Harper Collins Publisher.

Nafisi, A. (2003). *Leer Lolita en Teherán.* Barcelona: El Aleph Editores.

Pakman, M. (2011). *Palabras que Permanecen, Palabras por Venir: micropolítica y poética en psicoterapia.* Barcelona: Gedisa.

Parker, I. (2007). *Revolution in Psychology: Alienation to Emancipation.* London: Pluto Press.

Schilt, K. (2003). 'I'll resist with every inch and every breath': Girls and zine making as a form of resistance. *Youth and Society, 35,* 71–97.

Schreuder, B. (2001). The violation of inner and outer boundaries in political persecution. *Journal of Applied Psychoanalytic Studies., 3,* 231–242.
Šebek, M. (1996). Aggression in society and on the couch. *Free Associations, 6,* 477–492.
Taylor, J., Gilligan, C., & Sullivan, A. (1995). *Between voice and silence: Women and girls, race and relationship* (p. 1995). Cambridge: Harvard University Press.

Index

M. Llorens, *Politically Reflective Psychotherapy* , Latin American Voices,
https://doi.org/10.1007/978-3-030-57792-6